CANADIAN

REAL ESTATE

6TH EDITION

CANADIAN REAL ESTATE

6TH EDITION

RICHARD STEACY

First published in 1984 by
Musson Book Company.

Published by Stoddart Publishing
30 Lesmill Road,
Don Mills, Ontario
M3B 2T6

6th Edition

No publication can keep up with the mortgage rates — the rates used in this book are a guide and an example only.

Canadian Cataloguing in Publication Data

Steacy, Richard, 1919-
  Canadian real estate

ISBN 0-7737-2042-I

I. Real estate business — Canada. 1. Title.
II. Title: Canadian real estate.

HD316.S73 1981   333.33'0971   C81-094402-2

To my sons,

Charles Richard Graham Steacy

William Harold Denham Steacy

and their mother, Mary

ACKNOWLEDGMENTS

The author sincerely thanks the following, and acknowledges their generous time and patience in helping with my research:

Lorne S. Speck, staff director, membership services, Canadian Real Estate Association, for his preparation of the chapter "Metric Real Estate".

Richard Boden of the Mortgage Insurance Company of Canada, for his help in preparing the chapter "The High-Ratio Mortgage".

The State Farm Insurance Companies for its permission to use the material in the chapter "A Comparative Guide for Househunters", which is an excerpt from its publication "Finding the Right Home for You".

Mr. John Marsh, a foremost hotel broker in Toronto, for his help preparing the chapter "Buying a Hotel".

The Insurance Institute of Ontario provided the advice in the chapter "Property Insurance".

The advice contained in the chapter "Condominium Ownership" is taken from extracts from "Home Ownership through Condominium" published by Central Mortgage and Housing Corporation, Ottawa.

CONTENTS

Dedication
Acknowledgments
Foreword

CHAPTERS

FOREWORD

With the exception of the current $1,000. tax free allowance on investment income, home ownership as a principal dwelling is the only tax-free investment we have in Canada. This fact is not lost on many investment minded consumers who are shrewdly looking to the future.

To the majority of single persons, apartment living is the way to do it. I don't agree. Every single who has lived in an apartment for the last few years would be much much better off financially if they had purchased a home. Look at the roaring increase in the cost of housing during those years — but it is not too late! There is absolutely no point in looking back and saying — "If I had only - etc." Look ahead.

When I read about couples who say they just can't afford a home despite the fact that they have substantial incomes it is enough to make me shudder. What they are really saying is that they don't want the responsibility of owning a home and the debt structure that goes with it.

What do they do with the money? Fancy cars, exotic holidays, expensive booze, jazzy clothes? Sure, we would all like a touch of that, but home owners have their feet on the ground — their ground.

If a man under forty doesn't own a home, where is he (or she) going to live when he is 65 or 70? In the poor house? They have fancier words for such places now, but it is still the poor house.

In many cases it is the poor taxpayer who is footing the bills because old so-and-so liked the good life, and he ran out of money and steam at the end of the line, with nowhere to hang his hat.

Don't let that happen to you. If you don't own a house, BUY ONE. Go right out and do it. If you can afford a new car you can afford to buy a house. You don't have to live in it if you don't want to. Rent it. The rental income from today's house can be about 8% of its value. A house worth $60,000. can rent for about $400. a month — 8% of its value.

The costs in mortgage differential and taxes will be offset and overcome by the increasing value of the house. I don't have to remind you about the staggering increase in house prices during the past few years.

If you buy and sell a house without living in it, the net profit of the sale will be taxed at capital gain rates and not as income tax rates. The financial gain during the period of your own occupancy will be tax free.

The mortgage debt even protects against inflation. One borrows healthy dollars this year, and repays the debt with cheaper, depreciated dollars later. The mortgage repayment will be cheaper and cheaper as time goes by: today's dollar would be worth 50 cents in ten years with a 7% annual inflation rate . . . . .

Buy a house and ten years from now you'll be well on the road to financial independence when you are one of our "senior citizens".

There are tens of thousands of retired couples living in small houses they paid for over a period of about 25 years. All paid for now, so they don't have to go begging for a place to live. The Provincial and Federal allowances keep bread on the table, the taxes paid, the house heated, and something for self respect. Where would these old couples be today without their home? Why, we wouldn't be able to keep up with the demand for subsidized housing. It is not only good economics, it is good citizenship.

So you be independent. Get out there and do yourself a favour — buy a house. If you already own your own home, then buy some land. Even an acre or two in the country.

How could Grampa know, when he planted that black walnut tree 50 years ago, that a tree buyer would offer the present owner $7,000. for it? SEVEN THOUSAND DOLLARS for one tree!

There are about 60,000 real estate agents in Canada. In buying, selling, leasing and mortgaging, these agents should be able to take care of themselves.

But what about the 25,000,000 Canadians who are not real estate agents?

A good method of providing yourself with additional real estate ammunition is to read about it. This book will provide you with helpful information in one volume that would take weeks of research to find (if you knew where to look). It will describe short cuts, things you never thought about, pitfalls to avoid, hints on making money, saving money, and using it wisely, and ideas for establishing a firm foothold in the greatest money-making business in the world — REAL ESTATE.

When you lend money to a bank or trust company, with a modest return to you in the form of interest, the borrower uses your money to lend it to somebody else at a higher rate of interest, and that somebody else uses your money to make more money.

A great deal of this money is used to finance real estate, so instead of lending your money to "A" to lend it to "B" to use it to make HIS pile in real estate, eliminate the middleman and get a piece of the action yourself.

Richard Steacy

1

IN THE BEGINNING

The first man known to plant a flag on what is now North American land was an Italian from Venice, popularly know as John Cabot, in the year 1497. He was sponsored by King Henry VII of Great Britain, so the land claims Cabot made were on behalf of the British.

Before 1600 there was no set way of spelling proper names, and one may find in contemporary documents several variant spellings of the same name. It is therefore difficult to state what was the correct, original spelling of Cabot. The librarian of the British House of Lords gives us Cabote, Cabotto, Shabot and Cabot, but however we spell the man's name, he was the one who did it.

The land Cabot discovered didn't look very inviting; too many rocks and trees, but the fishing was something else. Cod fish by the millions; just dip down a basket and scoop them in. When word got back to England about the excellent fishing off North America, commercial fishermen got onto a good thing, traffic started, and business boomed.

So we can thank an Italian and the cod fish for generating the initial rush of interest in this land of ours.

Thirty-seven years later (1534) the King of France got into the act and he sent Jacques Cartier over, who made his own claims for France.

In establishing the British and French colonies, settlers were recruited and land holdings in North America began. The French gave large tracts of land to seigneurs, who in turn broke it in parcels and granted rights to individuals, who in turn paid the seigneurs farm produce, or money, for this favour. The British land grants were outright grants, and the grantees owned them, whether they obtained them by paying for them or not.

For more than two hundred years there was a great amount of territory being captured, recaptured and ceded between the British and the French, who finally ended it with the Treaty of Paris in 1763, which ended the Seven Years' War.

Under the terms of this Treaty, France agreed to cede Canada on condition that Britain guaranteed the inhabitants the right to practise the

Catholic religion according to the Roman rite. King George III agreed to this insofar as the laws of Great Britain allowed, and the one chapter in twenty-five of the Treaty of Paris that dealt exclusively with Canada saw Louis XV cede to Britain all French territory as far as the western plains.

The inhabitants could choose to leave the country within 18 months, during which time they could sell their property to British subjects, or they could stay, becoming subjects of Great Britain.

The King issued a *Proclamation*, imposing English criminal and civil law on the inhabitants of New France.

The inhabitants, accustomed to French law, were most unhappy about this, and after much representation to George III, the *Quebec Act* (1774) established the Province of Quebec, an area that included part of what is now Ontario, and provided for a Governor and Legislative Council with rights to make ordinances.

The Quebec Act revoked the Proclamation of 1763, insofar as it concerned civil rights and property, and re-established the French law as it existed before the Proclamation. It provided for the continuance of the criminal law of England, as introduced by the Proclamation.

When war broke out between Britain and her American colonies, a large number of British subjects emigrated to the Province of Quebec. They settled chiefly in the western part of the Province, along the banks of the St. Lawrence river and around Lakes Erie and Ontario. Serious complaints were made by the new British settlers about the state of affairs in the Province of Quebec, and a demand was made for a constitution resembling that to which they had been accustomed.

The result was the *Constitutional Act* (1791) which separated the Province of Quebec into Upper Canada and Lower Canada, each having its own Governor, Legislative Council and Assembly.

English common law was introduced in Upper Canada in 1792, by its first statute, the Property and Civil Rights Act, which stated that the area had been settled principally by British subjects, who were unaccustomed to French law, and repealed the provisions of the Quebed Act regarding civil rights and property, replacing them with English law.

Under the Constitutional Act, Lower Canada retained its French law of real property, except that grantees would be entitled to grants in free tenure if they wished. (Feudal rights and duties were abolished in 1851).

Conflic ensued between the English and the French. Rebellion broke out in 1837 and the Constitution of Lower Canada was suspended. A High Commissioner was appointed to adjust the relations and government of the two Provinces.

The result of this was the *Union Act* (1840) which united Upper Canada and Lower Canada into the single Province of Canada.

French civil law continued in the area of the former Lower Canada and English common law continued in the area of the former Upper Canada. English criminal law was in force overall.

The *British North America Act* of 1867 was an Act to unite the Provinces of Canada, Nova Scotia and New Brunswick.

Three provinces went into the BNA Act and four came out of it: The Province of Canada became two provinces — Ontario and Quebec.

The newly formed Dominion of Canada's motto was ''From Sea to Sea'', which wasn't fulfilled until British Columbia joined in 1871, after being promised a railway, which it got. So from sea to sea our great country began.

Canada is the second largest country in the world, with an area of nearly ten million square kilometres. About 7% of the land is economically viable for farming, which means that on paper we have 700,000 square kilometres workable land for 23,000,000 people, or about 33 square kilometres each. Which sounds great until we see the population in crowded urban centers living on top of each other. Do you know that we have inhabitants who have never seen a COW?

So we have a land of vast population contrasts. Some have so much land they need a telescope or an aeroplane to give it the once over, while others are so crowded they can't stand the proximity of their neighbours.

The prime objective of this book is to get you involved in some of this land of ours, to own some of it. If I can accomplish this, my writing has been worthwhile.

Don't let me down.

2

LAND TENANCY

Land is considered to be permanent. Real. So we have an estate that is real. Real Estate.

Real estate is landed property, and landed property is land. So "real estate" only refers to land.

Put a building on the land, and we have real property, which includes the land *and* the building.

Terminate *real property* and we have *realty*.

Land, generally speaking, is held by the Crown-In-Right-Of the Provinces in Canada. Reference to this will be found in Section 109 of the British North America Act of 1867. When we hold land, we do so subject to the rights of the Crown, and this is why expressions such as the following include the word "tenant".

Tenant in Fee Simple: Fee — from the feudal term fief (tenure of land subject to feudal obligations). The feudal system was in effect in Europe during the middle ages, based on the holding of land in return for services to a lord by a vassal. Simple — unaffected. Therefore, this is real estate in its most untrammelled sense. It is an estate granted absolutely to a person and his heirs, forever.

Joint Tenancy: There are four unities here:

(a) Unity of Possession: Each entitled to undivided possession of the whole of the property, and none holds any part separately to the exlusion of the others.

(b) Unity of Time: The interest of each joint tenant must vest at the same time.

(c) Unity of Title: Each person must obtain title under the same instrument.

(d) Unity of Interest: The interest of each is identical. Joint tenancy is land ownership by two or more persons. If one person dies, his interest in the estate passes to the survivor(s). Joint tenancy can be severed and turned into a tenancy in common.

4

Tenancy in Common: There is just one unity here, and that is the unity of possession. It is ownership by two or more persons, but if one of them dies, his share passes to his *estate*, and *not* to the survivor(s) of the tenancy.

Historically, all land was owned by the King, who in turn granted it to his nobles. The land owner kept the proof of ownership in his own possession, from the time of the original grant from the King, or patent from the Crown. When he sold or mortgaged, he handed over all the documents.

In the early 1700's, registry offices were set up in counties in Britain. The documents themselves were not registered, but a note or memorandum was registered. These were registered alphabetically under the owner's or mortgagee's name, a system which was found to be most unwieldy.

Canadian land registry offices were established under authority of Upper Canada Statute 35, George III, Chapter 5, passed August 10, 1795, and entitled ''An Act for the public registering of deeds, conveyances, wills and other incumbrances which shall be made, or may affect, any lands, testaments or hereditaments within this Province.''

The alphabetical system was changed in most parts of Canada before Confederation, when abstract books were set up as we know them today, and documents themselves were registered against lots and plans.

Registration of a deed in a registry office does not necessarily imply absolute ownership. Competent persons can examine documents registered, or ''search title'', and give an opinion as to status of title. Although the opinion may be considered reliable, it may be quite impossible to state definitely that the title is clear.

Recognizing this, a government guaranteed system of registration was introduced in parts of Canada in 1885, known as ''Land Titles'', or the ''Torrens system'', a history of which is covered in the next chapter.

Real estate in the Province of Quebec is handled a little differently from the rest of Canada. All lands in Quebec, generally speaking, are held under free tenures. The owner of land holds it as absolutely as it is possible for anyone to hold it, and can dispose of it freely.

The owner may be an individual, or a group of individuals owning in equal or unequal shares, or a legal entity such as a corporation.

In all of Canada, with the exception of Quebec, a real estate purchase and sale, and conveyancing, will be handled for you by a lawyer.

In Quebec, it will be handled by a legal practitioner known as a Notary, whose chief duty is to draw up and execute deeds and contracts. A Barrister or Solicitor in Quebec is not allowed to do this, just the Notary. Which makes it easy to find a good real estate lawyer!

An interesting way to spend an afternoon is to do a bit of ''Title searching'' in a registry office or land titles office. Trace the history of your own property, and all the ownership and encumbrances before you came along. Most enlightening.

3

LAND TITLES REGISTRATION

The Land Titles, or ''Torrens'' system of registering property has been described as South Australia's greatest export.

Land registration systems are very ancient, and probably go back to Babylon. They were common in medieval Europe. The pattern for the earliest Australian systems were registers of deeds introduced in some English counties in the time of Queen Anne. But before the middle of the last century there was no system of land registration anywhere in the world which included all the desirable features of the ''Torrens'' system. It spread to North America in the 1880's, and a similar system was taken up by Germany and other European countries, by the French North African and other Mediterranean colonies, and by most of the British colonies and dependencies throughout the world.

It appeared in Canada when the Province of Alberta was part of the North West Territories, in 1886, under the Territories Real property Act, and spread to British Columbia, Saskatchewan, Manitoba, Ontario and the Yukon Territory.

The system removes all risk from defective deeds by enacting that the ownership of the person whose name shows in the register book shall be paramount. Registration makes his ownership conclusive, and the Provincial Governments and Territorial Governments guarantee it where used.

A person deprived of land through the operation of the system does not suffer loss, and if he is the victim of fraud he can recover. possession of the land. If an innocent third party has become registered as proprietor, the victim can proceed against the wrongdoer, not for land, but for pecuniary damages, as the third party's title will be indefeasible. If that action fails, the victim can recover compensation from the Government.

Compared to registry office systems, land titles transfers have no complicated covenants as in deeds. The whole title, and everything it is subject to, is all on one page. Long descriptions are not required — by using reference plans short descriptions are used. Land titles saves a great deal of time in ''searching title'' since it is all on one page.

7

There can be no adverse possession under land titles.

Here is a summary of its use in Canada.

Yukon Territory and Northwest Territories, purely Torrens.

British Columbia: With the exception of certain Crown lands, and a very small percentage of complicated titles, all lands are under the Torrens system.

Alberta: Pure Torrens.

Saskatchewan: About half of the land in Saskatchewan has been brought under Torrens.

Manitoba: Estimated that over 85% of the settled land area in the Province, and perhaps 95% of individual land holdings are under Torrens.

Ontario: The Land Titles Act governs all land granted in the northern part of the province since 1887. In the south, an estimate has been made that there are about 2,300,000 parcels of land, of which 15% are under Torrens.

In Newfoundland and the Maritimes, it is being considered.

Quebec does not use it.

The person directly responsible for the system was Sir Robert Richard Torrens, a former Premier of South Australia, who conceived the idea of applying the simple method of registration of shipping to the registration of land. He was the author of the "Real Property Act", an act to simplify the laws relating to the transfer and encumbrance of freehold and other interest in land. It was assented to on January 27, 1858, and took effect on July 1st the same year.

4

PROVIDING PROOF OF OWNERSHIP

Here is a summary of five basic means available to a property owner to reassure him of his rights to property.

1. If the property is registered in a Land Titles office, the title documents are guaranteed by the Provincial government, and the office will provide the rightful owner with a certificate of title. This certificate is conclusive proof of ownership and is indefeasible.

If an innocent third party has become registered as owner, the victim can proceed against the wrongdoer; not for land, but for pecuniary damages. If that action fails, the victim can recover compensation from the Government.

2. If the property is registered in a registry office, in many areas the property owner can apply to the Land Titles office for a certificate of title, despite the fact that the property is not registered in the Land Titles office.

For a prescribed fee, the director of titles will authorize a title search in the registry office, and, after a thorough investigation, if satisfied that the applicant does indeed own the property, will issue a certificate of title. This has the same protection and guarantee as though the property were registered in Land Titles, but with a time limitation.

When one is ''searching title'' on this property in the future, it would be necessary only to go back in time until the date of the certificate of title. Everything registered after that would be subject to the same rules in registry; the strength of the registered documents standing on their own merits and not being guaranteed by the Government.

3. In buying real estate, the purchaser's interest will be protected by a lawyer in the change of ownership.

Although registration of documents in a registry office has no guarantee of validity as in a Land Titles office, a lawyer, upon completing his search and satisfying himself that there is a sound indication of title, will state this in writing to the purchaser on completion of the conveyance of title.

Provincial statutes require this registry office search to be made through a number of years past: In Ontario, for example, a 40-year search will suffice.

If registration is under Land Titles, the new owner will, of course, be provided with a certificate of title.

4. Commercial title insurance is available to all property owners, mortgagees, and tenants.

It is protection against financial loss through such defects as those arising from fraud, forgery, conveyances by minors or persons of unsound mind, demands of missing heirs, rights of divorced persons, errors in registration, etc.

Under the terms of a title policy, if the title is attacked, the insurance company will defend it in court at its own expense and, if a loss is suffered, the insured will be protected. There are three types of policies available:

Owner's Policy: Insures estates of ownership, occupancy and possession and remains in force as long as the insured or his heirs have any interest in the policy.

Mortgagee Policy: Insures interests held by lenders as security for the payment of a debt. Liability is reduced as mortgage payments are made, and ends with the final payment of the debt.

Leaseholder Policy: Protects a tenant against loss or damage sustained by reason of eviction or curtailment of his leasehold interest through title difficulties.

5. Adverse possession is something that probably would seldom occur to property owners in establishing rights to ownership.

In Ontario, for example, the statute of limitation here is ten years — which means that simply by occupying your own home continually and unopposed for ten years can be ample proof of your right to ownership.

This can also apply to an unbroken chain of ownership. For example, if you purchased a house from one who had occupied it continuously for seven years, and you, as the new owner continued the unbroken chain of occupancy for three years, this would constitute your ten years rights of ownership, providing you had irrevocable proof of the the former owner's occupancy, which could probably be established by obtaining a signed affidavit to this effect from the former owner.

5

UNDERSTANDING INTEREST

Hundreds of years ago loans were regarded as forms of help that one owed his neighbour in distress. To profit from the distress was considered to be evil and unjust.

The noun *usury* is from the latin *usura*, meaning the ''use'' of something; borrowed capital for example. Usury was once defined as ''where more is asked than is given,'' and was prohibited by the Church and State. It was considered to be a form of robbery. Collecting interest today is not considered to be robbery, but if the interest is excessive, it is considered to be usury.

It was gradually accepted that a loss could occur through lending — the latin verb *intereo* means ''to be lost'' — interest was a loss, and the word interest gradually came to mean the compensation due to a creditor because of a loss incurred through lending. This loss was considered to be the difference between a lender's current position and that in which he would have stood if he had not made the loan.

In early times, loans were interest free, but incurred the penalty of interest if not repaid promptly. Lenders then saw the light and adopted the practice of charging interest from the beginning of the loan.

Today we have two types of interest: (a) simple, or fixed interest, and (b) compound interest.

If one borrows money and agrees to repay it plus 10% interest when the loan is repaid, the principal amount of the loan would be repaid plus the 10%, regardless of the repayment date. This is simple interest — interest on principal (the amount borrowed).

However, if one agreed to repay the loan at 10% interest *per annum* a loan is immediately created with compound interest, because if the loan is not repaid at the end of the year, the 10% interest due will be added to the indebtedness, and when the loan is repaid at a later date, interest will be paid on the new outstanding balance of the loan, which requires interest to be paid on interest.

11

Always remember that the more frequent the compounding, the greater the yield to the *lender*.

If the interest were compounded twice-yearly, or semi-annually, here is how it would look on $1,000. at 10%.

1st period (6 months) $\dfrac{10\%}{2} \times 1,000.$ = $ 50.00

2nd period (6 months) $\dfrac{10\%}{2} \times 1.050.$ =   52.50

                                                     $102.50

So the lender, receiving his interest at the end of the year, receives a return of 10.25% on the 10% loan.

If the loan interest were compounded quarter-yearly, here is the result:

1st period (3 months) $\dfrac{10\%}{4} \times 1,000.00$ = $ 25.00

2nd period (3 months) $\dfrac{10\%}{4} \times 1,025.00$ =   25.62

3rd period (3 months) $\dfrac{10\%}{4} \times 1,050.62$ =   26.26

4th period (3 months) $\dfrac{10\%}{4} \times 1,076.89$ =   26.92

                                                     $103.80

The lender receives 10.38% on the 10% loan.

The foregoing illustrations of actual return only apply if the loan interest is repaid once a year.

If the interest were paid at the end of each period, and the lender simply put the money in his pocket, the money in his pocket draws no interest so he would be getting 10% a year regardless of the compounding. For example, if the lender received the interest in two periods, the borrower would pay $50. interest at the end of each six months. The first $50. would not be added to the loan and therefore interest would not be paid on the $50. as in compounding.

On the other hand, if the borrower paid the periodic interest out of a pile he kept in a shoe box, he wouldn't *pay* any more than 10%, because money in a shoe box earns no interest.

This is basically why compound interest is said to produce an "effective yield."

The lender, to receive his 10.25% on the 10% loan would either (1) receive the interest at the end of the year, or (2) *immediately* re-invest the periodic payment of interest on the same terms as the loan on which he received the interest. Only then would he get his 10.25%, and make the compounding effective.

Interest rates (or factors as they are sometimes called) are easy to establish, providing the payments are to be made *with the same frequency*. To establish the periodic interest rate on a loan in which the interest is compounded monthly, simply divide the annual rate of interest by 12. If the interest were compounded quarter-yearly, divide the annual rate by four, and so on.

Calculate:	from the latin *calculus* which means pebble or stone
(synonymous)	used in counting. *Calculus* from the *latin calx*, which means small pebble. *Calculate* means *compute.*
Compute:	from the latin *com* which means together, and latin *puto* which means reckon.
Reckon:	from Old English, Swedish, Danish, etc., which means *count.*
Compound:	from *compounen* (to put together). Composed of two or more parts; not simple.
	Synonymous with Amalgamation, combination, mixture.
Simple Interest:	That interest which arises from the principal sum only.
Compound Interest:	That interest which arises from the principal with the interest added at stated times, as yearly, twice-yearly, etc. *Interest on interest.*

6

PUTTING THE BITE ON THE BANK

One dictionary definition of a bank is that it is a "pile", and the way today's Canadian banking institutions are piling up profits, it appears to be a very apropos description.

Never lose sight of the fact that a bank is in business to make money, and nobody but nobody knows how to do it better than a bank. Everything it does is geared to make money, and considering that the net assets of Canadian banks are increasing at more than 20% a year, it would appear that they are the all-time champions in the art of piling it up.

Manufacturers and insurance companies have been forced by the government to return a part of immoderate profits to the consumer, and corporate presidents may be forgiven for wondering why they should be singled out and not the banks. The 20% is a *net* increase; compound it for four years and the banks double in size.

Aside from their little gems such as charging you $3.00 for a phone call to say that your account is overdrawn, banks basically amass their profits by lending money. But to get some of that money requires planning, a step-by-step methodical planning for many.

Banks may be the same in the nature of services provided for the public, but individual branches are as different as day and night because of the ability of some managers to have rapport with customers, while others don't seem to know the meaning of the word. I would assume that a critical banking error is for a manager to allow a customer to leave his office without reaching rapport with the customer. We have all seen the differences: one a gregarious, affable guy who leaves a customer on a friendly plane, whether the answer is yes or no to a loan request, while another seems to think that he is doing one a favour by actually allowing him to cross the threshold of his office.

There are several things one can do to open the door to a bank loan, but before setting your plan in motion, "case the joint" in a bank and watch the personnel carefully. Make two or three forays and change a bill, take your time and see if there is a happy spirit in the way the clerks go about their business. Their attitude is generally affected by the personality of the manager, so watch for him and see how he conducts himself. If he appears to be a sourpuss, his clerks won't be doing much smiling, so think twice about doing your business here. Unless of course you are a sourpuss yourself, then you just might hit if off.

When you have found a happy branch, open a current account. Banks love to have customers with current accounts because they pay no interest on the money piling up in the account. And keep the account active. Deposits and withdrawals every other day. Banks like to see an active account because it charges for every movement in the account.

In establishing a credit rating at a bank, it is important to borrow money when you don't need it. This is the best time to approach the bank, because you will be relaxed and secure in the knowledge that if you don't get it, you are not going to worry about it. And if you can't get it when you don't need it, it will certainly be the time to switch banks fast — if you can't get it when you don't need it, what chance would you have if you *did* need it?

When you borrow when you don't need it, simply pay it back on time, and your good record of prompt payment will go on your loan record sheet to your credit. The interest you pay on the loan will be your nominal cost of establishing your credit rating at the bank.

The most important part of your planning to tap the bank is to ensure that the manager knows you. Clerks are nice to banter with, but the manager is the important one who says you get it or you don't. A clerk can't authorize a loan, and even the chief accountant is restricted in what he can do. So channel your charm and rapport for the manager.

The first time I used this system, it worked like a dream. I found a bank with a big, cigar chomping manager who was all over the place keeping everybody happy, and I noticed that when he approached his clerks they actually seemed to be glad to see him.

So I put my plan into effect, and after three or four weeks of keeping my current account busy and passing the time of day with the big man, I walked into his office one day, sat on the edge of his desk and said I would like to put the bite on him for a couple of thousand. He just reached for the magic drawer in his desk where managers keep their demand notes, and I knew I had it made.

Over the next two years, I built up my credit rating with the branch to fifteen thousand dollars, which was the manager's personal loan limit. Bank managers are given authority to lend up to a certain amount on their own authority, and the amount depends on the size of the branch. Any loan over his limit must be referred to a higher authority, so don't pick on the smallest branch in town if you can avoid it.

Well, while all this was going on, I was astute enough to establish a current account at another bank, in case of contingency, and had good rapport with its manager. This was fortunate thinking, because one day my manager at bank No. 1 was promoted, and a new man was sent in to take charge.

My brother Charles, the Air Force Colonel, once showed me the instrument panel of a zippy fighter aircraft. Staring at the pilot, with stark reality, is a large button stamped with the word PANIC. Push this button and there is no turning back. Out you go, parachute and all, and what you leave behind comes crashing down.

With decades of experience in doing business with Canadian banks, I am rapidly reaching the conclusion that newly appointed, and caretaker bank managers, are supplied with these buttons as part of their rations in the kit of new management.

Many of you reading this will recall with horror your own experience with a new manager: demand loans were recalled, overdrafts were cancelled, cheques bounced, and with it you suffered temporary frustration and anger. But you survived.

My notes were being honoured, the overdraft wasn't causing the giant corporation any pain, my cheques were being cashed, and everything was at peace in my small banking world. Then BANG. The new guy pushed the panic button which shot me out of the front door and everything I had built up inside came crashing down. But I had my parachute which worked beautifully.

It was my custom to drop into the bank on a Friday to pick up a couple of hundred for my wife's weekend shopping and pocket money for the following week. Consider then, my frustration on black Friday when I walked in for my weekly ration and was advised that my overdraft was too high so ha ha no money today.

The annoying part of this was that I had just made a deposit!

However, with my parachute I landed gently in the manager's office at bank No. 2, put the bite on him for a few hundred with ridiculous ease and survived. Bank No. 1 was later paid off with gusty glee.

I still have a reserve bank in the wings in case the head office decides to promote my man and install one of those guys with a panic button.

Don't think for one minute that a bank feels it owes you any loyalty. Business is business, and if a bank suspects that you are coming onto hard times it will drop you like a hot brick. And then what do you do?

Why, you just trot along and see your pal at bank No. 2.

7

CAPITALIZATION

To capitalize something is to convert it to capital, *capital value*. It is essential to understand it clearly before venturing into any type of real estate investments.

If you pay one thousand dollars for a bond or other security, and receive one hundred dollars interest once a year, it is obvious that the investment has a return of 10% per annum.

But what happens to the value of the bond if you, the holder, wish to sell it?

If a buyer can be found who will be satisfied with a 10% return, the bond could be sold for its original purchase price, one thousand dollars.

But what happens if a buyer can't be found at 10%, one who would not be satisfied with 10%? What would the bond be worth if the ultimate buyer received 12%? That is, what should the selling price of the bond be if the $100. annual return is to represent 12%, and not the original 10%?

Take a look . . . . .

$$\frac{\$100.00}{12\%} \times \frac{100}{1} \qquad \textit{\$833.33}$$

And if the market pendulum were swinging the other way, and a buyer could be found who would be satisfied with a return of 8%, then what? Take another look . . . . .

$$\frac{\$100.00}{8\%} \times \frac{100}{1} \qquad \textit{\$1,250.00}$$

In this case, the constant $100. annual return represents 8% of the bond's new price. Get the idea?

Now, the same principal applies when we look at the ''cash flow'' of an investment in real estate, such as a small apartment building.

Cash flow is what is left after municipal taxes and all operating expenses related to the property have been paid, including the mortgage payments.

To illustrate:

Annual gross return (rental)	$50,000.
Less Taxes and Operating Expenses	18,000.
	$32,000.
Less annual payments on $200,000. mortgage, interest and principal:	25,000.
CASH FLOW	$ 7,000.

Now then, if a buyer for this property can be found who would be satisfied with a return of 8% on his invested cash, what will its approximate selling price be, cash to mortgage?

Here we are . . . . .

$$\frac{\$7,000.00}{8\%} \times \frac{100}{1} \qquad \$87,500.00 \text{ cash}$$

To which we add the principal balance of the mortgage ($200,000.) and the price is $287,500.

If an 8% buyer cannot be found, and we can only come up with a 10% buyer, then we have:

$$\frac{\$7,000.00}{10\%} \times \frac{100}{1} \qquad \$70,000.00 \text{ cash}$$

To which we add the principal balance of the mortgage ($200,000.) and the price is $270,000.

See how it works? When looking for a real estate investment, a first consideration will be the return required on the cash invested.

When selling, or acquiring any investment, the purchase price must at least produce a return that will reflect current market rates at the time of the transaction.

Periodically we hear about those "perpetual" bonds sold by the Federal Government many years ago which produce about 3% interest. The present owners are stuck with them, and if such bonds were offered for sale, the buyer would wish to acquire them at current rates of return.

If current rates are 9%, here is what one might expect to receive for $1,000. worth — the $1,000. being what the original buyer paid. Remember now, the $1,000. bond pays 3%, or $30. per year.

$$\frac{\$30.00}{9\%} \times \frac{100}{1} \qquad \$333.33$$

18

That's all the bond would be worth today, $333.33.

Consider some of your own securities. If they yield 6%, what are they worth to a buyer today if the current rates available on similar securities are eight or nine per cent? Now that you understand capitalization, figure it out quickly with one of those marvellous little calculators we can buy today for less than ten bucks.

8

LEVERAGE

Leverage is the act of lifting an object with as little exertion as possible. In the area of money, it is the act of making as much as possible with as little as possible.

The most prominent and profitable leverage in real estate is in buying property with a view to selling it shortly after the purchase. The less one invests in such a venture, the more one makes!

Buy property for $50,000. cash and turn it over quickly for $55,000. cash. Profit: 10%

Buy property for $50,000. with $5,000. down, turn it over quickly for $55,000. and the profit is 100%.

See how it works? The profit here is based on the amount of cash invested; not what the property cost.

Take the $50,000. purchase, resold quickly at $55,000. with different down payments. Here is your profit on the investment.

Cash Invested	Profit
$ 5,000.	100.0%
7,000.	71.4%
10,000.	50.0%
12,000.	41.6%
15,000.	33.3%
20,000.	25.0%
25,000.	20.0%
30,000.	16.6%

See, the less one invests, the more one makes.

The foregoing are round figures. There will be acquisition costs (principally legal fees) and in selling, more legal fees — and possibly a real estate agent's selling fee.

20

So the cash invested will have to include the acquisition costs, and the net return will have to be what is left after selling costs.

Then you will have to consider the capital gain tax on what you made.

Take the purchase with $5,000. down for example. Say the acquisition costs total $500. Now we have invested $5,500.

Assuming the property were resold quickly for $55,000. and we were lucky enough to make a private deal without paying anyone a selling commission, we will still have to pay our legals — say $500.

We sell for $55,000. cash to the mortgages totalling $45,000. We knock off $500. for legals, leaving us with $9,500. cash.

Cash realized in selling	$9,500.
Less cash invested	5,500.
Gain:	4,000.
Return on cash invested:	72.7%

If we had to pay a selling commission of 5% of the $55,000. ($2,750.) we would show a net gain of $1,250. resulting in a return of 22.7%.

Even paying our taxes, it will still show a very nice return on the money invested.

The income tax we pay will depend on our tax bracket. If the bracket is 35%, for example, we would be taxed 35% of ½ of $1,250. or $218.75, leaving us with a $1,031.25 net cash gain on the investment of $5,500. — a tax free return of 18.75%.

We sold the property for 10% more than its purchase price, and made 18.75%. Not bad, not bad.

Well, you say, how does one buy property at a price that will justify a sudden increase of 10% in its market value? Why, do it the way others do it — make offers, plenty of them.

Review the chapter on speculation.

9

THE MORTGAGE DEED

Where would we be without the mortgage? Living in cramped shacks, no doubt.

Who would have believed three or four decades ago that a labourer can today live in such luxurious surroundings, complete with broadloom?

Don't curse the mortgage lender. Bless him. He makes it all possible, and at a much cheaper rate than the loans on cars and a few thousand other items.

When we sign a mortgage deed, we borrow money. The rate of interest on this money is lower than money borrowed for other necessities (and luxuries) in life.

Who pays cash for a house? Usually someone who has just sold a house that was all paid for over a number of years. And how was this possible? By a mortgage or two of course.

To you who have built up your large equity in your home, remember that it was a mortgage lender who made it possible.

And to you who have yet to own a home, and want one, grit your teeth and prepare to sacrifice a bit like the rest of us. It will be worth it.

Who's Who?

Mortgagee and mortgagor. You will find them throughout this book, also referred to as lender and borrower.

When you are a tenant in a building, you are a lessee.

When you receive a gift, you are a donee.

When you purchase goods, you are a vendee.

Notice that each one of the foregoing are ones upon whom a right is conferred. The right to occupy a building, the right to own the gift and the right to the goods purchased. Everyone on the receiving end is the one with the EE on the end of the name.

When one lends money to a real property owner, the property owner signs a mortgage deed and give it to the lender. This is the lender's proof of security. The lender, receiving the mortgage from the borrower is therefore the one to whom the right to the security is conferred. The mortgagee. The one with the EE on the end of its name.

Perhaps an easier way to remember who's who is to remember that the one with the OR on the end of the name is the one who has title to something.

The lessor owns the building which the lessee occupies.

The donor owns the gift he is giving the donee.

The vendor owns the goods he is selling the vendee.

And so it is with the borrower in a mortgage deed. He owns some real estate which he is using as security for a loan, and is therefore the one who has title to something, the property.

The mortgagor. The one with the OR at the end of the name.

MORTGAGOR	Borrower	
MORTGAGEE	Lender	*(don't forget)*

Defining a Mortgage

We all know what a mortgage is. Right? Wrong.

The noun mortgage comes from two French words, ''mort'' (dead) and ''gage'' (pledge). The pledge becomes dead when the loan is paid off, or, as some say, the real estate pledged becomes dead (lost) due to failure to pay. Take your pick.

A mortgage is contained in a document called a deed. A mortgage deed is what we have.

A deed is a document that contains a contract, or agreement, that is signed, sealed, contains proof of its delivery, and is effective on the date of delivery (to the lender).

It is signed by the borrower in English Common Law. In Quebec by borrower and lender.

It is often signed under seal. The seal is old hat — it signifies that the borrower was conscious of what he was doing when he signed the deed. So he signs it and sticks a seal on it.

The one signing places the seal with his signature. If one signed a deed and weren't conscious of the seal — in other words if the seal were placed on the deed after he signed and left the room — it wouldn't mean a thing. He must know about the seal at the time of signing.

You will find deeds in a Registry Office with seals and without seals. As a matter of fact some court judgments on the subject have said seals are unnecessary *period*, so if your lawyer tells you you don't need a seal, don't ask me to argue with him. But we must admit at least a seal does make a deed look better.

Proof of delivery. Signing a deed in the presence of one's solicitor and giving the deed to the solicitor is considered to be proof of delivery, because solicitors act in trust. So the one signing is trusting the solicitor to deliver the deed to the rightful party, and that's good enough.

It is effective on the date of delivery — which would be the date the signature goes on because that is done in the presence of a solicitor who is accepting delivery of it on that day for the lender.

There is a difference in Quebec and the rest of Canada in the handling of a mortgage deed and what it means.

In English Common Law (all of Canada except Quebec) there is, strictly speaking, only one legal mortgage. This may sound a bit confusing, but it is really very simple.

English Common Law says that the legal mortgagee is *entitled* to the *title* deed.

There could be only one person *entitled* to the *title* deed in this statement, so he would be obviously the mortgagee who is the one who received the *first* mortgage deed signed by a borrower using the *title* deed as security. Once this mortgagee is entitled to the title deed by law, no one else could be entitled to it.

So a legal mortgage in English Common Law is a first mortgage — but only a first mortgage registered against property in a *land registry office*. This requires a bit of further explanation.

There are two basic systems of land registration — the registry and land titles offices.

In land titles registration, the mortgage is a *charge* against the property, and therefore the legal mortgagee is not entitled to the title deed; he can't get it, because the mortgage is a charge on the property. Only in the registry office is he entitled to it.

O.K. So a legal mortgage in English Common Law is a mortgage of first priority in a land registry office. Well, what about all the other mortgages? Aren't they legal? Sure, but they are not called legal mortgages.

When one signs a first mortgage to be registered in a registry office, he is left with what is known as an equity of redemption. He has the right to redeem his property by paying off the mortgage.

When one borrows additional funds, and signs another mortgage deed, he is borrowing against his equity in the property, and so this mortgage is called an equitable mortgage. So is a third and a fourth mortgage.

So a first mortgagee in a land registry office holds the (strictly speaking) legal mortgage, and the junior mortgagees in a land registry office hold

24

equitable mortgages. But they are all legal. If it sounds like a lot of hocus pocus it is not intended to be, because apparently that is the way it is.

The legal mortgage is where we get the definition of a mortgage in that it is a conveyance of real property as security for a debt, and when the debt is repaid the property is returned, or reconveyed to the borrower. But not always.

You see, if there happens to be a second (equitable) mortgage registered against the property, the minute the first (legal) mortgage is paid off and discharged, the second mortgage automatically becomes the first (legal) mortgage.

Well, what about Quebec?

Now, here is a Province that really knows how to define a mortgage. In Quebec a mortgage is called a deed of loan with hypothec. And get this — the Quebec Civil Code goes on to define hypthec as being a LIEN ON AN IMMOVEABLE. (which really is a first class definition of a mortgage without all the gobbledygook of English Common Law.)

In Quebec no mortgagee is entitled to a title deed because all mortgages are a charge (lien) against property.

There we are. A mortgage is one of three things — (a) implied conveyance of property to the lender, or (b) an equitable lien (or charge) on property in favour of the lender, or, in Quebec, a lien on an immoveable.

I like the last definition. Because that's really what a mortgage is all about.

What's in a Mortgage?

The essential element in a mortgage deed is a covenant to repay the debt, plus interest.

Most basic. The lender puts up the money for one purpose and one purpose only — to obtain a financial return on the investment satisfactory to the lender. An exception to this may be Aunt Sally helping out Cousin Joe, but generally speaking, the name of the game is money. As much as possible, as safely as possible, as securely as possible.

The borrower wants to get the money as cheaply as possible, but mortgage markets being what they are, he hasn't got much choice in the public sector. The private sector is the one where a borrower can pay less for the use of borrowed money, and also where he can get a real hosing and pay the most.

So the mortgagor and the mortgagee reach an agreement as to the size of the loan and its terms, and then get formal about it by proceeding with the business of preparing a deed and entering into a legal contract.

A mortgage deed may start right off at the top calling itself an indenture. It is an interesting word, which simply means an agreement between two or more parties, but its history of terminology is interesting.

Many years ago, before carbon paper and all of today's common means of copying, such an agreement would be penned in duplicate (two original copies) and then the copies would be placed evenly, one on top of the other, and a wavy line, or indentation, would be cut along one side of the copies. Each party would receive one, and of course the idea was that when the two were placed together, the wavy cutting would match and this was supposed to establish authenticity.

Don't tell me. Already you are thinking what fun a slick forger with a pair of shears could have. Anyhow, that's where the word indenture came from.

A mortgage to be registered in a land titles office will have the word CHARGE on it, so it will be easily identifiable as to its registry.

The names of the borrower(s) and lender(s) will be in it, that's for sure, and a legal description of the property secured as collateral for the loan.

It will clearly state the principal amount of the money OWED by the mortgagor. You will notice that I did not say the principal amount of the money BORROWED. On can borrow, say, $9,000. and have a bonus of $1,000. tacked onto it, producing a $10,000. debt, although the borrower never sees the $1,000. bonus until he hands it over to the lender at a later date.

Watch the bonus deals, they can be especially expensive. The borrower not only owes the bonus he never saw, but he pays interest on money that doesn't exist for the duration of the loan.

The mortgage will clearly state the rate of interest charged on the loan, but it is here that perhaps the biggest bones of contention exist because of the various means lenders decide to take in extracting the interest. Ensure that your mortgage, if you are the borrower, CLEARLY states that the interest will be compounded either annually or semi-annually, not in advance, and with no more frequency than that. Many lenders, especially private lenders, will extract interest compounded monthly, which is more expensive.

The term will be there. This is the length of time the borrower has the use of the money (subject, of course, to default in the loan).

The repayment amount will be shown as monthly, quarter-yearly, half-yearly or annually. It can take many routes, the most common of which are:

(a) A payment covering the interest only.
(b) A fixed payment covering the interest and a portion of the principal amount of the loan.
(c) A fixed principal payment, plus interest.

If a mortgage contains a stated fixed amount at regular intervals to cover ''interest and principal'' be sure it is large enough to at least cover the interest. Believe it or not, mortgages ARE sometimes thoughtlessly written and when a calculator goes to work on it, it is discovered that the payment actually is a little short of covering the interest!

A court judgment ruled, so I have been told, that in one such mortgage held by the vendor of a property, the vendor's lawyer obtained a court order to have the sale cancelled because, apparently, the effect of the payment not covering the interest was that the vendor had not actually sold the property, but had given the purchaser an option to buy it. Before the purchaser exercised the option, I suppose by rectifying the error, the vendor cancelled the purchaser's right to the option and got the property back. Read this again and remember it . . .

The responsibilities of the borrower will be spelled out, and basically they are to maintain the payments, keep the property insured, keep the property in a good state of repair, and not misuse it.

The borrower's rights will be shown, such as to have quiet enjoyment of the property and to be free of the lender's rights when the debt is finally paid.

The lender's rights will be shown, and they are quite lengthy. For example, the rights to possession of the property on default by the borrower, and legal recourse to seize the property. These are the most serious. There are many others, such as what happens if the borrower is lazy about paying municipal taxes? The lender can pay them and add the amount to the mortgage debt, plus interest. Ditto for insurance.

One could go on and on and on about the contents of a mortgage, but the foregoing are the basics. I suggest you obtain a blank copy of a mortgage deed and study it. The document will be a long winded legal affair, but it is necessary to be legal in detail about such a contract; after all, there is a sizeable amount of money involved.

The mortgage will be signed and witnessed, and everybody is in business hoping nothing goes wrong.

How a Mortgage is Registered

There are two basic systems of registering real property and mortgages in Canada. I say two *basic* systems, because the Province of Quebec has a system that embraces a part of each of two systems used in the rest of Canada.

It was in Upper Canada (later Ontario) that the first land registry office was established in Canada. August 10, 1795 to be exact.

27

Early registry offices used an alphabetical system to register title and mortgage deeds, but it became a bit cumbersome so was changed to a system using abstract (history of ownership) books where the documents were registered against lots and plans.

The registry office system with abstract books is a lulu. If it is in your area, and your property is registered there, do a title search sometime and learn what frustration really is. You will hop from page to page and book to book all over the place, and drive yourself up the wall going to the root of title to your property.

In registry offices nothing is guaranteed. For example, when property changes hands the legal practitioner acting for the purchaser will say in his closing letter that he is of the *opinion* that the title is good and marketable, but can't guarantee it.

It is in this registry system that we find the legal mortgages referred to earlier.

Well, in 1858, in South Australia a man named Robert Richard Torrens came up with an obviously better system of registration for title and mortgage deeds. The Government Land Titles Office, which guarantees title documents accepted for registration.

This system today is used in the Western Provinces, and parts of Ontario, If it is in your area, take a look. You will find everything pertaining to one parcel of property all in one place nice and neat. No jumping from book to book.

Mortgage deeds are registered against title and stamped for time and date. As a matter of fact the first mortgage recorded in Canada had the time on it — 11 a.m., April 13, 1796.

In the Registry Office the senior mortgage is the Legal mortgage, as we have discussed. All junior mortgages are equitable mortgages — the seniority being established by the time and date of registration.

In the Land Titles Office the mortgage is registered as a charge against title.

In Quebec, a Registry Office system is used which in one respect is similar to Land Titles — the mortgage is a lien (charge) against title, although no title registration is guaranteed by the Province of Quebec as in Land Titles registration.

When you pay off a mortgage, get a discharge certificate from the lender, and ensure that the discharge of the debt is recorded on title. Otherwise the mortgage registration will just stay there.

It is the lender who registers the mortgage on title, but it is up to the borrower to remove it.

10

AMORTIZATION

Amortize means to deaden.

To amortize a loan is to extinguish it my means of a sinking fund; in other words, an allowance of payments over a period of time will be made to reduce the debt to zero.

The most common method of amortizing a mortgage is to have the repayment schedule computerized to ensure that all monthly payments are identical, with each payment containing the amortized principal amount, plus interest on the outstanding balance of the loan.

To illustrate this, the following is the first year's repayment schedule of a 20-year, $20,000. loan, at 10%, compounded semi-annually, each line representing one month's payment, and each payment being exactly $190.34.

Payment Number	Interest Payment	Principal Payment	Balance of Loan
1	163.30	27.04	19972.96
2	163.08	27.26	19945.70
3	162.85	27.49	19918.21
4	162.63	27.71	19890.50
5	162.40	27.94	19862.56
6	162.17	28.17	19834.39
7	161.94	28.40	19805.99
8	161.71	28.63	19777.36
9	161.48	28.86	19748.50
10	161.24	29.10	19719.40
11	161.01	29.33	19690.07
12	160.77	29.57	19660.50

In the beginning, each payment is practically all interest. As the loan progresses, each payment contains less interest, and more principal. Each monthly payment still remains the same, with minor adjustment on the last payment (to take care of the fractions).

Note the allowances for principal payments durings the final year of this loan:

229	17.66	172.68	1989.91
230	16.25	174.09	1815.82
231	14.83	175.51	1640.31
232	13.39	176.95	1463.36
233	11.95	178.39	1284.97
234	10.49	179.85	1105.12
235	9.02	181.32	923.80
236	7.54	182.80	741.00
237	6.05	184.29	556.71
238	4.55	185.79	370.92
239	3.03	187.31	183.61
240	1.50	183.61	.00

One thing to be quite clear about is that regardless of the differences of principal and interest in each payment, the borrower only pays interest on the outstanding principal balance of the loan at the time of each payment.

As the loan progresses the borrower is making larger principal payments, because there is less principal on which to pay interest.

If this loan were amortized with equal principal payments, plus interest, this is how the monthly payments would vary:

1st month: $ 83.33 principal plus
$163.29 interest ($246.62)

120th month: $ 83.33 principal plus
$ 81.64 interest ($164.97)

240th month: $ 83.33 principal plus
$ .68 interest ($84.01)

The obvious disadvantage with this method is that the highest payments are in the beginning, when the home owner probably needs all the available money to support his family.

With rising interest rates, the only possible way to keep monthly mortgage payments down is to lengthen the amortization of the loan.

Unfortunately, this financial rubber band can be stretched just so far.

To illustrate, note what happened when National Housing Act loans were extended to a maximum amortization of 40 years:

Take a 40-year N.H.A. loan of $25,000. When one becomes a mortgagor in such a deed, a 1% insurance fee (in favour of the lender) must be added to the loan.

This produces an N.H.A. mortgage of $25,250.

Using an interest rate of 10%, compounded semi-annually, the monthly payment is $210.41.

If this loan were amortized at the previous maximum level of 35 years, the monthly payment would $213.17.

A difference of *two dollars and seventy-six cents.*

By taking advantage of this $2.76 monthly saving, the borrower will bind himself not only to a further five years in the loan, but to an additional debt of more than *eleven thousand dollars!*

And N.H.A. regulations, by allowing the interest to be adjusted every five years, could mean an even bigger difference if interest rates increase.

At this point some mathematical genius will undoubtedly point out that if the borrower invested the $2.76 each month, compounded at 10% for 40 years, he would end up with about $11,000.

However, such an investment would be highly unlikely.

The following illustrates the repayment of 30, 35 and 40-year amortized N.H.A. mortgages of $25,250, 10%, compounded semi-annually. The total amount of interest to be paid will stagger you.

	40 year loan	*35 year loan*	*30 year loan*
Monthly payment:	$ 210.41	$ 213.17	$ 217.83
Yearly cost:	2,524.92	2,558.04	2,613.96
Total cost:	100,996.80	89,531.40	78,418.80
Total interest paid:	75,746.80	64,281.40	53,168.80
Principal amount owning at end of:			
5 years	$ 24,922.78	$24,710.25	$24,351.32
10 years	24,389.79	23,831.09	22,887.47
15 years	23,521.65	22,399.00	20,502.96
20 years	22,107.55	20,066.25	16,618.85
25 years	19,804.10	16,266.45	10,292.07
30 years	16,052.00	10,077.01	
35 years	9,940.24		
40 years			

Do not confuse the *amortization* of a loan with its *term*. If one is told that a mortgage is amortized for 20 years, it must *not* be assumed that it has a 20-year term. The following chapter will explain.

11

THE MORTGAGE TERM

The term of a mortgage is the period of time a borrower has before the lender can demand the principal balance owing on the loan, subject to mortgage default by the borrower.

It is very important to clearly understand it.

A few years ago, it was a common practice of lenders to make loans for long periods of time, such as 25 years, at a fixed rate of interest.

With the shrinking value of the dollar, and the increasing yo-yo behaviour of interest rates, this did not make economic sense. Today, a mortgage with a term of more than five years is uncommon. Some of them are as short as six months.

If you were the borrower with a repayment schedule amortizing a loan over a period of 20 years, and the mortgage had a five-year term, it would mean that despite the 20-year amortization, you would have to repay the outstanding principal balance of the loan at the end of five years. Unless, of course, the lender agreed to renew the loan.

Take a look at the following table in a $20,000 loan, 9½%, compounded semi-annually, amortized over 20 years:

Principal balance owing at end of:

Year 1	$19,640	Year 11	$13,420
Year 2	19,240	Year 12	12,420
Year 3	18,820	Year 13	11,320
Year 4	18,340	Year 14	10,120
Year 5	17,820	Year 15	8,800
Year 6	17,240	Year 16	7,360
Year 7	16,620	Year 17	5,760
Year 8	15,920	Year 18	4,020
Year 9	15,160	Year 19	2,100
Year 10	14,340	Year 20	0

You will notice that in 20 years the loan will be extinguished, but here is where the five year term will grab you.

At the end of the five years, the lender wants his money, namely $17,820. To repay the loan, you probably will have to commit yourself to another mortgage, and borrow the rounded balance of $17,800. If you commit yourself for a further five-year period (same amortization and rate) this is what your outstanding balance will be over the next five years in round figures:

Year 1	$17,479
Year 2	17,123
Year 3	16,749
Year 4	16,322
Year 5	15,859

At the end of this five year period, when you have to repay the loan, you may repeat the process. We'll do this just twice more, to take us to the end of four five-year terms.

Third five years: ($15,800 loan)		Fourth five years ($14,000 loan)	
Year 1	$15,515	Year 1	$13,748
Year 2	15,199	Year 2	13,468
Year 3	14,867	Year 3	13,174
Year 4	14,488	Year 4	12,838
Year 5	14,077	Year 5	12,474

Each new five year term will result in smaller monthly payments because the principal amount of each succeeding term will be less.

If one keeps up the pattern of the five year terms by starting each new term with the outstanding principal balance of the previous one, and amortizing the loan over 20 years, it will take more than 100 years to reduce the loan to zero.

Whereas if the term of the mortgage had been 20 years, it would have been reduced to zero in that time, although the monthly payments would have remained constant (and larger) than under each renewed five year term.

If the 20 year mortgage is to be retired, or paid in full in 20 years, then each time the mortgage is renewed, the principal balance owing must be amortized for no longer a period than the remaining number of years in the original amortization.

Examine the chart and remember it.

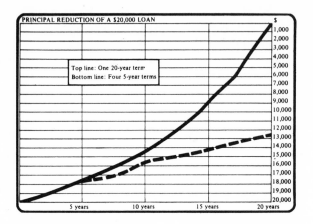

PRINCIPAL REDUCTION OF A $20,000 LOAN

Top line: One 20-year term
Bottom line: Four 5-year terms

$
1,000
2,000
3,000
4,000
5,000
6,000
7,000
8,000
9,000
10,000
11,000
12,000
13,000
14,000
15,000
16,000
17,000
18,000
19,000
20,000

5 years   10 years   15 years   20 years

12

COSTS OF ARRANGING A MORTGAGE

The two most misunderstood charges to a real estate buyer are the legal fees in obtaining a mortgage loan, and the insurance fee added to many mortgages.

A lawyer is entitles to reasonable compensation for his services, and considering the work involved in acting for a purchaser, the generally accepted tariff appears to be fair.

In acting for a purchaser, there is one necessary aspect of the lawyer's work that surely must drive some of them ''up the wall''. That is when a property is registered in a Registry Office.

In a Land Titles Office (not used east of Ontario) all title documents registered are guaranteed by the Provincial Government, but not so in the Registry Office. Hours and hours of patient sifting through abstract books can be required, going from page to page and book to book, the lawyer all the time being acutely aware that there just might be something wrong in the chain of title that will interfere with the client's enjoyment of the property at a later date.

The legal fees in acting for a purchaser can amount to about 1¼% of the cost of the average home. This is for the lawyer's services, and in addition to this, there will be adjustments to the date of closing made on such things as the municipal property taxes, hydro and water charges, insurance, and if oil heated, the cost for a full tank.

Then there will be a charge for a land transfer tax, which the Provincial Government gets.

There will be a charge made by the registry offices for every document registered. If the property covers parts of more than one lot, it costs more.

Some mortgage lenders will deduct a portion of future municipal taxes from the mortgage principal, which can be annoying to one's pocketbook, resulting in more cash to be coughed up by the buyer. Also, many mortgage lenders require an up to date survey, and if one is not available, this can cost hundreds of dollars.

Then there will be a final check made with the Sheriff's office to see if any last minute liens or charges have been made against the property, for which there will be a nominal charge.

The average buyer, after paying for much of the foregoing, can be forgiven if he finds himself in a state of shock upon being presented with an additional bill for third party mortgage charges. The following are the three basic areas of financial escalation in mortgaging costs for the borrower, and will clearly indicate just how you can save money in mortgaging.

A common method of mortgaging in buying real estate is for the purchaser to ''assume'' an existing mortgage, one already registered against the property. The one assuming the mortgage is agreeing to basically maintain the payments and be jointly responsible for the debt with the one who originally signed the mortgage deed.

Assuming a mortgage when buying real estate normally incurs no extra financial charges to the buyer — it is already there.

Another method is for the seller to agree to ''take back'' a mortgage from the purchaser for part of the purchase price. This is another cheap way to get a mortgage.

Such a mortgage has several advantages. It requires no credit check of the borrower, no appraisal fees to be paid by the borrower, smaller legal fees than other mortgaging, instant knowledge that the ''mortgage application'' has been approved, and in many cases can be secured at a lower rate than third party mortgages, with longer terms. Furthermore, they ususaly have ''open'' repayment privileges.

The most expensive method of mortgaging is a for a purchaser to arrange a mortgage from a third party, such as a bank, insurance or trust company.

Charging an inspection fee of about $75 does not seem unreasonable, but the financial crunch comes when a lawyer presents his bill for legal fees and disbursements.

Legal tariffs in mortgaging can be just as much proportionately as they are for services in closing the purchase. The reason for this is that many of the services performed in mortgaging are identical to services in closing. For the lender's protection, the title must be searched in the same manner, right down to a last minute visit to the sheriff's office.

Lending institutions usually prefer to retain the services of their own approved lawyers, which is understandable. This results in a complete job being done in the title search, etc., in addition to the one done by the purchaser's lawyer for closing purposes. Result — the additional fee.

If a purchaser is fortunate enough to have his own lawyer do the legal work in the third party mortgage, the combined fee for mortgaging and closing will undoubtedly be much less than the separate fees of two lawyers. It therefore follows that it can be advisable for a purchaser to determine what lawyers will be acting for the mortgage lender, and retain him to also close the purchase.

Or better still, have one's own lawyer arrange for the funds through a lender who will allow him to act in the mortgage.

One thing to keep in mind is that the mortgagee (lender) pays for absolutely nothing, with the exception of a small charge for registering the mortgage. The borrower pays all costs, the simple reason being that if the lender paid for any part of it, his investment would be "watered down". When a lender advances money at 10 percent he wants 10 percent, and he *gets* 10 percent.

The second puzzling charge confronting a borrower is the mortgage insurance fee. This charge is found in two type of mortgages, National Housing Act loans and loans insured by the Mortgage Insurance Company of Canada, for example.

When a mortgage is obtained that amounts to no more than 75 percent of the value of the property, it is generally accepted that there is sufficient equity in the property to require no monetary insurance.

But when the loan amounts to as much as 95 percent of the purchase price, it is understandable for the lender to consider that the borrower, having a 5 percent equity in the property is a risk that requires additional assurance that the loan will be secure. This assurance is realized by having the loan completely insured, and the borrower pays the premium.

The insurance premium is not normally paid for directly out of the borrower's pocket. It is added to the principal amount of the loan and the total will be registered principal sum in the mortgage deed, although M.I.C.C. will accept a direct payment. The lender then sends a cheque matching the premium to the insurer, Central Mortgage and Housing Corporation, or the Mortgage Insurance Company of Canada.

If the loan is repaid before the mortgage term expires there is no provision for any rebate of the insurance premium.

Regardless of the source of mortgage funds, the lender will require the borrower to have the security adequately covered by property insurance. It is mandatory, written into the mortgage deed, and paid for by the borrower.

Summary . . . Consider the following:

(a) **Property where there is a mortgage already registered at current rates or lower. If you can't come up with the cash to the mortgage, see if the vendor will hold a second at a reasonable rate of interest.**

(b) Property where the vendor will take back a mortgage for a large part of the purchase price.

(c) If you must go to a third party for a mortgage, retain the mortgagee's lawyer to close your purchase, or have your lawyer act for the mortgagee (lender) if possible.

(d) Be wary of short term mortgages that have to replaced. It can be expensive.

13

AVERAGING THE INTEREST RATE

If you wish to know what your annual rate of interest is on a combination of mortgages, here is how to do it:

Take the per cent of each mortgage to the total debt (of 100%) and multiply by its rate of interest. viz:

Example		*Principal Amount*
1st mortgage:	8%	$16,000
2nd mortgage:	14%	4,000
Total mortgage debt:		$20,000

$$\frac{16,000}{20,000} \times \frac{100}{1} = 80\% \times 8\% = 6.4\%$$

$$\frac{4,000}{20,000} \times \frac{100}{1} = 20\% \times 14\% = 2.8\%$$

Total: *100% (average)*   9.2%

Example		*Principal Amount*
1st mortgage:	8.25%	$12,544
2nd mortgage:	10.50%	3,724
3rd mortgage:	13.00%	3,332
Total mortgage debt:		$19,600

$$\frac{12,544}{19,600} \times \frac{100}{1} = 64\% \times 8.25\% = 5.280\%$$

$$\frac{3,724}{19,600} \times \frac{100}{1} = 19\% \times 10.50\% = 1.995\%$$

$$\frac{3,332}{19,600} \times \frac{100}{1} = 17\% \times 13.00\% = 2.210\%$$

Total: *100% (average)*   9.485%

(Sometimes you're not as bad off as you think you are . . .)

Here is another way to do it. Follow the figures I have given you in the second example, and round out the interest on an annual basis:

	Principal			Interest
1st mortgage:	$12,544.	@	8.25%	$1,034.88
2nd mortgage:	3,724.	@	10.50%	391.12
3rd mortgage:	3,332.	@	13.00%	433.16
	$19,600.			$1,859.16

Now, just divide the interest by the principal and multiply by one hundred:

$$\frac{1,859.16}{19,600.00} \times \frac{100}{1} = 9.485\%$$

Same thing, see?

14

A COSTLY ERROR
IN PRIVATE MORTGAGING

In mortgaging done by conventional lenders such as banks and trust companies, the mortgage deed will contain a statement showing that the interest is compounded twice-yearly. This automatically complies with the Federal Interest Act, which states:

"Whenever any principal money or interest secured by mortgage of real estate is, by the mortgage, made payable on the sinking fund plan, or on any plan under which the payments of principal money and interest are blended, or on any plan that involves an allowance of interest on stipulated repayments, no interest whatever shall be chargeable, payable or recoverable, on any part of the principal money advanced, unless the mortgage contains a statement showing the amount of such principal money and the rate of interest chargeable thereon, calculated yearly or half-yearly, not in advance."

I would not think that the foregoing reference to a "statement" means that it must be shown in total in one paragraph in the mortgage deed. A statement means "something stated", and I would assume that providing the information required is *somewhere* in the mortgage deed, it would qualify as being stated. So the conventional lenders ensure that their deeds comply by having it printed as a part of their forms.

In private mortgaging, it is quite common to find that although the mortgage deeds naturally state the annual rate of interest in the loan, no mention is made of any frequency of compounding, or calculating the interest. Most of these private mortgages require monthly payments, and this is where a costly error may be found.

To arrive at the interest to be paid for the period (month) the lender quite often simply divides the annual rate of interest by twelve. Which isn't right, if the mortgage is to comply with the Interest Act. After all, dividing the annual rate by twelve means that the interest is being compounded monthly. A mortgage showing an annual rate of 12% would not comply

41

with the Act if the interest were compounded monthly, producing a rate of 1% per month.

This error arises in mortgages that require the payment to be blended — as $200. per month, including principal and interest, for example.

Take a $12,000. 12% mortgage, payments $200. each month. I @ P.

If the lender divides by twelve to arrive at the interest to be paid for the first month, here is what we see:

$$\frac{12\%}{12} = 1\% \text{ of } \$12,000. = \$120. \text{ interest}$$

The payment will therefore be $120. interest and the balance, $80., credited to principal.

The second month will show that the principal balance owing is $12,000. less $80., or $11,920. Here is the second month's breakdown:

$$\frac{12\%}{12} = 1\% \text{ of } \$11,920. = \$119.20 \text{ interest}$$

The payment will therefore be $119.20 interest and the balance, $80.80, credited to principal.

Still with me? Now, if this mortgage interest were compounded yearly, here is what the first month would show, breaking down the $200. payment:

$12,000. × 0.948879 = $113.86 interest, and the balance of the payment ($86.14) would be credited to principal.

The borrower, in the foregoing example of compounding monthly, pays $6.14, or 5.39% more than he should, in one payment alone!

The interest factor of 0.948879 was obtained from the tables in this book, which can come in quite handy.

Examine your mortgage deeds carefully. As a borrower, you just might save a bundle, and as a lender, you just might save yourself a headache.

15

MORTGAGE ACCELERATION SAVINGS

Mortgage payment acceleration is one of the greatest means available today to force oneself to save money.

The example used is a repayment schedule of the first 12 months of a 40-year National Housing Act 10% mortgage loan of $25,000 (plus 1% insurance fee which must be added to the loan), with each payment being $210.41.

Payment No.	Interest	Principal	Balance Owing
1	$206.16	$4.25	$25,245.75
2	206.13	4.28	25,241.47
3	206.09	4.32	25,237.15
4	206.06	4.35	25,232.80
5	206.02	4.39	25,228.41
6	205.99	4.42	25,223.99
7	205.95	4.46	25,219.53
8	205.91	4.50	25,215.03
9	205.88	4.53	25,210.50
10	205.84	4.57	25,205.93
11	205.80	4.61	25,201.32
12	205.76	4.65	25,196.67

When a mortgagor reaches the 12th payment of this loan he has the privilege of paying an additional amount of principal, not in excess of 10% of the original amount of the mortgage.

The additional payment made under this privilege is not made in a round figure such as exactly $100. It is a payment that will reach a future balance of the loan. For example, the principal balance owing at payment No. 32 is $25,095.36.

The difference between the balance owing at the 12th payment and the balance owing at the 32 payment is $101.31. By paying the lender this amount, 20 payments of $210.41 each are eliminated. This amounts to $4,208.20.

The chart illustrates the savings that can be effected by making various additional mortgage principal payments at the end of the first year.

Additional Payment	No. of Payments Eliminated	Payment Dollars Eliminated	Balance Owing	Time Left on Mortgage
$101.31	20	$ 4,208.20	$25,095.36	37 yrs., 4 mos.
201.38	37	7,785.17	24,995.29	35 yrs., 11 mos.
301.91	52	10,941.32	24,894.76	34 yrs., 8 mos.
407.48	66	13,887.06	24,789.19	33 yrs., 6 mos.
508.04	78	16,411.98	24,688.63	32 yrs., 6 mos.

16

PAYING OFF THE MORTGAGE

There are four types of repayment privileges in mortgages in mortgage deeds — your mortgage will conform to one of them:

Corporate Borrowers

The Interest Act precludes any prepayment privileges in a mortgage where the borrower is a joint stock company or other corporation, and in any debenture issued by any such company or corporation.

If the mortgage is one with a 20-year term, the mortgagor is bound to its deed for 20 years.

However, if the lender wishes to allow the borrower to repay the loan before its maturity, it is his privilege to do so. This can be written into the deed, or otherwise negotiated.

If the prevailing interest rates at the time of a request to discharge such a mortgage are much higher than the rate in the mortgage, this would probably create no problem. The lender would obviously be glad to have his money returned in order to re-invest it at a higher rate of interest.

Conventional Loans

Here I refer to loans made by such corporations as insurance and trust companies, banks, and other large lenders in loans other than N.H.A. mortgages.

Again the Interest Act applies. Whenever any mortgage is not payable until a time of more than five years after the date of a mortgage (a mortgage with a term of more than 5 years) the borrower is entitled to repay the principal balance owing at any time after the first 5 years.

With this prepayment, an additional interest charge equal to 3 months interest of the mortgage balance is to be made.

The Interest Act states that the balance may be paid in such circumstances ''together with three month's further interest *in lieu of notice*''.

One might assume that if a borrower gave the lender 3 month's notice of his intention to repay the loan, no additional interest would be required. But with no guarantee that the borrower will in fact repay the mortgage in three months, such notice is not acceptable by lenders, and the additional interest must be paid.

National Housing Act Loans

There are two basic types of N.H.A. loans. The ''direct'' loans made by Central Mortgage and Housing Corporation, and loans made by approved lenders of C.M.H.C.

If the mortgage money comes directly from C.M.H.C., the prepayment privileges are very generous. At any time after the date of the mortgage, the borrower may repay any or all of the principal balance owing at any time without paying any interest penalty.

If the mortgage money comes from an approved lender of C.M.H.C. and the loan is not in default (i.e., payments have been kept up to date), the borrower has the privilege of paying an additional amount of principal, not in excess of 10% of the original amount of the mortgage, on the first anniversary of the date for adjustment of interest (when the mortgage is one year old).

A similar amount of principal may be paid on the second anniversary date. In each case, three months' interest must be paid on the amount of any such additional payment — these two repayment privileges are not cumulative.

When the mortgage is three years old, and on any monthly installment date thereafter, the borrower may repay the whole amount owing, or any part of it, together with three months' additional interest on any such additional payment.

''Open'' Mortgages

It is quite common for a property owner to accept a mortgage as part of the purchase price of the property he is selling.

The majority of the ''purchase mortgages'' will contain a clause allowing the mortgagor to pay any part (or all) of the mortgage at any time, or on any payment date, without requiring the borrower to pay any interest penalty.

The obvious reason is that the lender would be delighted to get his money.

In addition to the above, of course, conventional and private lenders can (and often do) insert additional repayment clauses in deeds.

Paying the Mortgage Off Early

If one is a mortgagor with a 5 year term mortgage and wishes to pay it off at the end of year one, what then?

The lender can really sock it to the borrower because the debt plus interest has another four years to go. However, not all lenders are ogres, and the most common penalty I have found is such cases is six months' interest.

Why Pay Off The Mortgage?

This question has often come up. A mortgagor has about $20,000. principal balance owing on a mortgage which has not reached the end of its term.

A repayment privilege is that it can be repaid at any time without notice or bonus.

Now, the mortgagor finds himself with a financial windfall and wonders if he should leave the mortgage alone, or pay it off.

The answer is a matter of simple arthmetic: Let us assume that:

(a) The rate of interest in the $20,000. mortgage is 9%

(b) The mortgagor could safely invest his money at 10%

Investing $20,000. at 10% produces a round $2,000. annually.

The current income tax regulations allow $1,000. of interest income to be tax-free, leaving $1,000. of the $2,000. subject to tax.

If one is in a 40% tax bracket, the Government will take $400. of this, which will leave a tax free net income of $1,600. on the investment.

$1,600. is 8% of $20,000.

So, in this example, one would receive a net return of 8%, and pay the mortgage at 9%, which would cost money. If the mortgage were paid off with the $20,000. there would obviously be a saving.

Take the same example with a $50,000 mortgage, at 9%, and a $50,000. investment at 10%.

Return @ 10%	$5,000.
Taxable: $4,000. @ 40%	1,600.
Net return on $50,000. investment:	$3,400.

Now, the picture is a little bleaker. The net sum of $3,400. represents a return of 6.8%, or less than 7% on the $50,000. investment.

The money comes in at about 7%, and goes out at 9%. Obviously, this is going to cost about $1,000. a year right out of the mortgagor's pocket, so the mortgage should certainly be paid off.

The principal consideration here should be — what would you do with the money if you didn't pay off the mortgage? Could it be used to better advantage? Possibly buy some realty, or an old masterpiece?

The choice is yours, but if it is a matter of weighing invested capital to produce a fixed return, use the foregoing examples to fit your own particular circumstances, and the answer to the question will be quite clear to you.

17

RENEWING THE MORTGAGE

For years the mortgagor has been doing his best to keep up the payments on the loan, and now the mortgage is nearing the end of its term. This is when the mortgage must be paid off, replaced or renewed.

Well, most of us can't pay if off, so that's out.

Replacing it with a new mortgage from a different lender can be costly. A new set of fees all around, so we logically look to the lender in our present mortgage deed.

If one has a record of making payments on time, or reasonably so, there will be no problem with large institutional lenders. However, many borrowers have been late with a payment or two or more, and some may have even gone through the traumatic experience of a court action, or something approaching it. Such things will naturally make one feel that the lender will be most reluctant to renew the loan — but not necessarily.

One of the advantages of doing business with a large lender such as a bank is that this lender likes to keep a high profile in its public image, plus the fact that it is in business to make money, and therefore it will be reasonable in assessing renewal.

I know of one borrower who had a record of being consistently late in making mortgage payments to a bank, although the payments were always brought up to date eventually. This borrower began wondering about the chances of renewal when, one day, about 6 weeks before the term expiry, an offer from the lender to renew the loan was received in the mail. Right out of the blue, and most welcome. Here is how it was handled:

The lender, in assessing the loan, naturally knew of all the late payments, but it also knew that they were brought up to date. So it offered to renew the mortgage loan at a rate ¼ of one per cent *above* the rate it would have charged if the borrower had made his payments on time.

The renewal had a face value of about $38,000. which meant, in round figures, that the ¼% increase carried an additional cost of close to a hundred dollars a year. The total cost over a five year term would be just about what the costs of *replacing* the mortgage would be, so the borrower accepted it. The only other additional cost was a reasonable $30. administrative charge.

If this borrower had had a first class record of payments, the cost renewal of this mortgage loan would have been just $30., and at the prevailing rate at the time of renewal. Stick with your present lender if you can — you will probably save money.

With offers of renewal from large lenders there are options available, such as a reduction in the amount of renewal, or possibly an increased amount.

An agreement for a penalty-free mortgage may be obtained for agreeing to pay ¼% *above* that offered in the renewal agreement.

This means that during the life of the term (usually five years) the borrower can make additional lump sum payments to reduce the debt, without being charged an interest penalty. This is worth considering, and is simply a matter of arithmetic. The savings could be substantial if one wished to pay off the entire loan before maturity, which normally could be very costly.

If one wished to have a reduced term in the loan, such as three years, it will probably be available at ¼% *less* than one with a five year term.

Also, mortgage debt insurance can be instantly available covering the life of the mortgagor, reasonably, and without a medical. The insurance payment is made with the monthly loan payment.

The foregoing is what one can expect from large corporate lenders. But what about those ''private'' mortgages?

That's where you take your chances on renewal, unless it is written into the mortgage deed.

One thing to remember in renewal: Ensure that the *amortization* of the renewal loan does not exceed the remaining number of years in the original loan. Otherwise, you'll never get it paid off.

18

BUYING A MORTGAGE

The most common mortgages bought and sold are the ''second'' mortgages. There is no mystery about them and they are, if properly purchased, a sound and profitable investment.

Before buying one, however, there are a few guidelines to follow to help one arrive at not only a sensible decision about which one to buy, but also to ensure that the price is right!

The four prime areas that require scrutiny are (1) the real estate used as security, (2) the equity in the property, (3) the covenant, or the ability of the mortgagor (borrower) to repay the loan and (4) the details of the mortgage terms.

Whenever a mortgagee (lender) is asked to loan money, the property involved will be inspected and appraised to ensure that there is sufficient tangible security for the loan. The mortgagor pays for the inspection.

In considering the purchase of second mortgages one cannot very well have an appraisal done on all the real estate involved. This would require a fee to be paid for each mortgage considered.

The alternative is for the mortgage purchaser to inspect the property himself. In this inspection, it is wise to carefully check not only the condition of the building, but also to note how the title holder (owner) is maintaining it.

Regardless of any documents produced to show evidence of what the current market value of the property is, the mortgage purchaser should, if possible, make comparisons and inspect properties that are offered for sale in the same area that are of a similar plan and size to the one secured by the mortgage.

Also, check with the hydro authority, municipal buildings department and registry office to see if there are any outstanding work orders issued against the property. If there are, the work will have to be done, and the cost of repairs or renovations must be considered in the value.

Mortgage seniority is established by the time and date of registering

50

the mortgage deed. A second mortgage ranks second, so that the mortgagee of first priority has first claim to the dollar value of the security.

Other, but junior mortgages may be registered against the property, but the second mortgage will take precedence over these.

The equity in a property is its market value, less the total amount of all mortgages and other financial charges registered against the property. It is therefore important to know something about the mortgagor and his ability to repay the loan, because his only stake in the property is this equity.

If there is very little equity, it does not necessarily mean that the mortgagor will be any more lax in his payments than one with a larger equity, but regardless of the tangible security, a mortgagee likes to have some reasonable assurance that the debt is going to be paid, and paid according to contract.

The financial decision in purchasing a second mortgage must be based on two prime factors: (1) the rate of interest, and (2) the terms of the loan.

Second mortgages, having a secondary position, normally require a higher rate of return than first mortgages. If the current rate of interest, for example, is 14% on secondary financing, then the rate in the mortgage considered must be adjusted acccordingly.

The hard-headed mortgage buyer will demand it, and a rule of thumb method of rapid calculation will be:

Assuming the rate of interest on an existing second mortgage is 9%, and one wishes to have it produce 14%, the 5% difference will be multiplied by the number of years remaining in the term of the mortgage, or to its maturity, when the principal balance is due and payable.

The result will be the discount at which he will purchase the mortgage. Some illustrations are shown in the chart.

By purchasing a mortgage in this manner, two obvious bonuses will be secured: (1) the additional interest extracted from the mortgage is obtained in advance and (2) this additional interest is based on the present outstanding principal balance of the mortgage, and not on a reducing balance which occurs as the loan payments progress.

Examples of One Method Mortgage Buyers Use in Discounting Second Mortgages

Mortgage Principal	Rate of Interest	Interest Required	Difference	Mortgage Term	Discount
$2,000.00	10%	14%	4%	3 years	12% ($ 240)
3,000.00	9%	15%	6%	4 years	24% ($ 720)
4,000.00	8%	13%	5%	5 years	25% ($1000)
5,000.00	10%	14%	4%	2 years	8% ($ 400)

To know the *exact* price one should pay for a mortgage to produce a specific yield, write to *Consumers Computer Limited,* Box 400, Willowdale, Ontario. A tailor-made analysis will be made for you for a few dollars. If you are *selling* a mortgage, it is also important to obtain an accurate market valuation of the mortgage. Don't sell it for anything less than you have to. The foregoing illustrations are not precisely accurate, and are used only as a rough guide to illustrate discounting.

REMEMBER THIS: If you are going to be a mortgagee in a purchase mortgage with the intention of selling it, keep the interest rate as close as possible to current market rates, and the term down to three years if possible.

19

CANADA'S NATIONAL HOUSING ACT

Canada's federal government has been involved in housing development since the depths of the depression.

In 1935, the Dominion Housing Act was passed, principally as a means of providing jobs, but also to help improve the quality of Canadian housing and to establish building standards.

Under the Dominion Housing Act, the federal government provided one-quarter of the money for high-ratio mortgages with private lenders providing the balance. The objective was to make it easier for people to build and buy houses by supplying bigger mortgages — and make possible smaller down payments than would be available from private lenders.

Between 1935 and 1938, about 5,000 new houses were put up with the financing provided in part under the Dominion Housing Act.

Then, in 1938, the first Act was replaced with the new National Housing Act which provided more mortgage money and which, for the first time, offered loan assistance for the construction of housing for low-income families.

But the federal government really didn't come into its own in the housing field until the Second World War. Housing starts fell off during the war, so when hostilities ended there was an enormous backlog of demand. To help meet this demand, a new National Housing Act was passed in 1945.

Central Mortgage and Housing Coporation, a Crown Corporation, put up 17,000 new houses for veterans and took over ownership of all other wartime housing so that, by 1949, the government agency owned 41,000 houses. Most of these wartime houses have since been sold to former tenants.

Under the 1945 National Housing Act, postwar housing construction entered a real boom period. In the early years, lots of private money also was available for mortgage financing. Canada's output rose from 64,400 new houses in 1946 to 92,350 in 1950, when almost half of the year's total production was financed under N.H.A.

By the early fifties, however, private mortgage money sources began to dry up — the boom had been so explosive that most "conventional" money was fully committed.

So in 1954 the National Housing Act was again overhauled, this time establishing a system of insurance of N.H.A. mortgages so that these mortgages became an attractive alternative to bonds as long-term investments. Under this system, the full amount of the mortgage was provided by a private lender and the government guaranteed, first 98%, and finally the full loan amount (the borrower paid the insurance fee that provided this guarantee). In this way the government for a while stopped actually lending money, except as a last resort, for housing and simply made it 100% safe for private lenders to provide the funds.

At around the same time, the Bank Act was changed so that, for the first time, the chartered banks were allowed to make long-term mortgage loans. This provided tremendous new funds for home building.

By 1958 the number of housing starts in Canada had risen to the unprecedented total of 164,000.

Since then things have become more difficult for builders and buyers alike. Land costs, wages and materials have all risen, driving the price of new houses up, to say nothing of rising interest rates.

Because the banks were limited by law to charging 6% interest, they virtually stopped putting money into N.H.A. mortgages in 1959 when rates started rising. The other lenders, life insurance and trust and loan companies, still had money to put into mortgages, but they put more and more into higher-paying private mortgages, less into the low-paying N.H.A. variety.

So, although housing starts reached an all-time record of 166,565 in 1965, the supply of private money for mortgages began to dwindle away.

To keep the industry going and to put roofs over Canadians' heads, the Government changed the Bank Act again to allow the banks to lend mortgage money at interest rates higher than 6%. Even more significantly, the government has pumped vast amounts of public money directly into housing as private funds started staying away. By 1967, the federal government was holding, through C.M.H.C., about three *billion* dollars worth of mortgages.

During the past few years further amendments were made to the Act, and today the help provided by C.M.H.C. is varied and extensive. Here are the current provisions for home ownership loans:

The down payment must be within your financial means and the monthly payments on your mortgage plus municipal taxes and other continuing charges such as heat, electricity, maintenance costs, (and condominium

54

cost, where applicable) should be covered comfortably by your housing budget. Whether you build or buy your new or existing home the financing terms and conditions will be the same.

NHA Loans

National Housing Act loans are available for the purchase of a newly-built home or the purchase and improvement (if required) of an existing dwelling.

The type of dwelling that may be bought or improved includes a single-detached house, a unit of row housing, a duplex, a unit in a condominium or one or both units of a semi-detached dwelling. Cooperative housing associations wishing to purchase new or existing housing projects may also obtain NHA loans.

Loans may also be made to builders for the construction of houses for sale or for financing houses acquired as 'trade ins' which are to be resold to a buyer who intends to occupy the dwelling. The buyer makes a down-payment to the builder and assumes responsibility for repayment of the mortgage.

Types of NHA Loans

● *Approved Lender Loans*

The National Housing Act provides for loans by approved lenders. These are private companies such as chartered banks, life insurance companies and trust and loan companies authorized by the Federal Government to lend under the terms of the Act. A list of these companies is available from any Central Mortgage and Housing Corporation office.

● *Direct Loans*

Direct Loans from CMHC are available only in those areas not normally serviced by approved lenders. For information regarding your particular locality, you should discuss your requirements with the nearest office of CMHC.

Loan Amount

The amount of loan you may obtain will depend on the "lending value" of your property, the maximum loan permitted and your annual income.

Lending value is the value of your proposed house and lot as established by CMHC. The lending value for mortgage purpose is not necessarily equal to the actual price of the house.

Loan maximums are established by the Corporation on a local or regional basis. The maximum loan available in any particular area may be obtained from the local office of CMHC serving that area.

As a general guide, annual payments to be made for principal and interest on your loan and for municipal taxes and 50 per cent of condominium fees, if applicable, should not exceed 30 per cent of your annual income. In establishing your total annual income, the lender may consider a portion or all of the income of your spouse.

Cash Requirements

You will have to provide a down payment equal to the difference between the NHA loan and the total cost of your house and lot. The minimum requirement, 5 per cent of the lending value, must come from your own resources. If you cannot provide the total in cash, the amount in excess of the 5 per cent minimum may be borrowed from other sources only if the repayment, when combined with your mortgage payment, does not exceed 30 per cent of your income. If you already own your building lot its value will reduce your cash requirements as will the value of any labor you plan to do on your new home.

Interest Rate

The interest rate for loans made by approved lenders is negotiable between the borrower and lender.

Taxes

Under NHA arrangements, your monthly payment to the lender includes an amount equal to one-twelfth of the estimated annual taxes on your home.

When you receive your tax bill from the municipality you forward it to your lender for payment. Some lenders arrange with the municipality to have tax bills sent direct to them for payment and then mail the receipted bill to the home owner.

The monthly amounts collected are based on an estimate of your taxes for the year ahead. Where taxes prove to be higher or lower than the estimated amount, the lender will adjust the tax portion of your monthly payment accordingly.

Repayment of Loan

Most NHA loans, are made on a five-year term basis with the repayment amortized over a period of 25 to 40 years. For this type of loan the interest rate and related monthly mortgage payments will be constant for five years after which the borrower must renegotiate the interest rate with his lender. Monthly mortgage payments will then be adjusted to reflect the new interest rate.

Some NHA loans are however arranged with a repayment term of from 25 years to as long as 40 years.

Prepayment of Loan

After you have made 36 regular monthly payments you may pay off all or part of the balance owing on your loan. At the time of the 12th and 24th payments you may make a prepayment of not more than 10 percent of the original loan amount. Whenever prepayments are made your lender may ask for a three months' interest bonus on the amount paid off in advance. Any prepayments you make will, of course, reduce the amount of interest charges on your mortgage loan, and without altering the monthly payments, will reduce the repayment period.

Application for Loan

A loan application cannot be approved if work has gone beyond the first floor joist (including subfloor) stage of construction for one and two-unit houses. Application should be made to one of the approved lenders.

Application Fee

An application fee of $35 must accompany your application to the lender. If your loan is not approved, the fee will be refunded. It will also be returned if requested within 30 days, if the amount of loan approved is smaller or the term shorter than you applied for and you wish to cancel you application. Should you cancel the application for any other reason the fee is not refunded.

Mortgage Insurance Fee

All NHA approved lenders and CMHC are insured against loss on the loans they make through the operation of a Mortgage Insurance Fund established under the authority of the act. The fee, usually one per cent of loan principal, is included in the loan amount.

Insurance of this type must not be confused with mortgage life insurance which provides for payment of the outstanding balance in case of death of the mortgagor. Mortgage life insurance, if desired, may be obtained from most life insurance companies or arranged through your lender.

Other Charges

In addition to the application fee and mortgage insurance fee, the approved lender may deduct from your loan, or bill you for costs involved in obtaining a surveyor's certificate or its equivalent showing the location of your house on the lot, and for legal work performed for the lender. You will also be required to pay the accumulated interest on mortgage advances made during construction.

Start of Construction

It is a condition of loans under NHA that a construction stage inspection be requested within four months of approval of the loan.

Loan Advances

Construction of your house may be started when your loan has been approved. The loan will be advanced to you in at least four instalments as the house reaches various stages of construction. The amount of each advance is based on the percentage of work completed.

Inspections

While your house is being built, CMHC will make a number of construction inspections. These are NOT full architectural or engineering inspections. They are made to protect the investment of the lender by ensuring that your house is built in reasonable conformity with the plans and specifications and the housing standards prescribed by CMHC. They also serve to check construction progress for the purpose of loan advances.

Home Buyer Assistance Programs

Assistance programs involving payment reduction loans and the recently-introduced Graduated Payment Mortgage loans, are available in most areas in Canada. To determine what may be availabe to you from either federal or provincial resources check with the CMHC office nearest to the area in which you plan to buy or build.

20

THE HIGH-RATIO MORTGAGE

Prior to 1964, a Canadian buying a house under conventional mortgaging had to come up with either one third of the value of the house and a lot in cash or put down less cash and assume, or obtain, a second mortgage. This second mortgage usually carried a fairly high rate of interest.

Consequently, many were unable to realize their dreams of owning their own home. In 1964, high-ratio mortgages became available and the picture changed dramatically. For six years, until 1970, variations and refinements made the high-ratio mortgage an important part of the housing scene.

In March of 1970, amendments to the Canadian and British Insurance Companies Act, the Foreign Insurance Companies Act, the Trust Companies Act, and the Loan Companies Act were passed by the Parliament of Canada. Lending institutions operating under this legislation, as well as the chartered banks, are now authorized to make mortgage loans over 75% of value provided the excess is insured by a policy of mortgage insurance, issued by an insurance company registered under the Canadian and British Insurance Companies Act. The Mortgage Insurance Company of Canada (M.I.C.C.) leads the field in providing such a service.

In 1973 the private mortgage insurance industry expanded with the creation of two other companies, the Sovereign Mortgage Insurance Company and Insmor Mortgage Insurance Company. These companies merged in 1977 to form Insmor Holdings Limited which subsequently merged with M.I.C.C. Investments at the end of 1981. M.I.C.C. is the sole remaining private mortgage insurer in Canada.

Since 1964, more than 400,000 families have bought their own home using the M.I.C.C. insured high-ratio mortgage plan. Under this plan, the mortgage lender is insured against loss in the event of default by the purchaser.

Using an M.I.C.C. high-ratio mortgage, a house may be purchased with as little as 10% down to one 90% mortgage. The loan amount obtainable is based on a formula as follows:

90% of the first $80,000 of value
80% above $80,000 of value

A mortgage insurance premium is payable by the borrower. It does not have to be paid in cash, but may be added to the mortgage, the current premium being .9% of the loan amount to 60% of value, 1.2% from 60 to 75% of value, and 1.5% over 75% of value. These rates apply to a 20-year policy paid on a one-time basis. In addition, M.I.C.C. offers renewable policies at the option of the lender. These short-term (one- to five-year) policies have lower premium rates.

The following example illustrates loan amounts, homeowner equity, and mortgage insurance premium:

Home Value: $100,000	
90% of $80,000	$72,000
80% of $20,000	$16,000
Mortgage available:	$88,000
Insurance Premium of 1.5%	1,320
Total mortgage:	$89,320
Home Value	$100,000
Less Total Mortgage	89,320
Cash Equity Required	$10,680

M.I.C.C. high-ratio mortgages are available to finance the purchase of a new or existing home, to finance the construction of a new home for sale or occupancy, and to refinance an existing mortgage to obtain cash, consolidate existing housing debt, or carry out home improvements. The interest rate on such a mortgage today, all across Canada, is generally the going market rate of interest on conventional loans. There is a complete lack of red tape, and no special procedures are involved. The low down payments make buying easier. The larger mortgage amount also makes selling easier, should the homeowner decide to move.

The advent of the insured high-ratio mortgage has opened up the housing market to a large number of Canadians who could not save the large down payment required, or who were unwilling to or unable to pay the high interest rates demanded on many second mortgages. Thousands of homeowners would undoubtedly be still paying rent, unable to enjoy the pride of ownership of their homes if it were not for this service.

High house prices and high interest rates make it difficult for some, and impossible for others, to buy. Home ownership has never, except for a fortunate few, been easily attained. Land costs, labour costs, interest rates, and house prices will no more return to levels of the part than will the costs of autos, hamburgers, or golf balls. However, we can hope that items making up the end price of housing will stabilize, perhaps even ease somewhat. We can also hope that items such as mortgage interest rates, which affect the carrying costs of housing, moderate as inflation eases.

Most mortgage lenders follow the general rule that a borrower should not commit himself to pay more than 30% of his gross salary for his mortgage payments and taxes.

Example:　　　Gross monthly income:　　$1,500.
　　　　　　　　　　　　30%　　　　　　450.
or 32% if space heating costs are included

Therefore, someone with an income of $1,500. a month (before deductions) should normally not pay more than $450. per month on his mortgage, including taxes. The lender also looks at the borrower's other debts, credit rating etc. when reviewing a mortgage application. A portion or all of the spouse's income can be used, depending on stability and quality of income.

When the affordable monthly payment has been worked out, the affordable mortgage can be determined. Assume that the monthly payment is $495. and taxes are $75. per month. The amount available for mortgage principle and interest is then $420. a month. What amount of mortgage will payments of $420. a month repay?

At an interest rate of 15%, an amount of $12.46 per month would repay $1,000. in 25 years. Assuming that you can obtain a mortgage at 15% on a 25-year repayment plan, then $420. per month would handle a mortgage of:

$$\frac{\$420.}{12.46} \quad X \quad \$1,000. \quad = \quad \$33,708.$$

Application for a high-ratio mortgage loan is made in the normal way to any M.I.C.C. approved lender (i.e. banks, trust companies, credit unions, life insurance companies, savings and loan companies, caisses populaires).

At the end of this chapter there is a list of services offered by M.I.C.C.

For detailed information of this service to homebuyers available from coast to coast in Canada, write to:

The Mortgage Insurance Company of Canada
Suite 1600, Box 12
Eaton Tower
1 Dundas St. West
Toronto, Ontario
M5G 1Z3

MICC MORTGAGE INSURANCE PROGRAMS

	First Mortgages			Second Mortgages		
	Homeownership & Vacation Properties	Rental Projects	Commercial, Industrial & Farm Properties	Homeownership & Vacation Properties	Rental Projects	Commercial, Industrial
Application fees (1)	$75.00 per loan	¼ of 1%, minimum $300	¼ of 1%, minimum $300	Same as for 1st mortgage	Same as for 1st mortgage	Same as for 1st mortgage
Maximum loan to value ratio (2)	90% of first $80,000 of value 80% above $80,000 of value	85%, but negotiated on a deal basis	85%, but negotiated on a deal basis	Same as for 1st mortgage	Same as for 1st mortgage	Same as for 1st mortgage
Maximum loan Premiums (3)	Nil .9% to 60% of value 1.2% to 60-75% of value 1.5% over 75% of value	Nil 2% for a 5-year policy, increasing by ¼ of 1% for each additional 5-year period up to a total of 20 years	Nil	Nil Same as for 1st mortgage	Nil	Nil
Insurance of progress advances	Yes	Yes	Yes	No	No	No

1. Normally paid by the borrower.
2. Refers to the maximum allowable ratio of 1st and 2nd mortgage in relation to value of real estate.
3. Normally paid by the borrower.
   First mortgages — Single premium based on loan amount.
   Second mortgages — Single premium based on total of outstanding balance of first and second mortgage, subject to maximum as indicated.

63

21

THE EXISTING MORTGAGE

This mortgage is already there, registered against the property. Without reference to interest rates, it is the cheapest way to get a mortgage.

When purchasing property that already has a mortgage registered against it, which the buyer would like to use in financing the purchase, a part of the purchase agreement would say something like ''the purchaser agrees to assume an existing first mortgage now registered against the property'' — with the details of the mortgage following this statement.

Well, what is the buyer really saying when he ''agrees to assume'' the mortgage?

All he is really saying to the vendor is that he will maintain the mortgage payments without the permission of the mortgagee!!

The vendor (or a previous owner) is the one who signed the mortgage deed and has the covenant and responsibility to repay the debt. The covenantor is not released of his obligation simply because he transfers his property equity to someone else.

So the buyer assumes the mortgage, takes possession of the property and continues making the payments required by the mortgage. As long as the payments are received in time, the mortgagee is happy and not the slightest bit concerned about the new guy.

When one buys a property and assumes an existing mortgage(s) consider the financial and other advantages —

(a) no mortgage application

(b) no credit check (very seldom)

(c) no waiting

(d) no mortgage appraisal fee

(e) no ''arranging'' fees

(f) no legal fees

It can save a buyer hundreds of dollars, and, when the term expires, the buyer who is paying the mortgagee on time will have an excellent chance of obtaining an immediate renewal of the loan, providing it was originally obtained from a conventional source. Private lenders often do not wish to renew mortgage loans.

A buyer, especially one who is in no particular hurry, would be well advised to restrict his house hunting to properties that have mortgages already registered against them that would suit him.

If one finds a property with an acceptable mortgage against it, but it falls a short of loan requirements, study the availability of secondary financing and then average the interest rate in the total mortgage package. But if this route is taken, ensure that the TOTAL costs of the secondary financing is clearly understood.

The best and cheapest way to obtain secondary financing is covered in the following chapter, where the vendor lends a helping hand.

A point to remember here is to read the actual mortgage deed if you intend to assume a mortgage. Some deeds have a non-transfer clause in them which means that if the secured property is sold, the mortgage must be paid off and of course if this is the case, you can just forget it and look for another one.

22

THE PURCHASE MORTGAGE

Who says it is hard to borrow money?

A man with a horrible credit record would have difficulty floating a loan at his bank for a few hundred dollars, but the same man can borrow as much as FIFTY THOUSAND DOLLARS or more quite easily when buying a home.

How? Why, he simply borrows it from the one selling him the home.

No credit check (or at least very seldom) no waiting for results of a mortgage application, instant approval of the loan, no problems. How about that?

It is the purchase mortgage. The mortgage held by the one selling the property. If one is looking for a top deal in a mortgage, here is where it is really possible.

When looking through the listing files of a real estate broker, this financing will be indicated on the listing by the notation ''V.T.B.'' (Vendor Take Back) usually followed by ''at current rates'' which of course refers to the current market interest rates.

What usually happens though, is that the buyer will make his offer to the vendor with the interest rate shown as lower than market rates, and often gets the deal.

There are two basic reasons for a vendor to agree to lend the buyer the money secured by the mortgage.

(1) It is considered to be a good investment. A mortgage on property that is security familiar to the vendor, which produces a higher yield than other usual investments.

(2) It makes the property very saleable because of the financing available to the buyer.

The purchase mortgage does not necessarily have to be one first mortgage. The majority of purchase mortgages are second mortgages, which are created after:

(a) The buyer assumes an existing first mortgage.

(b) The buyer arranges a new first mortgage, OR a vendor might agree to hold two mortgages, a first and a second, the larger the first mortgage and the smaller the second, the reasons being:

(1) Two separate mortgage deeds create two separate securities.

(2) The vendor, holding the two mortgages, could perhaps give one to a relative, or use them as security in borrowing money on two separate occasions. Some people follow the old adage ''don't put all your eggs in one basket'' (read the chapter on derivative mortgages).

Any way one looks at it, a property offered with the vendor helping with the financing can be a sweet deal.

In taking advantage of this financing, ensure that there is an ''open'' privilege clause inserted in the mortgage deed which will enable the borrower to repay any part or all of the outstanding principal balance at any time (or on any payment date) without notice or bonus.

23

N.H.A. LOANS

These are called N.H.A. mortgages because they come under the concept of Canada's National Housing Act (administered by a Crown Corporation called Central Mortgage and Housing Corporation).

The money is borrowed from "approved lenders" of C.M.H.C. such as banks and trust companies.

The interest rates are not set, but are often available at about ¼% lower than conventional loans.

Here is what happens if one arranges a N.H.A. mortgage through a bank, for example:

The bank will require a loan application (naturally) which it will thoroughly examine, particularly in the area of the applicant's credit worthiness.

If the application is approved by the bank, the bank will agree to lend the money to the borrower, and when the mortgage is "closed" (when the borrower takes possession of the property) send the money, through its lawyer, to the party entitled to it, such as the one selling the borrower a house.

In addition to the principal amount of the loan, the borrower will agree to pay an insurance fee equal to 1% of the amount of the loan, which will be added to the principal amount of the mortgage.

The bank also puts up the money for this insurance fee (which it loaned to the borrower) and sends it to Ottawa, to C.M.H.C. which places it in an insurance fund.

This mortgage insurance, paid by the borrower, is for the benefit of the lender, the bank.

If an eventual default occurs in the repayment of the mortgage, and if the bank (lender) ends up with the title deed to the secured property, it can then recover its loan from the insurance fund.

However, in today's market, this is rather unlikely. By the time such default occurs, the value of the property will have probably risen, and instead of allowing a foreclosure, the borrower would probably sell the property, pocket a profit, and pay off the lender.

Even if the lender did end up with the title to the property, it is unlikely that it would look to the insurance fund for compensation, which would be less than the market value of the property seized.

An advantage therefore of the N.H.A. mortgage is in favour of the lender, because the loan is insured on the lender's behalf at no cost to it. The slight saving for the borrower of about a quarter-point in interest is just about offset by the required cost of the 1% insurance (over the normal five year term of the loan).

In addition to the recurring 10% annual principal prepayment feature, a N.H.A. mortgage is "open" in three years, and may be paid off (with a 3 months' interest penalty) before its term expires.

C.M.H.C. Direct Loan

The Central Mortgage and Housing Corporation has money available for borrowers in smaller communities and in the country where "conventional" mortgage loans are not usually available.

The rate of interest in the loan will be a shade lower than N.H.A. loans obtained through banks etc. in larger centres and the money comes directly from C.M.H.C. and not from the approved N.H.A. lender.

One chief advantage of such a mortgage is the generous repayment provision. Any part or all the principal balance of the loan may be repaid at any time after signing the deed, and no interest penalty will apply.

If you out in the sticks or in a small town, write Central Mortgage and Housing Corporation Ottawa, Ontario, and ask if such funds are currently available for your area.

24

THE CONVENTIONAL MORTGAGE

This mortgage is called conventional because it is the customary, prevalent and most commonly used method of obtaining a mortgage loan.

When an agreement to buy a house is made, a conditional clause is often inserted in the agreement giving the buyer about ten days to arrange a new mortgage.

Immediately on acceptance of the purchase agreement by buyer and seller, the buyer makes application (usually through the suggestions of the real estate broker who made the sale to a mortgage lender such as a bank, insurance or trust company).

It is a sound move to follow the suggestion of a real estate broker in making the application, because the broker is on top of the money market and knows not only where the best flow of money happens to be, but where he can get the fastest action in the application (which adds a little glue to the sale).

If the buyer is a person of means and one with an excellent credit rating, he could buy the property without the conditional clause simply because he would have no difficulty in obtaining financing. Vendors are more willing to sell without conditional clauses in the sales agreements.

It is quite common to have a 10% annual principal prepayment clause in today's conventional mortgage, and the term will probably be for five years.

25

THE BLANKET MORTGAGE

The original concept of a blanket mortgage probably began with a house builder.

The builder obtains an agreement with a lending institution to cover (blanket) it financially in the construction of a multiple housing project.

The original mortgage deed signed by the builder will cover the entire project, and as the construction of houses progresses, the borrower will be given loan advances to pay the bills.

Finally, when the houses reach the selling stage, a buyer for house number one will appear and sign an agreement to buy the first house from the builder, subject to credit approval.

The builder then marches the buyer down to the blanket mortgagee's office where a mortgage application is processed. If approved, the one house sold is taken off the covenant in the builder's blanket mortgage and a single mortgage for the house buyer's signature is prepared.

The builder and his lender proceed in this fashion until all the houses are sold, and the original blanket mortgage which covered the entire project is reduced to zero and discharged.

This is a very favourable method for large lenders to place funds, because they can do it in large chunks initially which will be reduced and spread over hundreds of individuals eventually. It makes for easier and faster accounting of the lenders' budgets because of the size of the initial mortgages.

26

THE UMBRELLA MORTGAGE

When a borrower wishes to float a loan secured by a mortgage, the equity in the proposed realty to be used for security sometimes is not large enough to satisfy the lender.

If the borrower owned more than one parcel of realty, he could borrow against each parcel but this would normally require separate mortgage deeds.

So, sometimes the borrower will put up more than one parcel to secure the loan, and sign just one mortgage deed to cover all the parcels used for security.

The mortgage will be registered on title against each parcel so secured.

One mortgage. One payment. Voila, the umbrella mortgage, which umbrellas more than one parcel.

A clause would probably be in the mortgage deed covering the eventuality that the borrower may wish to sell one or more of the secured parcels of property. This clause would stipulate the principal reduction and possible penalty required if carried out.

27

THE PIGGY BACK MORTGAGE

Here's an example:

A homeowner has a first mortgage registered against his property. He wants to borrow some money so gets it from a private source and signs a mortgage deed that is registered as a second mortgage.

In this deed, there will be a clause requiring the mortgagor to do one of the following:

(a) Provide the mortgagee in the second mortgage with monthly payments made payable to the first mortgagee, which the second mortgagee will post immediately to the first mortgagee.

(b) Provide the mortgagee in the second mortgage with proof positive that the monthly payment on the first mortgage has been made. It will require that the proof be supplied within a specified period of time.

In other words, the second mortgagee is constantly on the borrower's back to ensure that the senior mortgage is always in good standing.

Piggyback!

28

THE DERIVATIVE MORTGAGE

It is called a derivative mortgage because the security in the mortgage deed is derived from the value of a senior mortgage owned by the borrower in the derivative mortgage deed.

Assume one is a mortgagee (lender) in a second mortgage deed with a face value of $5,000.

The owner of the deed wishes to borrow $3,000. and considers selling the mortgage, but he has a problem. The interest rate in the mortgage is a few points below current secondary rates and he finds that he can only get $4,000. for it in a sale.

Well, it would be more prudent for him to borrow $3,000. at bank rates and use the second mortgage for security. This would save him a bundle, depending on the length of the loan.

So he effectively mortgages his mortgage.

A note would be created having a third mortgage charge on the second mortgage owned by the borrower.

It will be registered on title against the second mortgage which is registered against some property.

If the second mortgage were paid off, the registered charge would serve as a caution to advise all interested parties that there is $3,000. (plus interest) owing against the second mortgage.

So, when the second is paid off, the third gets his first and the balance is paid to the second mortgagee, who is the mortgagor in the third. Get it?

If you own a mortgage and need money think twice before selling your deed. Maybe you would be better off borrowing against it.

29

THE GRADUATED PAYMENT MORTGAGE

Basically, this mortgage is intended to help young people keep the initial carrying costs of a mortgage to a minimum, by allowing the borrower to pay less in the beginning, and more later.

Payments in the early years of this mortgage do not cover the full amount of interest due on the loan, and therefore the outstanding principal balance will increase, creating what is known as negative amortization.

The borrower is effectively borrowing additional money during the early years of the mortgage which is used to reduce the monthly mortgage payments during these years. This additional borrowed money is added to the mortgage and is repaid by increasing the payment amounts in later years.

To illustrate, study the C.M.H.C. illustration on page 90 . You will note that the normal monthly payment for the $35,000. mortgage would be $319. Under the graduated payment plan, the initial monthly payments are $240., increasing by 5% a year for ten years, at which time the payment reaches a peak of $382.

The shortage in the early payments is added to the principal amount of the loan pushing it up to $37,385., or $2,385. more than the original amount of the loan. From the sixth year it starts to go downhill.

The U.S. Dept. of Housing and Urban Development introduced this type of mortgage, and agreed to insure the loans on behalf of U.S. bank lenders. Hundreds of thousands of such mortgages have been authorized in the U.S.A., and, although a similar plan is now available for insurance by our own C.M.H.C., there appears to be resistance to it here in Canada.

The resistance is principally from lenders, who undoubtedly feel that the plan counts on a fairly high level of employment and inflation to keep it going without creating problems for the borrower (and lender). An important asset a mortgagor has is the knowledge that the mortgage payment will remain steady for a number of years, which, of course, the graduated payment plan does not provide.

However, for a mortgagor "on the way up" a substantial reduction in initial mortgage payments can be attractive. It enables one to obtain title to property now that otherwise might be out of reach.

Furthermore, the future, higher payments will be made with deflated dollars.

GRADUATED PAYMENT MORTGAGE
PAYMENT CHARACTERISTICS

$35,000 MORTGAGE   25 YEARS AMORTIZATION AT 10¼%

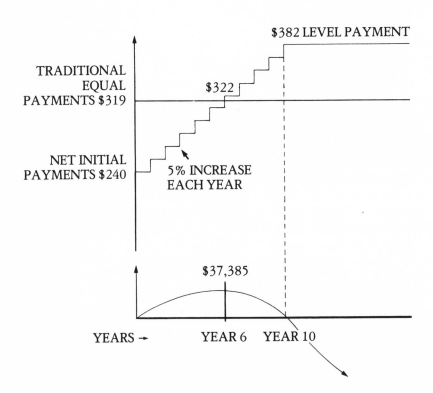

30

THE LEASEHOLD MORTGAGE

Not all building owners own the land on which the building stands.

The owners of some very large buildings in Canada lease the land under the buildings, which is called leasehold property. Leasehold property creates a leasehold mortgage.

Before a builder signs a ground lease, he will have an irrevocable mortgage commitment for his building. The mortgage requires an assignment of the ground lease, or sub-lease, and the terms of the ground lease will be satisfactory to the mortgagee, or there is no lease.

The principal sum of a leasehold mortgage is understandably less than it would be if the mortgagor owned the land.

If the mortgagee takes his mortgage under assignment of the lease, a situation is established between the lessor and mortgagee whereby the mortgagee becomes responsible for the terms of the lease, including that of paying the ground rent. The mortgagee would be liable for all breaches of covenant that might occur.

Under a sub-lease arrangement, the requirement would be that the mortgagor would hold the last day of the term of the lease in trust for the mortgagee, in order to allow the mortgagee to control the last day and thereby control the renewable term. This is necessary, because although the mortgage term is usually of shorter duration than that of the lease, it could be possible for the mortgagee to have not received his final payments by the end of the term.

A leasehold mortgagee will most certainly protect himself fully to ensure that there is no termination of the ground lease, and will therefore have an agreement with the lessor to allow the mortgagee time to remedy any default on the part of the lessee.

The mortgage will contain a clause stipulating that a default by the mortgagor under the terms of the ground lease will automatically become a default under the mortgage.

The leasehold mortgage will require that the lessee pays the ground rent to the mortgagee, who in turn will pay it to the lessor, or require the lessee/mortgagor to produce receipts promptly.

This will answer the question: "which has priority, the ground rent, or the mortgage payment?"

31

SHAFTING THE MORTGAGEE

There is a new game in town played by the mortgagor and mortgagee. The expert in the game is obviously a graduate of Shaft University (Shaft U for short).

The Shaft U graduate is the borrower in, say, a $60,000. mortgage deed with a five year term at 11%. The mortgage is two years old.

The mortgagor wants to pay off the mortgage because he is selling and the buyer doesn't want a mortgage, or he came into a financial windfall and doesn't want the debt, or any one of a dozen other reasons.

He discovers that the mortgagee is willing to accept a payoff and provide a discharge certificate, but wants six month's interest for the privilege, which could cost the borrower more than three thousand big ones. The mortgage term, having another three years to go, could cost the borrower a lot more, but in this case the lender is being reasonable. But three thousand is three thousand, and the borrower decides that he could make better use of the money than handling it over to the lender.

So the mortgagor starts his game. He does a bit of play acting and lets the lender know that he is sorry, but he can't make the next payment, which of course is a lot of hogwash. The lender is a bit disturbed by this, and the borrower merrily goes on ignoring the lender.

Finally, the borrower receives a warning letter from the lender's lawyer, which he promptly tosses in the garbage. Another letter, ditto.

And thenn, WHOOPEE, a sheriff's officer arrives at the mortgagor's door and serves him with a writ of foreclosure. Hooray. This is just what the borrower was waiting for!

You see, in the writ the lender can just claim arrears of interest, plus principal, but NOT the six month's penalty he wanted to pay off the mortgage. So the borrower pays off the writ, plus a couple of hundred to the lawyer, and he has just saved himself a bundle.

Well, one can image what this sort of behaviour would cost and save if the mortgage were a big one like maybe a couple of hundred thousand.

However, some lenders are catching on to the game, especially the ones holding the big mortgages, and if they suspect the borrower is playing this little game, they will sue him for the ARREARS owing and NOT for foreclosure. This keeps the affluent borrower on the hook and if he now wants to pay off the mortgage it might cost a bit more than the six month's interest.

If the mortgagor played this game to pay off the mortgage, and there was a junior mortgage registered behind the big one, he would obviously have to move quickly in paying off the writ. The junior mortgagee could march in and bring the arrears of the first mortgage up to date and charge the amount to its mortgage, plus a legal fee, which would put the mortgagor back in square one.

However, don't quote me. Better you should *check with your lawyer* first!

32

FORECLOSURE

Missed a couple of mortgage payments? The lender bugging you, putting on the pressure? You are short of cash and worried? Naturally.

A situation like this is bound to create anxiety, perhaps even cause one to wake up at 5 a.m. in a cold sweat, but the mortgagor, the borrower in a mortgage deed, can loom largely as a formidable opponent in an action by a mortgage lender.

The remedies and means available to a mortgagor to hang onto his property are quite fair. Unfortunately, not all the remedies are spelled out in a writ of foreclosure or a notice of sale delivered on behalf of the lender to the hapless borrower.

This is not written to be of any help to the lender, most of whom don't need any advice. The large lenders have a well-oiled legal machine at their disposal. It is written to help the borrower who is worried about maintaining a roof over his head.

For the thousands of homeowners worried about an unknown horror that might take place and possibly leave them on the street, here is some advice on what can be done. In this, there are two principals, the mortgagor-borrower-defendant, and the mortgagee-lender-plaintiff.

The following is the practice in Ontario, and outlined to illustrate at least one Provincial Government's rules of the game. It must not be construed or read as legal advice; it is based on practical observations by the author.

The two chief means employed to force a mortgagor to pay principal and interest arrears are (1) foreclosure, and (2) mortgagee's power of sale.

The *power of sale* is usually employed when the market value of the property is insufficient to cover the mortgage debt, or close to it. The reason is that when a property is sold by the mortgagee, the mortgagee has recourse to sue the borrower for any balance owing on the mortgage that was not realized from the proceeds of the sale.

If the mortgagee sells the property without notice to the mortgagor, it is worth noting that a *land titles office* will NOT accept its registration (which will probably surprise some wiseguy money sharks).

A *final order of foreclosure* cancels the mortgage debt completely. If the lender sold the property after foreclosure, and the proceeds of the sale did not erase the mortgage debt, the lender could not look to his former mortgagor to make up the difference.

However, the equity (difference between market value and mortgage debt) held by a mortgagor will be lost to him by foreclosure, but if the property were lost under power of sale, any surplus from the sale will be paid to the former owner-mortgagor.

If there appears to be sufficient equity in the property to adequately satisfy the mortgage debt, it is customary for a mortgagee to proceed by way of writ of foreclosure.

Being served with such a writ can be a traumatic experience for one unaccustomed to the appearance of a sheriff's officer at the front door. After the initial shock, when one has settled his jangled nerves and mustered the courage to read the contents of the writ, it is quite normal at this stage to bite your nails and reach for a drink (and you might as well have a double), because the writ states quite clearly that the plaintiff is suing for not only the arrears, but the entire total amount of the mortgage principal.

The first indignant thought would be that if one fell behind in the payments, how could it be possible to pay the entire thing off?

But take heart. Help is at hand.

The help is the law. Section 20 of the Ontario Mortgages Act comes to the rescue of the harassed homeowner. The following outlines the recourse available to the defendant:

The interest and principal payment *arrears* may be paid within the time limit specified in the writ, and the action will be dismissed.

For example, if one is four payments behind, hustle around and borrow the money, make the payments, plus a small amount of interest owing on the late payments, plus about $150. costs, and you are right back where you were before you were sued. But keep up the payments or the lender might get mad and do it again.

If the defendant cannot raise the money to pay the arrears, there are two things that can be done.

Instruct a lawyer to prepare a ''notice D.O.R.'' and a ''notice D.O.S.''

The D.O.R. is the mortgagor's request to have an opportunity to redeem the property. This notice is served on the solicitor for the plaintiff, which you can do yourself. If the solicitor refuses to accept service and acknowledge receipt of the notice, it can be left in his office with one of his employees.

Noting the name of the employee, the next step is to sign an affidavit of service, which is a sworn statement that the notice was left with the lawyer's employee.

Then go to the office of the Supreme Court of Ontario, pay a nominal fee and file the notice and affidavit. It will be recorded.

Once this is done, the defendant can breathe a sigh of relief, because he has just been granted a six month's moratorium during which time he doesn't have to pay anything to the plaintiff.

However, the plaintiff's lawyer is not going to take this sitting down, so he will immediately act to protect his client by obtaining a judgment for the entire mortgage debt. The court, on the other hand, will stay proceedings in the judgment for a period of six months.

The six month's period does not start from the day a defendant files the D.O.R., it starts from the day the mortgagee obtains the judgment of foreclosure. If the mortgagee or his solicitor does not act promptly, the six months could stretch to eight or nine.

During or at the end of the six month's period, the defendant must pay all the interest and principal *arrears* owing on the mortgage. If this is not done, the plaintiff will obtain a *final* order of foreclosure, and game over.

When the arrears have been paid, the defendant-mortgagor may go on making his normal mortgage payments, but don't miss one! Remember, the plaintiff obtained a judgment, and the court stayed proceedings. If payments are missed, the court, upon application, may remove the stay, and that means foreclosure, out, you've had it.

At the time of filing the D.O.R., the defendant should seriously consider filing a ''Notice D.O.S.'', the opportunity to have the property sold in the event that it is impossible to pay the arrears owing on the mortgage during the six month's redemption period granted by the court.

Remember, a final order of foreclosure not only cancels the mortgage debt, it also conveys the equity in the property once owned by the defendant to the plaintiff. If one had a substantial interest in the property over and above the mortgage debt, this would be a serious loss.

The D.O.S. will prevent such a thing happening. This will mean that although the plaintiff will obtain a judgment of foreclosure and sale, it will stop the final order of foreclosure and force the plaintiff into a sale of the property at the end of the six-month period if the defendant has not been able to pay the arrears.

If the action ends in a sale of the property, here is the order of payment from the proceeds of the sale:

1. The costs incurred in selling the property.
2. The interest owing on the debt.

3. The principal owing.
4. Money owing subsequent encumbrancers.
5. Anything left goes to the one who lost the property.

In the hungry thirties, provincial governments passed mortgage moratorium acts, which allowed a borrower to make no principal payments on the mortgage debt. As long as interest payments on the loan were maintained, he was secure. With today's countless numbers buying homes with about a 10% (or even 5%) down payment, a rising tide of unemployment would certainly create problems for mortgagors, but such government help wouldn't really be much help because with a 90% mortgage debt most of the mortgage payments would be interest anyhow.

If you are served with a writ of foreclosure, or a notice of sale of your property, *call a lawyer immediately and have him spell out your legal rights for defence.*

33

CAVEAT EMPTOR
(let the buyer beware)

Most real estate is bought, sold and leased through licensed real estate salesmen working under the direction of real estate brokers, who effectively operate clearing houses for the salesmen.

All brokers, large and small, from the giant trust companies to the small one-man brokerage offices, operate under a Provincial license. All are subject to the same rules of conduct.

When one is in the market as a buyer, the salesman's initial job is to introduce the potential buyer to property. Don't be offended by a few pointed questions that may be asked of you by a salesman, he is just doing his job by "screening", paving the way to a better working relationship. This screening is most important, because it will enable the salesman to better fit you and properties together, principally in the area of finance, which will save you both a lot of time.

However, regardless of whether you inspected property privately or through an agent, it is a good idea to have a check-list of points to remember *before* considering an offer to purchase the real estate. Read the following carefully — it may save a few headaches.

Zoning: What is the approved municipal zoning? On the property, on the street, in the neighbourhood? Look at a zoning map, then study the by-laws.

The fact that a house is being used as a rooming or boarding house does not necessarily mean that one could buy it and continue to use it as such. It may be used this way by the present owner under legal non-conforming use, which means that it was used as a rooming or boarding house *before* the area zoning was changed. There is an assumption that if a property is under "legal non-conforming" a buyer can continue the use providing there is no time break between the seller and buyer in the non-conforming use. But don't count on it. Get it in writing from the municipality.

Municipal zoning by-laws could be very important to you. Some neighbourhoods allow multiple roomers in houses, but perhaps you don't want this, with the possibility of a lot of transients in your neighbourhood. There are areas in cities that forbid a property owner to rent even one room — the houses must be occupied by the owner and his family and no one else.

A nice house could be on the fringe of industrial zoning, which isn't the best location. One might inspect such a property on a week-end when the plants are closed down, and smell nothing but the flowers. Then, to the dismay of the buyer, after he has committed himself to a contract he might find that the smell of operational industrial plants is not coming up roses.

A house might have a basement apartment leased to someone — be very careful about this one. You might find to your dismay that the apartment is not there legally, with the result that you would be deprived of its use as a source of income if the municipality decided to inspect the house.

Look carefully at all factors in zoning. Do not assume anything about what you see in the property. Be sure that it conforms with all municipal by-laws, and especially your intended use. If you don't, you could be one very sad buyer.

Condition of Property: Don't let a can of paint or a piece of wallpaper fool you. Check the condition of the structure itself, the heating plant and equipment, the plumbing, the wiring, and the roof. If you are unsure about something, get professional help and advice. It will be worth it. Review the chapter ''selecting your house.''

Work Orders: Ensure that the property will stand rigid inspection by the fire department, and that no part of the land or any building or other erection on the land has been confiscated, taken or expropriated by any Provincial, municipal or other authority with this right. Check to see that no alteration, repair, improvement, or other work has been ordered or directed to be done or performed to or in respect of the land or any building thereon. If this has happened, it will naturally affect your thinking about the offer.

Value: Perhaps you are one of the lucky ones, and have found the ideal property. Perhaps it is worth more to you than the listed price. Perhaps less. If you find *your* property, act quickly, but not hastily.

Most real estate that has been listed with a real estate broker has been listed realistically. Confirmation of the market value of a property you are interested in can be made by (1) viewing other comparable listings, and more important (2) seeing a list of comparable *recent* sales in the area, which can be provided by the agent.

''Hot buys'' are hard to find, basically because alert real estate salesmen are watching for them every day, and when one appears on the market it will be pounced on quickly by one of the agent's buyers.

Review the chapter "Don't be afraid to made an offer" for some guidance in price.

If you feel that a property you have found is just the last word as far as you are concerned, consider blanketing the opposition by offering a couple of hundred dollars *more* for the property than the listing price. Two hundred dollars can be peanuts spread over the years if you have found just what you want.

Remember that whatever your offer is, the agent *must* bring it to the attention of the vendor.

Terms: If you intend to pay cash for property, the seller will have to consider discharging any financial encumbrances against it that other buyers might agree to assume. If recent mortgaging has taken place, this could run into a sizeable sum getting the mortgagee to agree to discharge the mortgage. This will have a bearing on the price.

If you agree to assume the existing mortgage(s), ensure that you have all the facts. There could be an open or prepayment privilege not noted on the listing. The term could be shorter than you realize, which may not be brought to your attention until your lawyer checks it. Real estate brokers usually have all the mortgage details available, but just be sure.

If you are going to ask the seller to help with your purchase by holding a mortgage or two, always go for an "open" clause. Even if you won't want to discharge it at a later date without penalty, perhaps some future buyer may wish to do so. You might also include a clause in your purchase mortgage (one to the vendor) to the effect that if the mortgagee wishes to sell it, you are to have first refusal in its sale. If such a mortgage is sold, it is usually sold at a discount, and if you are in funds at the time, you could save some money.

It is very important to have no misunderstanding about what chattels go with the purchase price. Do not assume, for example, that a chandelier in the living room goes with the property because you saw it there. The owner might have other ideas without telling you and replace it with a light bulb. Then what will you do? Put it all in the agreement.

Be clear about any possible tenancy. Make it a part of your offer. The present tenant in that little flat on the third floor may look all right today, but is the seller going to tell you he gets drunk and noisy three nights of the week? He might even be the second mortgagee.

Don't expect to call for the production of any title deed, abstract, survey or other evidence of title except such as are in the possession of the vendor.

Allow yourself (your lawyer) as much time as possible to examine title. This will be at the buyer's expense. If within this time any valid objection to title is made in writing to the vendor, which the vendor is unable or unwilling to remove, and which you will not waive, the agreement will, notwithstanding any intermediate acts or negotiations in respect of such objections, be null and void and you will have your deposit returned without deductions.

When your offer has been accepted, all buildings and equipment on the property will remain at the risk of the vendor until closing.

Pending completion of the sale, the vendor will hold all insurance policies and the proceeds thereof in trust for the parties as their interest may appear, and in the event of damage to the premises, the buyer may either have the proceeds of the insurance and complete the purchase, or alternatively, require the vendor to use the proceeds to repair the damage so that on closing the buyer will acquire the property in its condition at the time of acceptance of the offer. It is possible that under these circumstances, the premises may be so damaged that the contract may be voidable.

The deed or transfer is prepared at the expense of the vendor.

The mortgages are prepared at the buyer's expense.

If the vendor is a trustee, the deed or transfer will contain trustee covenants only.

In the estimates of purchase costs, do not forget the costs that will be incurred by the services of your lawyer, and costs that will be incurred in the adjustments of insurance, rentals, mortgages, taxes, water, fuel and local improvements.

Do not commit yourself to something you cannot handle. Remember that, in addition to the mortgage payments and municipal taxes, the place will have to be heated, lighted, maintained in good repair, and insured.

When making out the deposit cheque to go with the offer, make it out in trust to the *listing broker* — not to the owner of the property if it can be avoided. The broker holds your cheque in trust for the seller, but if something on the seller's part makes it impossible for him to convey title to you, it is sometimes difficult to have your money returned if the seller has it in his bank account — he may have left on a three months' holiday. Your broker is always there.

34

HOW SAFE IS A TRUST ACCCOUNT?

Real Estate brokers are required by law to have a trust account, which is used to hold money in trust for others.

For example, the money could be rents collected on behalf of property owners who have retained the broker to manage property, or deposits on real estate transactions. Government inspectors keep a watchful eye on the movement of money in and out of the accounts, and woe to the broker who misuses the trust.

But what does a trust account mean to a bank?

It is simply another bank account — which leads one to ask just how secure the money really is in the account. Can a judgment creditor seize the money in a trust account?

A broker will have three accounts in a bank. One for his personal use, one for his general business use, and one for money held in trust. If a sheriff's officer arrived at the bank and produced a notice of seizure to the bank manager to seize the broker's money on behalf of a judgment creditor, what would the bank manager do?

Is your money safe in the trust account?

The bank manager, in his wisdom (and they are pretty smart cookies) would know that the trust account is there to hold money in trust for others, so here is what his response to the sheriff's officer would be:

Money from the broker's personal account and his general business account (if it is not a limited company) would be surrendered up to the amount of the seizure. If the broker's personal and general account were depleted by the seizure, what happens to the third account, the trust account?

The trust account is a different matter. The banker would accept the seizure, but would NOT surrender any money from the trust account. He would, however, put a "hold" on the account.

Whenever the broker wished to write a cheque on the trust account, he would have to satisfy the banker that the cheque really was, in fact, someone else's money that had to be paid according to the terms of the trust. Once this was established, the bank would honour the cheque and release the funds.

If the broker, for example, held a deposit on a real estate transaction for, say, $5,000. and the broker's commission were $4,000., when the sale is completed the broker could write a cheque for $1,000. to be paid to the vendor, but he could not write a cheque for the $4,000. commission to be transferred to his general account. This portion could be seized by a judgment creditor because when the sale closed it belonged to the broker.

So you see, your money held in trust by a real estate broker should be quite safe from seizure.

35

PRIVATE "FOR SALE" SIGNS

An approach to buying a home (or other real estate) that could be financially very dangerous is to knock on the door behind a private "for sale" sign.

The obvious reason for a private sale of property is to obtain as much money as possible from the sale, usually excusing the effort by saying one wishes to avoid paying a real estate sales commission, and therefore saving the buyer some money.

This can be dynamite to an unsuspecting buyer's pocketbook, especially to one who is of the opinion that he too is being clever in avoiding a real estate agent.

There is certainly nothing illegal or wrong in selling one's own property privately, but if you are considering such a buy, ensure that it is done properly.

The most vulnerable buyer is one who is searching for a house in an unfamiliar area. Values are not consistent from province to province, and certainly not from city to town.

A standard six-room brick bungalow in an urban fringe town with a market value of $60,000. could very well command as much as $10,000. more in the city and, not only that, the city property would probably be on a smaller lot.

A buyer, after searching in the city and becoming discouraged with its inflated market, could reasonably look to the suburbs and surrounding towns. Coming across a private "for sale" sign in a town on a comparable $70,000. city property could be an expensive experience. If he found the vendor asking $65,500. for the property, it might seem like a bargain, when in reality the market price locally might dictate a value of $60,000.

I am not suggesting that a buyer should ignore a private sign, because the home might be very suitable for his particular needs. What I do strongly suggest is that a true, and reasonable local value be determined.

This can be done by employing an established local real estate broker to do one of the following:

(a) Appraise the property. This will cost about $150.

(b) Act as a counsellor for the purchase, for a prescribed fee.

A vendor who is not actively engaged in real estate is not really qualified to appraise his own home — the basic reason being that he has a built-in inflated idea of what his own property is worth.

As a matter of fact, real estate brokers often enlist the aid of other brokers in valuing their own homes.

So an appraisal must be done to establish what the value is. If the private seller is doing a good job, he will have had an appraisal done to justify the selling price.

The potential purchaser, in objecting to paying for an appraisal is not being realistic, and if the seller objects to having one done, there may be a fly in the financial ointment.

The appraisal will only come into the picture when a purchaser has found a property he is genuinely interested in buying, and when one reaches this stage, it is better to be out $150. rather than three or four thousand, which could happen. If the appraisal should justify the private seller's price, then it would certainly be worth $150. to know that one at least did not pay more than the market value of the property.

Retaining a broker on a fee basis means that the broker would have to represent the buyer in negotiating the purchase, and this would cost more than an appraisal. If one did not wish a broker to go this far, at least the broker could draw up a proper offer, possibly with advice that could save the buyer money.

The local broker would know, through experience, what the market value of the property really is, and his advice in negotiating would be invaluable.

When you are the buyer, get a little help to ensure the price is right.

36

WHY BUYER NEEDS A LAWYER

Closing a barn door after the horse has run away is apropos to contacting a lawyer after one has signed a legal document, and a legal document of large financial proportions is an agreement of purchase and sale of real estate. One would be well advised to seek a lawyer's counsel *before* signing such an agreement.

This is when a lawyer's assistance may be the most useful, regardless of whether one is buying, selling, leasing or mortgaging. For example, here are some of the things a trained legal mind will think about on your behalf if you seek his advice before you sign an offer to purchase property:

Is the description of the property clearly stated?

Is there a private drive or a mutual drive?

What are your rights and responsibilities over a mutual driveway?

Are there any easements to which your property will be subject?

Where do you stand financially when the mortgagees have to be paid off?

Are there any hidden charges?

Does the purchase involve the sale of your present property?

If it is a summer residence:

(a) Is it leasehold, or freehold?

(b) Is there a right of way to a beach?

(c) Is there an assured right of way to the cottage from a public highway?

The time to be thoroughly advised is before you sign the contract. Your lawyer is the best one to advise you. He will perform the services of explaining and advising about the offer to purchase as part of the service of acting for you as a purchaser.

After your offer has been accepted by the vendor, your lawyer has a number of responsibilities:

To discuss with you the legal aspects as to how you will have the property registered:

93

(a) In your name

(b) In your wife's name

(c) To the two of you jointly, or as tenants in common.

(Here there can be complications, which your lawyer will explain)

To search title — are there any legal outstanding interests which will interfere with your full legal enjoyment of the property, or hold up a sale when that time comes? Title defects have a way of lying dormant for years only to come to light when you are selling the property.

To approve of the deed, affidavits, statutory declarations, and to prepare legal documents.

To attend to the proper registrations of the various legal documents when the purchase is closed.

To give an opinion as to your title and a complete report to you of the transaction.

A lawyer's training qualifies him to serve you by giving your legal affairs and problems patient study. He will advise on the laws of real estate and mortgages. He has the ability to explain fine print, knowledge of drafting legal documents, and above all can think and act for you in working out the terms and completion of an important legal contract.

It requires the professional judgment of a well-trained lawyer to advise and assist from the beginning to the final registration in purchasing real estate, and his help is no less important in selling or leasing.

If you wish to sign an agreement of purchase or sale, or an offer to lease, and cannot see your lawyer personally, at least read it to him over a telephone.

Do yourself a favour by letting him in on your plans from the beginning, before you sign. Remember, sometimes it is too late for help after you sign!

37

SELECTING A LAWYER

Finding a lawyer to handle a mortgage or real estate deal in Quebec and B.C. is a simple matter; just head for the nearest notary.

In Quebec, there are three categories of legal practitioners; the barrister, the solicitor and the notary.

Generally speaking, the barrister and solicitor both can give legal advice, prepare and draw up notices, motions, etc. for use in cases before the courts, but when the time comes to go to court, it is only the barrister who appears.

But don't call a barrister or solicitor to handle a real estate deal in Quebec. It is the Quebec Notary who is a very special person to anyone involved in real estate.

The notary is a legal practitioner whose chief duty is to draw up and execute deeds and contracts. No one in the Province of Quebec, other than a practising notary may, on behalf of another person, draw up deeds under private signature effecting real estate and requiring registration.

Well, you say, that's fine for Quebec and B.C., but what about the rest of Canada?

The legal profession has maintained a discreet silence in just what areas of law its people practice. It has not considered it proper for lawyers to advertise their special qualifications in law.

However, this is gradually changing. It has changed in parts of the U.S.A. with some results that are a bit shocking to the profession. Razzle dazzle and hoopla advertisements from lawyers, and on T.V.? Yep.

All this Yankee hoopla is not lost on the Canadian law societies, and probably is doing the societies a favour by providing them with no nos and restrictions on how far a lawyer can go when we eventually will see the rules changed here.

Lawyers in Canada will undoubtedly be allowed to advertise their special field of law sometime in the not too distant future, but certainly with reservation. Which will be a good thing for the consumer.

Right now we can go on personal experience, or personal recommendations. Real estate brokers are not supposed to recommend specific lawyers, but I certainly see nothing wrong in a broker having available a list of half a dozen lawyers in his area available for buyers and sellers; lawyers who the broker *knows* are specialists in real estate conveyancing. Just give a copy of the list to the consumer and say take your pick.

Of course, one can always walk into a large office building, check the directory, visit several legal offices and ask if they have real estate specialists available.

But however one selects the lawyer, it is quite possible to save money by getting a quotation on costs for handling the real estate transaction. Don't be afraid to ask — it is your money, so save a bit if you can.

Shop around.

38

HOW TO GET SERVICE
FROM A SALESMAN

There is an old saying in real estate — "all buyers are liars." It is not meant literally, but many people who go looking for a home or other real estate really don't know what they want.

Two-storey buyers buy bungalows, new-house buyers buy resales, detached-house buyers buy duplexes or doubles, downtown buyers buy in the suburbs, and so it goes.

The new salesman can't understand it. The buyer did say he wanted to be near the subway, and now he has bought in the country.

This can be disconcerting to a salesman who has patiently done his homework for days to find the "right" house, but it can be delightful for the salesman who suddenly made a quick sale. The latter got the buyer at the end of his search, when the buyer was fed up with house hunting and simply bought one, or suddenly found one he thought was ideal.

Everyone who is setting out to buy a house should accept the fact that perhaps he too has the same peculiarities. It is possible that because of them he might buy a house that he really didn't want.

Here are some suggestions on how to work with a real estate salesman to get the best possible service from him, or her, so that in the end you wind up with the house you really want.

Once you have settled on an area in which you feel you would like to live, visit the offices of real estate brokers in the immediate vicinity, preferably ones who are members of a local real estate board, because they have acccess to all the properties listed for sale through a multiple-listing service. This system not only provides the details of each property, but also a photograph.

Do not restrict yourself to one broker. Visit as many as possible, because brokers will have their own exclusive listings, which other brokers may not know about, and one of these listings could mean the end of your search. However, do restrict yourself to one salesman in each broker's of-

97

fice. He has access to all the listings in his office, and if he feels that you are his "exclusive" buyer, he will work harder for you.

When you have half a dozen salesmen from various offices assisting you, you might lean toward one over all the others for any of several reasons, such as his knowledge of the market, enthusiasm, deportment, etc. Do not ignore the calls from the others, because they could have your ideal property, but sticking to one can be helpful.

If you notice an advertisement in the newspaper, or a "for sale" sign on a house that looks good, regardless of the area or the broker's name, call your No. 1 man. He can get all the information for you, and introduce you to the property through the co-operation of the listing broker.

Your No. 1 man knows what you are looking for, and this can relieve you of the pressure of a new man trying to make a sale. This saves confusion.

By co-operating with one salesman, the salesman will feel that he has a red hot buyer who is really sticking with him, and will knock himself out to get results that will please you.

39

BUY OR RENT?

For some families, ownership of a home is like a love affair. They find exactly the right place in the right location. Home ownership has always been their goal. It will make them independent and respected.

For others, ownership has an economic value. A house is an inflation-resistant investment and a tangible incentive to save.

Others are less enchanted by ownership. They have neither time nor inclination to manage the unkeep of a house. They may find available rental properties best suited to their needs. They fear hidden or unexpected expenses sometimes connected with ownership, and possible shrinkage of capital of property as values go down.

Others do not have and may never have the capital to buy a house. Renting makes adapting to changing family needs easier than owning. Because real estate transactions take so much time, the mobile family wants no house to lessen its bargaining power for a new position or to lose mobility for other than occupational reasons. This, of course, can someitmes be contingent upon the lease.

The decision to own or rent is related to stages in the life cycle that begins at marriage and extends some time after the dissolution of the family. A typical sequence of changes upgrades shelter with increases in assets, age, and family needs. Net worth is normally highest after 35. Home ownership is greatest after that, and does not begin extensively before age 25.

The residential cycle may begin in a small rented apartment, perhaps after a couple has lived for a time with the parents of one. The next step may be a larger apartment, or the purchase of a small new or used house with equity. The family may sell this after about age 35 in favour of a larger, newer house.

Later, demands of children call for expansion by remodelling or even buying another house. If finances permit, a custom-planned house may be built at this stage.

It may be the last house until old age and retirement indicate a smaller house, a co-operative or rental apartment. The spouse remaining after death of one partner may remain awhile, but later may seek accommodation with children or other relatives, or in homes or projects for the aged.

Families move through the life cycle at varying rates, and with varying numbers of moves. When changed residential status is not caused by moving to a new position or upgrading accommodations, turning points usually come during the expanding and contracting phases. Changes in residence, rented or owned, entail changes, often abrupt and substantial in allocation of family resources. Whether as rent, mortgage installments, taxes or repairs, the residence claim is regular, and it is inexorable.

Home ownership is most often achieved with the help of mortgages. The average time required to pay off a mortgage on a house is about 25 years, which is about the same time it takes to rear a child from infancy to maturity and slightly longer than the couple has together after the children have left. If a family moves several times during this period, the feat of owning a home free and clear of debt is accomplished by enlarging the equity in succeeding houses.

A young family buying its first home often has little money, but if the buyers can carry a stipulated debt load, homes may be purchased with as little as 10% down (or less) through the availability of mortgaging that is default-insured by the buyer for the benefit of the lender.

Other avenues are open to those with modest down payments by the agreement of the seller to help with the financing by holding a mortgage or two as part of the purchase price.

Besides the down payment, buyers need closing costs — legal fees, mortgagee's service charges, and adjustments necessitated in balancing taxes, insurance, fuel etc. to the date of closing. These are items not to be overlooked.

There are pros and cons for both buying and renting.

Some morning when you are shovelling snow in front of your house wondering whether it is worth the effort, and you see your neighbour leaving his apartment building whistling cheerfully, you may think he had the answer. On the other hand, when the apartment building neighbour is feeling a bit cramped in July, and sees you entertaining friends with a nice outdoor barbecue in the garden, he may think you had the answer.

Here is an examination from both sides — renting and ownership:

Owning as Opposed to Renting

Pride of Ownership: This is ours. Our house. We can make a beautiful home out of it, or live in a shamble. We can keep up, or down, with the

Joneses. As long as we comply with the by-laws of our municipality, we can live just the way we want to live.

Apartment: We are restricted. We have to watch the noise; no loud parties after midnight. Turn down the television. No smelly cooking, it might offend the neighbours. Can't be ourselves. Sombody always complaining.

Children: A really big reason. One or a dozen, no matter. Pack them all in the house. Double bunks if necessary, but we'll get them in.

Apartment: No children allowed in many places, or they restrict children to an age group, or make you live on children-only floors.

Roominess: Lots of room to stretch. Get out of each other's hair. Workshop in basement for father, mother on main floor attending to her work, the children upstairs or in the rec room watching T.V. or doing their homework. Barbecues outdoors and gardening, very private parking.

Apartment: Cramped. Get on each other's nerves.

Pets: Just got a cute little pup that's going to be as big as a baby horse in a year? So what? If I can affort to feed it, I'll keep it.

Apartment: What? If you are going to have a dog lady, make it a small one. Or none at all.

Credit: Property ownership definitely is an asset when you want to put the bite on a bank or loan company. If you paid two thousand dollars down for the house, who is to say that the equity now isn't worth four?

Apartment: Renting goes on debit side of credit application sometimes, unless perhaps you have been in the building for a few years.

Stability: Real solid citizen. That's Mr. Smith, he owns 512 up the street.

Apartment: Oh, we live in an apartment.

Income Potential: Couple of extra rooms? Perhaps you can rent them, if the by-laws allow it. They will pay the taxes. Two rooms @ $20. a week each amounts to $2,080. a year. Probably enough left over to redecorate the house and pay the hydro.

Apartment: Nothing extra here. If you rent an extra room, it will probably only pay for your own rental on the extra room.

Possible Appreciation: Property values do go up, and how. For every dollar you credit yourself in paying off the principal on your mortgage, you could be adding another dollar in increased value.

Apartment: Nothing goes up but the rent.

Better Furnishings: When you have settled into a house, you feel that this is it; and you can safely spend more money on furniture and decorations because you feel that you will be there long enough to get the long range economic enjoyment out of it.

Apartment: Too many factors can cause you to move, so why spend a bundle on decorating the temporary premises with anything permanent?

Peace of Mind: Usually a responsible man living in a house will carry term insurance to cover the principal balance of his mortgage to ensure his family will be left with a debt-free roof over its head if the breadwinner is gone.

Apartment: What's going to happen to my family?

Permanence: It's nice to make friends out of compatible neighbours, people you know who have roots like your own. It is a nice feeling to open your front door and welcome friends into *your* home.

Apartment: Too many come and go.

Responsibility: A man needs it. Good citizens have it. A properly run household is like running your own small business. It takes planning, foresight and decisive action.

Apartment: Something wrong? Phone the superintendent, if he isn't too busy.

Civic Mindedness: Everything your municipality discusses concerning your neighbourhood concerns you. Join a ratepayers association, and your local homeowners association. They are stimulating and interesting.

Apartment: Oh, I don't know. So what if they are going to rip down those houses up the street or build something next door. I probably won't be here long enough to let it bother me anyhow.

Economy: You think about money when you own your home. You don't splash it around. Too many things you could use the money for on the house. Your principal payments on the mortgage force you to save, to gain equity.

Apartment: Let's have a party. I got a bonus today.

Renting as Opposed to Owning

Freedom: Ah, this is it. When I leave my apartment, I can just close the door and walk away knowing the superintendent is on the job. I can move into a new building as soon as my lease expires. Try something different with new surroundings.

House: Can't stay away too long. If I go on holidays, I have to notify all services and police that I shall be away for awhile, and put the bite on a neighbour to keep an eye on the place. Bit concerning. Stuck in same neighbourhood.

No Capital Tied Up: I can do what I want with my bank balance. It's flexible; there when I want it. I can invest it in anything I like, and readily.

House: Down payment tied up, and increasing equity in house.

Debt Free: Chunky mortgage commitments don't worry me, or maintenance or other service bills. All I do is pay the monthly rent, hydro (sometimes not even that) and telephone, with no extensions all over the place.

House: Always concerned about major disaster. New furnace? stove? fridge? roof? Other necessary expenses. Always something.

Freedom Loving Neighbours: I live in a building with some gorgeous chicks and nice neighbours. We really enjoy that pool. Carefree types with happy outlook on life. Company readily available.

House: Sourpuss neighbour next door. On other side can't communicate. I like to mix a bit.

No Children: Haven't any of my own. Can't stand them as a steady diet. Always under your feet. Noisy. They are on children-only floors.

House: Well, they are my own little darlings, but some of those kids they bring home from school. Phew!

Less Housekeeping: Small area to look after. Easy, once over lightly. Compact.

House: My wife is always complaining about all the work she has to do to make the house like a home.

No Pets: Boy, do I hate the sound of a yappy dog at 1 a.m. Especially when it's not mine! Not bothered with that. They're all on the pets-only floor.

House: The first thing the kids want when they can talk is a shagggy dog. I have to look after it and feed it, and pay the vet's bills. I can't tell them there is no room for it.

Save Money on Furnishings: I just have to provide modest furnishings. The owner supplied the stove and fridge, my living room was broadloomed when I moved in, and the drapes were in place.

House: At least five rooms plus stove and fridge. Wow.

Dollars and Cents

Take an average modest bungalow, detached, say 100 square metres, cost $65,000.

Compare its carrying costs with an apartment that will provide about the same room area. We'll have to consider the bungalow basement as a freebee, because there won't be one in the apartment.

Now, regardless of what the down payment and closing costs are on the house, the interest that we could have earned on this money, say 8%, will have to be shown as an expense under the house. Also, the mortgage principal, as it is paid, will be added to this.

Housing costs in your area won't be the same as mine, so you copy the following guide and fill in your own figures for comparison.

	House	Apartment
Rent	$	$
Insurance		
Water/Hydro		
Heat		
House Maintenance		
Grounds Maintenance		
Municipal Taxes		
Interest on Mortgages		
Interest on down payment and closing costs		
	$	$

From this you can draw your own conclusions. There are fringe benefits in both cases.

The apartment has a nice swimming pool and other amenities. The freedom of movement is there. The cash is in the bank.

The house has a nice garden and barbecue area for entertaining. It provides forced savings, roominess and roots in one's lifestyle. A big plus here of course, is the possibility of strong property appreciation.

The decision is yours.

40

SELECTING YOUR HOUSE

The Choice is Yours: Most of us have a number of houses in a lifetime. We increase our incomes; we move. We are transferred by our company; we move. We enlarge the family; we move. We decrease the family; we move. Count the number of moving vans the next time you are on the highway, and when are *you* going to move?

Let the choice be a good one or at least a thoughtful one, for even if you stay in a place only a short time it can influence you and your family's well-being, sometimes even involvement and identity, and happiness. A mistake, if you make one, can be corrected, but a mistake almost always leaves some kind of mark.

The Community: Before you make your choice, compare the costs of commuting in money, time and fatigue with the advantages and disadvantages of space, privacy, and quiet for yourself and your family.

Do not overlook differences in public amenities and municipal services, and in taxes and the cost of insurance and utilities. Choose, if you can, to live within the jurisdiction of a municipal govenment that has a master plan of zoning and development, and legislation to support it. During this period of increases in population and fast-growing cities, it is hard to forsee the future of a community or to influence its development. Without a plan, growth is chaotic and unpredictable.

Many families have built houses in the country only to find the city at their doorsteps sooner than they had expected. Many others have built or rented in city neighbourhoods whose residential character becomes eroded by conversion to incompatible uses. Do not buy or build a house on land that has a potential for industrial, commercial, or multiple-housing development except as a calculated investment. Seek a site protected by zoning.

You will find other advantages in legislation for planning. Visual quality — beauty and order — depends on the good will and sensibility of each property owner and the competence of the architect, but laws can control some of the influences that have contributed to the deterioration of the landscape — signs, billboards and utility structures. Some communities limit the location of billboards, the size of signs, and require that wires and pipes of utilities be put underground. Choose a community like this and one that is alert to the possibilities of such improvements.

Local government and public education are financed largely by taxes on real property. Tax rates and assessment practices vary among communities, but do not assume that communities with low taxes are necessarily more efficient. They quite often provide fewer or inferior services. The property tax has inevitable shortcomings, because it penalizes quality by rewarding shoddy property with low assessments.

Nothing is more important than good schools. They are not easy to develop. They are built by the efforts of dedicated people over long periods. Your children of school age get no benefit from long range improvements. They need good schools now. Good schools are expensive. Usually they co-exist with higher real property taxes, but differences in tax rates in communities with good schools and those with poor schools are seldom great enough to influence one's choice and are never worth the savings.

Communities with good schools usually are stimulating in other ways. So when you are looking for a place to live, look into opportunities for intellectual activity: libraries, museums, theatres, concerts, or perhaps even an amateur symphony or little-theatre groups. Mutual interests foster friendships more than geography does.

Look also for a beautiful place, or at least one that is not ugly. Visual quality, like a good school system, is not achieved quickly. It depends on long traditions of pride and long-continued programs of responsible public works. Street trees take years to mature. Established visual elegance in a residential community is literally priceless.

Consider also convenience to work, shopping, and schools in terms of distance and methods of transportation, for a house for most families today is a centre from which to commute to work. Children travel to school; parents to shops. Anticipate travelling costs in your estimate of housing costs.

The place you live often determines whether you need one or two automobiles or none. Sometimes it will be found to be cheaper to hire cabs while travelling within the community and renting cars on week-ends when you want to get away, rather than tying your cash up in the cost of owning an automobile or two.

The European lives in his city at large. Public and neighbourhood gathering places — piazzas, parks, sidewalk cafes, coffee-houses — serve as extensions of his house into which some social parts of life are projected. We have fences along our property lines, but we are experiencing a revival of interest in public amenities; especially in cities. Consider then the relationship between the kind of urban situation in which you live and the kind of housing facilities you may need or that are available.

Sometimes a neighbourhood is so attractive that it determines one's choice of community, but usually the community is selected first. Transportation may influence the second decision as well as the first. So, inevitably, will the housing situation. If you are interested in a particular kind of house or lot, or one at a certain price, you may find it only in a limited number of places. But, assuming there are alternatives, how to proceed?

Sometimes, when moving into a community, there is an advantage in renting for a while. Many qualities, especially the intangibles that have to do with sociability, common interests and even climate, cannot be understood without experience. Renting in an unfamiliar community will give you a clearer idea of the kind of house you want and the neighbourhood in which you would like to live.

Look for visual character. It is even more important in the neighbourhood than in the community, because the neighbourhood is closer to home.

Established neighbourhoods have at least two advantages. You can examine the houses and the landscape has had time to mature. Some of our best houses are very old, but middle-aged houses and neighbourhoods tend to deteriorate.

Judge the viability of an established neighbourhood before placing a new house there. If you don't trust your own evaluation, seek professional advice. New developments still under construction are harder to visualize, but plans can give some indication of their eventual completed appearance.

Houses for sale or rent and remaining lots in stable residential neighbourhoods command higher prices. So does property in thoughtfully planned and sensitively designed new residential areas that can reasonably be expected to develop admirably.

Your choice is difficult. Whether to accept an area that is not attractive and probably will not be developed attractively, or place a larger percentage of your investment in land and improvements to take advantage of a superior location, remembering that you will be able to do little to change the aspect of the neighbourhood.

Look for a location where you can walk to stores and shops, schools and a park. That may be difficult because much zoning legislation has produced antiseptic neighbourhoods, which by being unvaried are also lacking in services. Communities vary a great deal in the availability of facilities and programs for recreation. Do not overlook the importance of these for children.

107

Select a location that is free from unpleasant sources of noise, fumes and dirt and not near a main traffic artery, railroad, airport or objectionable industry. Noise travels surprising distances on quiet nights. So do fumes and dust on breezy days.

Consider the views. If the terrain is hilly, the views are more extensive, but construction costs will probably be higher.

What does the street look like? Purely local streets have advantages of relative quiet and safety. Subtly curved streets usually are more attractive than straight ones, but excessively curved patterns are puzzling to strangers and casual visitors.

What do the neighbourhood houses look like? Fencing? Landscaping? What is the orientation of the lot? Can you take advantage of winter sunshine, yet keep out excessive summer sun? What is the direction of the prevailing winds? Are cooling summer breezes accessible? Is the lot readily drained? What is the character of the soil? Is it subject to movement, settling, slides?

Check the zoning regulations. Find out what you can and cannot do there, the restrictions on the house itself and the kinds of room rental regulations in the area. Can you practice a part time profession or occupation, or build a swimming pool?

Ask whether there has been a recent flood in the neighbourhood. If not, and if it has survived a severe rainy season, its drainage facilities are adequate unless subsequently overloaded by new developments.

Inquire about provisions for collecting trash and garbage.

Is there a periodic water shortage, or is the supply adequate for house and garden?

Locations near an attractive and compatible development, such as a new college campus, golf course or public park exert stabilizing influences on nearby residential properties. If you follow these criteria and acquire a well designed and soundly constructed house, property values probably will be sustained. A house that is no more expensive than the average in the neighbourhood, and perhaps a little less so, is a conservative investment.

The House: When we acquire a house, we are inclined to think of the enterprise as an investment. A house can be ostentatiously out of place in its neighbourhood or too expensive for a given market to support, especially in small communities without diversified demands.

Experience does not support common assumptions about the effects of ethnic homogeneity. When a minority group moves into a neighbourhood, property values do not automatically decline. Sometimes they increase.

Of course, all the economic factors involved in the venture should be considered. The relative advantages of renting and owning; indirect costs, such as transportation; and the direct costs — the land and improvements, building, landscaping, furnishing, and operation (maintenance, taxes, insurance and what about the mortgage?).

Land costs are lowest in the country and highest in the central city, and vary with the desirability of the location and the extent of its improvement.

Do not overlook the costs of site improvements. As a prospective property owner, determine your liability to the municipality for current or future work. All things considered, it is better to live in a community that requires first-class utilities, drainage, street construction and lighting.

At the other end of the process, think of landscaping and furnishing costs. Families often find themselves with inadequate funds for these items simply because they follow site and structure in the sequence of acquisition.

Insurance costs vary with the quality and proximity of fire and police protection, but differences in premiums do not measure the advantages of adequate protection.

The building itself represents the largest single expenditure. Many variables influence its cost. For families with reduced incomes, cost will be critical and the alternatives severely limited, but for many others, several choices will be available at similar prices.

At this point, turn to considerations other than price to find measures of value. Who else can understand precisely how important to you are an escape to an unspoiled stretch of wilderness or the sound of music or the company of friends?

Existing houses, new or old, can be examined before the purchase. Building a new house, on the other hand, presents the opportunity to achieve a uniquely personal environment, given competent professional design — at least an architect, and preferably also a landscape architect.

Many houses could have been put up more economically had an architect designed them, but good professional service entails costs and so does custom building. Select your architect carefully on the basis of his work — one who is interested and experienced in house design. Select the builder carefully too. Most people assume that competitive bidding is the only way to solicit a reasonable price. Sometimes it is, but limit the bidders to good contractors. The best procedure, if you can manage it, and if your community is fortunate enough to have such men, is to select the best builder just as you selected the best architect. A man who takes a profession interest in his work usually quotes the same price whether he is bidding competitively or simply invited to bid.

If your house is being designed for you, its form has limitless possibilities. Take advantage of the opportunities to make it truly original, but avoid exotic excesses, which disrupt visual harmony in the neighbourhood and can make it difficult to sell in some unforseen future.

In the final analysis, the value of a house, regardless of its location, can be judged only in terms of its success as a personal environment for each member of the family in an emotional as well as a functional sense.

A Well Built House: How can you tell whether a house you are thinking of buying is well built?

First, get a copy of the plans and specifications. Compare what you can see of the house with what is shown on the plan. Sometimes plans are revised during construction, for better or for worse, unless the builder has registered his plans for mortgaging.

Some general features are not structural but still may be important to you. Among them are: Which way does the house face? Is the arrangement and size of rooms good? How about natural light and cross ventilation? Do the rooms provide enough wallspace of storage space? Does the plan permit some flexibility of living arrangements? These are partly matters of personal taste. Do they satisfy your family's needs or preferences?

From this we go to the structural parts of the house — the foundation, walls, floors, ceilings and roof. Start from the outside. Walk around the house.

Look at the foundation walls, which should extend well above the finish ground level. Watch for vertical cracks, which may indicate the structure has settled. Hairline cracks in the concrete are due to volume changes and have no great significance.

If the concrete is uneven or honeycombed, or has broken corners, it probably did not have enough cement or was carelessly placed in the forms — a sign of poor workmanship.

In block or stone walls observe the character of the joints. Use a pocketknife to pick at the mortar and see if it crumbles easily. If it does, it is a sign that too much sand or a poor quality cement was used. A nail driven into the joint will indicate if the mortar is skimpy there. If you wish to check the wall thickness, measure through a basement window.

The slope from the foundation at the grade line should be enough for rain to run off.

Basement windows wells must drain readily. Water from the roof should be carried away by adequate eaves troughs and downspouts of non-corrosive material. If downspouts are not connected to a storm sewer or other suitable outlet, splash blocks at the outlet will divert the water.

Check basement window jambs and trim to see if they fit snugly against masonry wall. The sills of all windows should have sufficient pitch to drain water outward. Here is a place where decay may have occurred — probing with a small screwdriver will soon tell you.

After a final look at the foundation walls to make sure the corners are even and walls are vertical, we can inspect the framed sidewalls. They may be covered with wood or composition siding, shingles, brick, stucco, stone, or other types of enclosing materials. All are good if used properly.

If the siding has been painted, examine the condition of the paint. See if the paint film is dense and opaque, or if the wood is showing through. Check for any gloss on the surface. Painted surfaces that are dull and chalky indicate that repainting is necessary.

The horizontal lap siding should be laid evenly, with correct overlap and tight butt joints. At the corners, the siding may be mitered or fitted snugly against vertical corner boards. An end of the siding board should not be exposed to the weather because it will soak up moisture.

Make sure the nails are of the non-corrosive type and that the space between the nailhead and the face of the siding has been filled in before painting. Simply scratch to find out.

Windows and doors should have a protective flashing of non-corrosive metal above them. They should be checked for weather-stripping. Check the sills for sufficient pitch for good drainage. A drip groove under the sill will permit the water to drop clear of the siding.

You have now had an opportunity to form an opinion on the quality of workmanship that has gone into the outside walls. Neat foundation walls, good metal eaves troughs and downspouts, snug-fitting woodwork, and provision for surface drainage all indicate the builder has made a conscientious effort to erect a house that will endure.

Signs that the builder has skimped are chipped or honey-combed concrete, loose mortar in the brickwork, large cracks between the ends of the siding and window or other trim, rust stains from an inferior grade of outside hardware, and thin or flaked-off paint in a nearly new house.

Now go inside the house. In the basement look more carefully at the foundation walls, post, and girders, and at the floor joists if they are not concealed by the ceiling material. The basement floor should be dry.

The basement floor should slope to the floor drain to permit quick runoff. A concrete floor should have a hard smooth surface without spalling, cracking or dusting.

The joists that support the floor above rest on the foundation walls and are supported by wood or steel girders. These girders in turn are supported by posts or division walls. If wood posts are used, they should be set on a concrete base block above the finish floor level.

When wood girders are built up by nailing several members side by side, make sure the members are well nailed together and that joints are over a post or a division wall.

Check to see that the ends of wood joists are not embedded in masonry or the concrete wall, as this practice may invite rot unless there is an air space at the sides and end of the beam.

111

The wood joist should be spaced evenly. Examine them for sagging, warping, or cross-breaks. Look carefully at any joists that have been cut for heating ducts or piping. Notches or holes on the bottom edge or near mid-span have the greatest weakening effect.

Check the area between the foundation wall and sill. Any opening should be filled with a cement mixture or a calking compound. The filling will lower the heat loss and prevent the entry of insects or mice into the basement.

Most construction in the living area will be hidden by various wall and ceiling finishes, but you can check the interior finish and such items as flooring, window, door and other trim. Examine the trim for any open joints, hammer marks, warped pieces or rough nailing.

Over the door where the side casings meet the horizontal, the joint is often mitered. If this joint is tight, as all joints should be, you have a pretty good sign of careful workmanship.

Note, too, if the baseboard fits snugly against the flooring and wall at all points.

Interior finishes are commonly of plaster or of such drywall construction as wood or composition material. You seldom see plaster cracks in a newly built home, because they develop slowly. In a house a year or more old, the absence of cracks indicates a well-built house. Of course, cracks can be concealed temporarily by wall paper or a coat of paint. Cracks extending diagonally from the corners of windows or doors may be signs of poor framing or that the house has settled.

As you walk over the floors, notice if they squeak or seem too springy. If the floor joists are big enough and the sub-floor has been laid correctly, neither fault should occur. If you wish to check to see if the floors are level, stretch a string across them.

If the flooring is exposed, hardwood flooring or the harder species of softwood are usually preferred. If carpeting is used wall to wall, the underlay may be of any material that presents a smooth and firm surface.

Look carefully for signs of nailing. Flooring of a standard thickness is tongued and grooved and is blind nailed along the tongue so that the nailing does not show. Small nailheads on the face or top of the flooring means that a very thin flooring has been used. Wood strip flooring normally becomes dry and cracks open between the strips in winter. These cracks, if they are not too wide, will close up in warmer weather.

Do not condemn floors in an old house simply because they are scratched and marred. Perhaps all they need is refinishing. If so, take this extra cost into account.

Perhaps the kitchen and the bathroom have tilework on the floor, on the wall, or wainscot. The tile floor should be smooth, without raised tile or depressed areas. Wall tiles should fit snugly around all windows, door trim and around the fixtures. Joists should be caulked tightly to keep water out.

Check the doors to see if they swing freely and close tightly without sticking. Is there a threshold under the exterior door to keep out snow and cold winds? Some of these doors may have metal weather-stripping. Are the interior doors hung so as to clear your rugs? Do they interfere with other doors? Do they latch readily and stay latched? Check all doors to see that they are not excessively warped.

Windows usually are of the double-hung type; the lower sash slides up and the upper one slides down. Open and shut all windows to be sure they work properly and there is not too much play in the sash. The weather-stripping should not interfere with the ease of operation. Don't forget to raise the window shades to assure yourself there are no cracked windowpanes.

Check window woodwork and plaster for water stains and signs of decay. Note the kind of glass in the window. Is it clear and flawless, or does it create distortion? Also see that the putty that hold the glass in is in good condition and is painted.

It is well to check the attic for the thickness of insulation between the ceiling joists and to see if there is a moisture barrier on the room side of the insulation. Check the attic ventilators. They should be open summer and winter. In summer, ventilaion helps to lower the attic temperature. In winter, ventilation removes moisture that may work through the ceiling and condense in the attic space.

Frost on the ends of nails in winter indicates insufficient ventilation and excess moisture.

Check the roof rafters or trusses to see that they are unbroken and that framing joints are right. Can you see any daylight under the eaves. Water-staining on the rafters or roof sheathing is a sign of a roof leak.

Questions that are more complex or that cannot be answered by comparison with standards may require the services of an architect. Find a man who has a good reputation and is well qualified; the cost of his services may be small compared to the toubles that can arise from a serious defect.

41

A COMPARATIVE GUIDE
FOR HOUSEHUNTERS

This chapter concerns the many physical aspects one may check on properties being inspected. The househunter using it can make his own comparisons from his notes.

By comparing the results, one will be able to make a decision as to which house is the right one.

Exterior Setting

Street Front: General appearance of neighbourhood. Other homes should be of like quality or better.

☐ Unpaved street or lack of sidewalks, storm and sanitary sewers may mean future assessments for improvements.

☐ If builder says he'll pave streets in new development, get it in writing.

☐ Check location of street lights, fire hydrants, if any.

Grounds: Determine lot's boundaries. Ask about easements.

☐ Note general quality of landscaping. Good lawn, plenty of shrubs, trees can be worth thousands. Lack of them will cost you money, work. If new house, get in writing what builder will provide. Look up: check for dead, dying trees. Their removal costly.

☐ Note condition of driveway, walks. Their length, grade important factors in wintry climes.

☐ Adequate outdoor lighting convenient, also deters prowlers.

☐ Visualize water runoff, drainage. Of special concern with low-lying houses. If in doubt, check grounds after heavy rain.

☐ Check for above-ground seepage if there's septic tank. Correcting condition is expensive. Leaving it is health hazard.

House Exterior: Be systematic. From ground, inspect all sides, top to bottom.

114

☐ Chimney: Note bricks, cap, flashing.

☐ Roof: If shingled, they should lie flat in even rows. Wide roof over-hangs offer both practical, aesthetic advantages.

☐ Gutters, leaders (downspouts) should be solidly attached, without signs of deterioration, clogging.

☐ Check general condition of exterior walls, paint.

☐ Look for rot on windows, doors. Check whether storms, screens installed.

☐ Foundation: Look for cracks, settling, low spots that collect water.

☐ Check number, location of hose connections.

☐ Waterproof, grounded electrical outlets handy, especially near patio, sundeck, porch.

Living Areas

General: Layout most important. Should provide free traffic flow.

☐ Keep family's living style in mind. Anticipate problem areas.

☐ Ideally, kitchen and living room should have southern exposure to get plenty of sunlight.

☐ Empty rooms can appear to be deceptively large. Get measure-ments, note placement of windows, doors, etc. to make sure your furniture will fit.

☐ If home has wallpaper you don't like, remember it can be chore for you to remove, expensive to have it done. Painting over usually less than satisfactory solution.

Kitchen: Probably most important single room. Also most costly on square foot basis. Keep in mind if it needs remodeling.

☐ Check layout, placement of stove, refrigerator, sink, counters for ef-ficiency.

☐ Ask what appliances come with the house, how old they are. See that they're in good working order. Frost-free refrigerator, self-cleaning oven a plus.

☐ If your present appliances to be installed, make sure they'll fit avail-able space.

☐ Adequate cabinet, counter space with plenty of work area critical factors. Measure, compare with what you now have.

☐ Ample electrical outlets also important.

☐ Kitchen close to garage, laundry room, family room, patio, can save steps.

☐ Ventilation over range a plus. Combination hood and exhaust fan most practical.

Living Room: Size most important factor, followed by layout, location.

☐ Measure, sketch rough layout to see if furniture will fit.

☐ Foyer preferable to door opening directly into room. Reduces drafts, provides privacy.

☐ In older house, especially, fireplace may not be in working order. Check.

☐ Coat closet should be handy.

☐ Check number, location of electrical outlets, wall switches.

Dining Room/Area: Measure, make sure it's big enough for your needs, furniture. Size of dining areas, in particular, often deceptive. Should be sufficient room for guests to circulate around table without crowding.

☐ Seclusion important. Screen, divider, even plants can achieve it in dining area.

☐ Consider convenience to kitchen, whether kitchen is visible to guests.

☐ Check number, location of electrical outlets, wall switches, adequacy of lighting. Dimmer switch a real convenience.

Bathrooms: Size, number of bathrooms important, especially for growing families. Quality of fixtures important too.

☐ Generally figure one bathroom for every 2 - 3 people, or two bedrooms per bathroom.

☐ Powder room near main living area great convenience.

☐ Look for leaks under basin, behind toilet, etc.

☐ Test water pressure adequacy by turning on all taps and flushing toilet. Drop in pressure can indicate problem. If so, have plumber check.

☐ Note condition of grout in tile walls.

☐ Check size of medicine cabinet.

☐ Lighting should be adequate.

☐ Electrical outlet for razor, hair dryer a convenience.

☐ Exhaust fan essential in windowless bathrooms. Frequently required by building code.

☐ Linen closet should be handy.

☐ Make sure door locks can be easily opened from exterior in case of emergency.

Bedrooms: Preferably isolated from main living area to minimize disturbing sounds.

☐ Size, closet space, ventilation important.

☐ Small windows high on wall dangerous in case of fire, especially for the very young or very old.

☐In children's rooms, think twice about windows far from ground, especially if nothing below can break fall.

☐Check number, location of electrical outlets, wall switches.

☐Ceiling fixtures useful, but many bedrooms don't have them.

☐Bedrooms with roofs immediately above (as in Cape Cods and finished attics) may be hot in summer, cold in winter.

☐If doors lock, make sure they can be opened from outside in emergency.

Basic Household Services

Electrical System: Check service panel, or entrance box. 100-ampere, 220-volt system absolute minimum today; 150-200 amperes, 220 volts may be needed if household's electrical demand high because of ranges, dryers, air conditioners, etc.

☐Circuits from box serve various parts of house. Should be minimum of 6, preferably 8 - 10, in average house. Spare capacity valuable.

☐Inadequate system not only hazardous, but affects appliance lifespan, performance. Old wiring especially dangerous.

☐Modernizing can be expensive.

Heating System: Heating is major household expense; ask to see bills from previous winter.

☐Check age of unit.

☐Both gas, oil have advantages, disadvantages. Electric heat generally too costly in most parts of country; A-1 insulation a must.

☐*Warm Air Heat* — Furnace should have blower, preferably belt-driven, easily removable filter. Humidifier a plus. Turn furnace on-off, listen for noisy ducts. Advantages to system: it warms house fast, can be adapted for central air conditioning. Continuous blower system advantageous.

☐*Hot Water/Steam Heat* — Furnace pipes usually take up less space. Furnace also may be used to heat water for faucets. But initial cost high, responds slowly to heating needs, lacks humidifier and may have unattractive radiators. Cast iron boiler, baseboard radiators best. Radiant heat in slab floor has many drawbacks.

☐*Hot Water Heater* — Check name plate for capacity, recovery rate. Both important. 40-gallon capacity adequate for average family; 30 gallons should be minimum. Unit should be able to heat at least 30 gallons 100 degrees in hour.

☐Check age of unit.

☐ Also check inside of burner compartment, floor beneath heater for signs of leakage.

☐ Gas heaters usually cheaper to install, operate than electric.

Plumbing: Inspect pipes in basement, under kitchen sink, in bathrooms. Copper, brass, bronze preferable. Some plastic pipes now being used, but not permitted in many areas.

☐ Grease trap especially important in homes having septic tank.

☐ Inadequate water pressure may indicate serious problem.

☐ Wells can be tricky. Purity, adequacy of water supply vitally important.

☐ Plumbing repairs expensive; system replacement even more so.

Air Conditioning System: Turn on to test cooling power, noise level.

☐ Look for name of manufacturer. Some off brands lack quality, adequate dealer servicing.

☐ Sizes required depend on area cooled, climate, insulation, etc. Generally one ton (or 12,000 BTU's per hour) needed for every 500 - 600 square feet. Insufficient capacity can be a problem.

☐ Water-cooled units can be costly to operate.

☐ Central system preferable to several individual units. Besides providing comfort, it's cheaper in long run, adds to home's resale value. Zone control thermostats also a plus.

Basement: Should be watertight. Look for wet spots, water stains, warped floor tiles. Musty smell can also be tipoff.

☐ Consider storage possibilities.

☐ Check floor for signs of heaving, cracking.

☐ Check joists for sagging. Inspect for rotted wood at point where joists rest on foundation. Also check for termites, but, remember, only an expert can really tell.

☐ Outside door great convenience.

☐ Heated basement a plus in cold weather areas, a necessity if basement's finished.

☐ 220-volt grounded outlet useful for power tools, etc.

Laundry: Location near living, sleeping areas saves lugging clothes up and down steps.

☐ Consider size, lighting of work area. Also placement of washer, dryer, etc. for efficiency.

☐ Find out whether laundry appliances come with house. If not, make sure yours will fit available space.

☐ Make sure dryer is properly vented.

☐ Electric dryers considerably more costly to operate than gas in most areas. Should have 220-volt grounded outlet.

☐ Shelves, counter space helpful. Ditto stationary tub, which many newer houses don't have.

Garage: Two-car garage a plus, even for one-car families, who'll get extra storage space for lawn mower, bikes, etc.

☐ Convenience to kitchen great help in carrying in groceries.

☐ Pull car(s) into garage, see how they fit. Garages in older homes built for smaller cars than many of today's. May be tight squeeze.

☐ 220-volt grounded outlet convenient for power tools, etc.

☐ Adding garage space can be expensive. Carport less costly, but still not cheap.

Attic: Consider accessibility, storage potential, possibility of finishing at later date.

☐ Louvres provide necessary ventilation, help cool home in summer, prevent condensation.

☐ Attic fan an asset in home without air conditioning.

☐ Wet spots, stains indicate leaky roof, expensive repair job, maybe new roof. Especially note area where chimney meets roof.

☐ Poor insulation or none at all, guarantees costly heating, cooling bills, plus likely discomfort.

Miscellaneous

Good insulation cuts cost of heating, cooling house considerably. Check normal requirements for your region. Weather stripping, storm doors, storm windows also money-savers. Double glazed (even triple-glazed) windows especially important in extra cold climates.

☐ Nobody ever has enough closet, storage space. Total up what you now have, compare with house you're considering purchasing.

☐ Although not a critical item, you'll probably want to check on TV reception, especially in fringe areas.

☐ Increasingly popular are such accessories as intercom, central vacuum, burglar, fire alarm.

42
WHAT'S THE HOUSE WORTH?

When viewing houses, you naturally wonder about value. Especially if one is moving from province to province, one city or town to another, rural locations, or in fact any move. Within cities there are also substantial differences in neighbourhood value.

Many househunters have been shocked when faced with large-city prices, after selling the home in smaller towns or rural areas. The first reaction is annoyance, and possibly anger, which is sometimes vented on the real estate salesman initially showing the moving househunter around his new locale.

The most obvious way to establish value is to inspect as many comparable properties as possible. This will familiarize you with local *asking* prices, which will provide an overview, but go into it further by asking the agent to show you recent *selling* prices.

The majority of real estate brokers maintain up-to-date files on sales, especially sales in their own territory. Also, many have access by subscription to a commercial service that can rattle off recent sales on a given street in a matter of minutes, by making a phone call. The information will also provide details of how each sale was financed.

Many real estate boards publish periodic volumes of sales for the benefit of members in providing better service to the public. So you see, the recent-sale information is readily available. All one has to do is ask.

Although recent-sale figures are a great help in determining market value, it is restricted in that if one is looking at six-room bungalows, the recent sales of two-story homes would not be of much help. The recent-sale figures of comparable six-room bungalows must be obtained, and if there are none, or few, or no sales recorded during the last year or two, then other approaches must be made.

Averaging is one. Brokers have records of the average monthly sales figures of *all* properties. If it can be seen that the average rise, for example, of *all* housing for the past year was 4% in the area, then this could be helpful. If the most recent sales of six-room comparable bungalows were a year old, then the 4% increase could be used as one guide in updating the figures.

Sales comparison figures on half a dozen comparable properties may be closely related, and driving past these properties will provide physical characteristics of each for comparison purposes, but you won't be able to inspect the interior of them. This is where averaging can help.

If the one you are interested in seems to be in average condition, fine, but if it is run-down and needs extensive work, or conversely it is in beautiful condition, these will be plus and minus facts for you.

All the foregoing, of course, is assuming that viewings are made of reasonably standard plans. If the house in question is one that is very dissimilar to your comparisons, it can create a problem in arriving at a value in your own mind. Perhaps the original cost of the house, if it is not too old, could be used as a basis for averaging over the years.

One thing is sure, though, and that is that the selling price on a house cannot be established until an offer to buy the place has been accepted by the vendor.

Review the chapter ''Don't be afraid to make an offer'' for additional help in getting a fair deal.

43

DON'T BE AFRAID TO MAKE AN OFFER

In 1867 the United States Government offered Russia $7,200,000. worth of 1867 gold for Alaska, and it was accepted.

Later, it was discovered that Alaska could have been purchased for five million dollars. In retrospect, paying 44% more than an acceptable price for Alaska was still a bargain, but at the time it must surely have made the U.S. negotiators think that they should have been a little less hasty with the offer.

Unless the heart rules the head, there is a certain amount of thought and discipline required before signing.

There is basically one of four price tags on every parcel of privately owned land in Canada. The highest is on the land that is not for sale.

Walk in cold on a man with his dream house, where he is comfortable, compatible with his neighbours, has a nice garden, is settled in the community and is supremely happy with his home and life style. If that man's home has a current market value of $75,000. how much would it take to get him out of there? Certainly a lot more than one would care to pay, and in some cases money would NEVER move him.

The next price tag down the scale is that of an owner who is "thinking of selling" but hasn't reached the point of making a firm decision about it.

An offer *could* be made to this owner. His $75,000. home *might* be purchased for slightly more than its market value, but if one fails with such an offer, the result will be a "free appraisal" of the man's realty and inflation of his property ego.

Now we are approaching a more reasonable situation. The house that is for sale; on the market. (the overpriced listings can be flushed out with a bit of viewing, so we'll ignore them).

How much does one offer for property on the market?

Do a little probing. Reasons for selling can have a great bearing on the price. Has the vendor bought another house? Is there a breakup in the family? Is the vendor leaving town?

Which leads us to the lowest price tag; distress selling. An example would be a vendor's desire to beat a final order of foreclosure on his property which he has not redeemed. At least something can usually be salvaged from his predicament by selling, if he can find a buyer in a hurry who will close quickly.

Once you know the circumstances surrounding the sale, you are ready to make an offer. How much?

This calls for some calculations on your part. If you bid too low, the vendor might react negatively or insist upon the full price, or perhaps reject the offer entirely which won't help with any attempted further offer.

A higher price might be grabbed immediately, and then you will be left wondering if you could have purchased the realty for a bit less. You will never be sure.

Armed with all the information you can get about the sale, and considering what you can afford, make an offer that is a little lower than what you sincerely believe to be fair under the circumstances.

It may not be accepted, but it it is not an insulting offer, you will undoubtedly find it counter-signed by the vendor with another price which you can accept, or negotiate further.

And if by some chance your offer *is* accepted, you can smile and consider yourself a shrewd buyer.

Of course, there are cases where you will rightfully offer a full price (or even more) for a property you absolutely MUST have, but remember that an offer is a most important step that requires very careful consideration, and one that can hurt or please your bank account.

Think it out well in advance, make a realistic offer, and you probably will be pleased with the result.

44

CONDOMINIUM OWNERSHIP

The first funds for condominium development in Canada were provided by Central Mortgage and Housing Corporation in 1967 when it made $4.3 million available to finance the construction of 296 condominium units. In part, these were trial projects. But by 1971, private lending institutions and some provincial housing agencies were also putting their money into this kind of housing and CMHC was able to reduce its direct participation. So the condominium method of ownership has had the support of both the public and private sectors of the economy. All the provinces and territories of Canada have passed legislation to make condominium home-ownership possible.

Condominium enables a person to share in the ownership and operation of a housing development while having negotiable title to his own unit. Condominium describes a form of tenure or ownership that can apply to many kinds of housing including single-detached houses, town houses, garden homes and high-rise apartment units.

Owning a condominium home includes a variety of important benefits:

1. The security of tenure of permanent home-ownership.

2. A better opportunity for those of average and modest income to buy rather than rent in areas where land costs are high.

3. The possibility of financial benefit to the owner in the event of resale at a better price.

4. The opportunity to have a say in the management of the affairs of the condominium as well as serving fellow owners by being a member of the Condominium Board of Directors.

5. The opportunity to enjoy services and facilities normally only associated with rental projects.

6. The availability of economies often available only to those who can purchase various commodities as a group.

7. The advantage of homeowner grants that are provided by some provinces toward initial purchase as well as annual taxes for home-ownership.

What Does Condominium
Home-ownership Mean?

Condominium housing can be an apartment or town house complex in which a residential unit is owned by the individual owner and in which the rest (common elements), including land, are owned in common with the other owners. The condominium legislation of each province provides a broad framework for the proper administration and management of each project as a whole. The project documents when registered, bring the project into being as the form of tenure known as condominium. This form of tenure is known as strata titles in British Columbia, and co-ownership of immoveables in Quebec. Condominium housing may be located on land which is held freehold, or on leasehold land which is subject to a long-term lease and the condominium corporation is tenant.

The Unit

In most provinces the part of the condominium which you will own outright is called the *unit*.

As a condominium owner you will have full and clear title to this unit which will be legally registered in your name. The definition of the elements and space you will own as a part of the unit may differ from project to project and a precise description will be provided in the documents prepared for each condominium.

Common Elements

The definition of *common elements* can be simply stated as 'all the property except the units'.

The common elements include lobbies, elevators, parking areas, roads and walkways, service equipment, recreation facilities, yards, plumbing, electrial systems and portions of walls, ceilings and floors and so on. Part, or parts, of the common elements may be designed for the exclusive use of one or more of the individual owners. These *limited common elements* may include balconies, patios, parking spaces and roof gardens, and the like.

The usual division of responsibility for maintenance and repair of elements in a condominium will be that owners maintain their own units, but that parts such as exterior walls, the basic stucture of the building and plumbing, electrical and heating systems, will be maintained by the condominium.

Common Expenses

As a condominium owner, you will be required to share with the other owners the costs of maintenance, repairs, alterations and improvements to the common elements.

Such payments, usually referred to as *common expenses*, can vary over the life of a particular condominium project depending on the extent of maintenance decided on by the owners, the amount of any reserve fund to cover unforeseen condominium expenses, the type of insurance coverage for the condominium and the arrangements for the management of the condominium.

Project Documents

These documents deal with the outlining of the 'goverrnment' or administration of a condominium project.

The documents that are registered with the land titles office to create a condominium are known as:

(a) a *description* and *declaration* in Ontario, Nova Scotia, New Brunswick, Newfoundland and Prince Edward Island.

(b) a *plan* and 'declaration' in Manitoba, Yukon and Northwest Territories.

(c) a *condominium plan* and *By-laws* in Alberta and Saskatchewan.

(d) a *strata plan* and *By-laws* in British Columbia.

(e) a 'plan of the immoveables' and a *declaration of co-ownership* in Quebec.

The requirements for the creation and operation of a condominium are generally similar across the country. Although the provincial condominium acts refer to these documents by different terminology, the condominium documents may be expected to contain the following information:

1. A commitment of the property to the condominium form of ownership;

2. A description of the entire project (including plans and drawings) indicating the location and boundaries of each of the separate units and of the project as a whole;

3. A determination of the percentage of each 'unit owner's interest' in the common elements;

4. A system of assessment for maintenance and operating expenses;

5. A statement of the fundamental rights and obligations of all parties involved; and

6. A description of the organization of the condominium owners.

The importance of the project documents is that they specify and regulate the constitution of each condominium and are intended to be of a lasting nature. A Declaration, for example, can only be changed or amended by the unanimous consent of all the owners and mortgage holders, except in Quebec where a 75% affirmative vote of the owners can amend the Declaration of Co-ownership.

By-laws

To ensure the successful operation of a condominium, it is necessary to formulate and observe rules concerning the use of the common elements, the conduct of members of the condominium and provisions for changes to the project and its rules. The various provincial acts provide for the establishment of by-laws for this purpose.

By-laws can be amended or revised by a majority vote of the owners as specified in the project documents.

The use of the term by-laws does not have the same meaning in every province. Some provincial acts clearly define what may be included in the by-laws and others are quite permissive in that they only ask that the corporation establish by-laws to provide for the control, management, administration, use and enjoyment of the units and the common property. These rules are known as:

'By-laws' in the Territories and all provinces except Quebec which does not have by-laws but uses the Declaration of Co-ownership instead.

Association of Owners

In order to carry on the necessary collective action involved in the operation of a condominium project, an organization of the owners is necessary. All provincial condominium acts require that an *association of owers* be formed to manage the property and affairs of the condominium.

The owners' association is known as:

(a) a *corporation* in Ontario, Manitoba, Alberta, Saskatchewan, New Brunswick, Yukon, Northwest Territories, Newfoundland, Nova Scotia and Prince Edward Island.

(b) a *strata corporation* in British Columbia; and the *co-proprietors* in Quebec.

The association of owners will have the power to carry out all the requirements of the provincial condominium act and the project documents. If the condominium is to be adequately maintained, the owners' association must have control over the parts of the condominium which are owned in common. In most condominium projects, the repairing and maintenance of buildings, the removal of snow, the maintenance of lawns and landscaping, driveways and walks, etc., will be managed by the association of owners.

The Board of Directors and Management of a Condominium

As a unit owner and member of the condominium you will have the responsibility of electing an executive or *board of directors* to direct the affairs of the condominium. The directors are elected primarily, but not exclusively, from among the members of the condominium and for the period of time outlined in the project documents. The board of directors will administer the *common funds* of the condominium and be responsible for project administration, regulation and maintenance.

The board of directors may employ any people and agencies it needs in connection with the control, management and administration of the common property and the exercise and performance of the powers and duties of the condominium association of owners.

Sometimes for the first year of operation or longer, the developer of the condominium project may enter into a management contract with the condominium corporation to provide the necessary management services. His experience with building management can be a valuable asset in the first years of a condominium's operation.

The condominium corporation may decide to hire the services of a professional management firm or it may decide to manage the project by itself and possibly invite the developer to act only in an advisory capacity on the board of directors. In a large condominium, because of the sophistication and complexity of the tasks involved, some form of professional management is almost essential.

The condominium management performs the services that ensure the orderly and efficent functioning of a condominium. It prepares the annual budget for the board of directors which, when adopted, becomes the program for the maintenance and upkeep of the project and the basis for the monthly common expenses. It also carries out the routine duties of invoicing and collecting common expenses, ordering repairs, making improvements and employing and training staff.

What Are the Costs Involved In Owning A Condominium Unit?

After the initial down payment has been made and the sale transaction has been closed, you will have two payments to make each month; mortgage payments (in Quebec, *hypothecary* payments) and common expenses.

Of course, if you pay cash for your unit, you will only have taxes and common expenses to pay.

Mortgage Payments

As a condominium owner, an individual mortgage will be arranged on your unit and you alone, as purchaser, make your payments directly to the mortgage lender. The monthly payments will usually include charges for the principal, interest and taxes.

Because you have your own mortgage with the lender you are in a position to negotiate new terms for the repayment or re-financing of your unit.

Under a National Housing Act loan, your monthly payments to the lender will include an amount equal to one-twelfth of the estimated annual taxes on both your unit and the share of the common elements apportioned to your unit. The tax bill is then paid by the lender and your account debited.

Assessment for Common Expenses

Common expenses will cover the operating costs of the common elements and are subject to re-adjustment if expenses increase or decrease.

Your unit will be charged a certain percentage of the project's total operating costs. This is established in the condominium declaration and may be determined by the original purchase price of each unit in relation to the value of the total project. You and your solicitor or notary should ensure that all items of common expenses to which each unit owner is to contribute are clearly spelled out in the project documents.

If the project is in operation the Directors or manager can quote you an exact figure for the common expenses. As a rule of thumb you might estimate monthly common expenses to be between .125% and .25% of the purchase price of your unit. For example, if your unit cost $30,000. to purchase you might expect your common expenses to be in the order of $35.00 to $75.00 per month.

The payments for the common expenses are usually made to the condominium and should cover the following items:

Insurance: find out what is covered by the policies of the condominium and arrange your own accordingly. The condominium normally carries public liability insurance, and fire insurance for the common elements and in most cases for all the units as they exist at the date of the first sales. The owner is usually responsible for insuring personl belongings and any improvements he makes to his unit after the registration of the condominium.

Maintenance and Repair of Common Elements: This covers costs for building repairs, maintenance and landscaping, recreational facilities and service equipment. Each owner is responsible for the cost of normal maintenance and repairs inside his unit.

Operating and Service Costs: The provision of heat, water, hydro and snow removal are some of the service costs which may be included in the common charges.

A Reserve or Contingency Fund: Money out of this common fund will provide for the replacement or major repair of common elements that become obsolete or wear out.

Management Costs: These are payments made to professional management firms or private individuals hired to administer all or part of the day to day functions of the condominium.

When Will You Legally Own Your Unit?

To gain title to your unit, the condominium must be legally registered at the land titles or registry office with copies of the description of each unit, the description of the entire condominium and the legal documents relating to the management of the condominium and the rights and responsibilities of the owners.

If you are thinking of buying a condominium unit which has not yet been registered, find out when the condominium is scheduled to come into being and what conditions remain to be met before the *registration* takes place. You can get this information from the developer or lender. After this, talk the whole thing over with your lender or lawyer before signing an *offer to purchase.*

If you move into your unit before the condominium is registered, you may have to pay a sum in the form of rent to the developer. The rent may, or may not, be used to partially reduce the price of your unit. It is only when the project has been legally registered, and you receive title to your unit, that your payments are made to your mortgage lender and the condominium association.

What To Look For In The Design Of A Condominium

As with the purchase of any home, there are several factors about design that you should consider.

The Location of the project should be reviewed in relation to distances to work, shopping, schools and transportation. Have a look at the present and projected development of the area surrounding the condominium.

Common Elements and Facilities such as open space, recreational areas and equipment and the quality and durability of the landscaping are important both from the aspect of their suitability to your needs and their long term maintenance costs.

Unit Design should be suitable for your present and future needs. The project documents, along with the condominium plan, will outline the boundaries of your unit and the areas to which you have exclusive use. Like the single family dwelling, you have the right to alter and maintainthe parts of the unit you own outright but you would have to receive permission from the board of directors to alter any part of the dwelling that are classified as common elements.

Privacy Arrangements are important, such as the distances between units, the fencing, planting and separation of your unit from walkways, roads and common areas. Adequate sound insulation of the surfaces between adjoining units is an important factor in multiple housing. Ask the developer about the provisions he has made to insure proper sound insulation.

Parking Facilities for both yourself and visitors should be looked at closely. Will you have long uncovered distances to carry articles from your car to your home? Is there parking space available for a second car or for a boat or trailer?

Storage Spaces for articles such as bicycles, sleighs, unused furniture, etc., within and outside your unit are as important to consider as the garbage storage and collection procedures from your unit and the project.

Quality of Materials should be looked at carefully since you will be paying for the upkeep of your own unit and will have to share in the upkeep of the common elements through your common expenses.

Some Additional Suggestions

Most people realize that buying a new home is going to be one of the largest financial decisions they will ever make. Before signing any papers, before paying any money, make certain you have all the available documents applying to your particular condominium.

Discuss the condominium documents with your solicitor or notary. Let him consider them thoroughly. At the same time, see your mortgage lender and house insurance agent to discuss your other legal and financial obligations.

Once these preliminary checks have been made, you are ready to sign and ''offer to purchase''. At this point, with the help of your solicitor or notary, you will have determined the date of occupancy and alternate arrangements in the event of delays in occupancy or of delays in registration of the condominium.

Further information and advice may be obtained from other condominium owners, the developer, an approved lending agency or bank that has handled condominium projects, or the local office of Central Mortgage and Housing Corporation.

45

OPTIONING PROPERTY

An option in real estate is an agreement whereby one has the right to purchase another's property at an agreed price, at some time in the future, with a time limit.

The purchaser (optionee) is not bound to purchase the property, but the vendor (optionor) is bound to sell if the purchaser "exercises" the option, thereby agreeing to the terms of purchase, which effectively turns the option agreement into a binding agreement of purchase and sale.

It is customary for a purchaser to give some cash to the vendor when receiving the option, which is retained by the vendor regardless of whether the purchaser ends up buying the property or not. If the deal closes, this cash is often credited to the purchase price on closing, although not always.

A common example of the foregoing is for "A" to give "B" the right to purchase A's property for $100,000. within one year.

"B" gives "A" $1,000. cash, which "A" keeps.

"B" may exercise the option at any time within the year. If "B" fails to do this, "A" keeps the thousand dollars and the agreement is automatically cancelled, unless, of course, there are renewable clauses in the option.

At this point, I wish to point out a red-flagged warning sign to a vendor. In the option to purchase within one year, it will say that when notice is given to exercise the option, the deal will close within, say, 60 days from that date.

This is where many vendors become upset. The vendor may assume that he will have one year from signing the option to move, not realizing that he will have just sixty days to move from the date of exercising the option. If the purchaser wished to move quickly on the purchase, he could exercise his rights within 24 hours, and the deal would close 60 days from then. It is important to understand this clearly.

It is a common practice to use the services of real estate agents in obtaining options. On some agents' option forms there will be a commission agreement on the bottom whereby the vendor agrees to pay the agent for procuring so-and-so to become the optionee, and if the property is purchased the vendor pays the agent. I don't agree with this, because in 99% of such agreements, the agent is really working for the purchaser, and it should be the purchaser who pays the agent.

Some agents may take the attitude that it is six of one and half a dozen of another, so what does it matter who pays? Well, it can matter quite a lot, and for this reason: I have found through experience that when approaching a vendor for an option, the reception is more cordial if the vendor fully understands that he won't have to pay a commission to the agent. All the money in the deal is his, so to speak, with no deductions.

So, if you are going to use an agent to help obtain your options, make your own agreement with the agent to pay him for his services. The arithmetic in the whole thing may not make any difference in the end, but it will smooth the way for negotiations if the agent asks the vendor for nothing.

If you are interested in optioning just one property, you will get your answer soon enough, but if the interest is in obtaining options on a number of properties, then there are certain guidelines I would suggest.

The first is to remember that very very few agents will be interested in spending a lot of time obtaining options for you without some ''front money'' — after all, you may end up dropping everything, and the agent knows this. He wants to be paid for work done.

So have a contract drawn up between you, the purchaser, and the agent. But before the contract, consider how you are going to proceed. A good example follows:

Assume there are 10 properties you wish to accquire. Before doing anything about them, check the ownership of each through your municipal offices. If it is found that more than one property is owned by the same party, it could be that someone else has his eye on eventual ownership of the ten, or at least eventually getting a bigger price than the others from some eventual buyer. Contact this multiple owner first and get his reaction to your plans — it could save you a lot of time.

If the 10 properties have 10 different owners, all living in the houses, you cannot assume that there will be clear sailing, because *somebody* is going to give you a hard time. So a testing of the market must be made. This is done with short term options with renewable clauses.

Instead of asking for one-year options, with a payment of about $1,000. to each vendor, ask for a 60-day option with a payment of about $200. to each vendor for the 60 days. In each option have renewable clauses, giving the purchaser the right the renew for six months at the end of the 60 days for $500. to each vendor, and a year renewal at the end of the six months for $1,000. Here are the reasons for this:

You will save money. If you were successul in obtaining options for seven of the ten properties and found that the remaining three were holdouts for sums that would create financial problems for your plans, you could forget the whole thing and drop it. At a cost of $1,400. Going for yearly options at $1,000. each would cost you $7,000. in dropping your plans.

The basic idea of the 60-day option is to find out how many properties you can secure. If things look promising at the end of 60 days with only a couple to go, you could renew for $500. each for 6 months. This will be the period in which you must obtain the remainder. Of course, maybe you'll be lucky and get the 10 during the 60 days, which would relieve you of any nervous strain in this part of the operation.

If this is the route to go, then the agreement with the agent could be to pay the agent about $200. each time he brings you an acceptable option. On closing, the agreement would stipulate a further payment from you to the agent, the figure being one you negotiate.

On one optioning job I did for a developer, he showed me the houses he wanted, and because of his ''packaging'' it for me, it was agreed to pay me $1,500. on closing each one, less my front money. This was less than a usual 5% or so, but was certainly fair because the developer set it up.

If, on the other hand, I did all the ground work for a project and took it to a developer, I would not only look for higher fees, but a bonus on completion of the project assembly.

Time is a big factor in optioning. It must be done as quickly as possible to forestall the probability of holdouts. People have a habit of varnishing the truth, and if a property were optioned at a price of $60,000. word of mouth might balloon this to $85,000. by the time it reached the ears of some listener who just happened to own one of the houses needed for the project. An agent must therefore be found who will work full time on your behalf.

As an example of what the application of option money can be, I approached an owner to secure a one year option at not more than $100,000. The owner sent me back to my client, the buyer, with a written agreement at $100,000. but stipulated he wanted an immediate five thousand dollars, and furthermore, the $5,000. was *not* to be credited to the purchaser if he closed. It would therefore cost the purchaser $105,000.

The purchaser agreed because he *knew* he wanted the property, would close the deal in one year, and a $5,000. payment meant that he could ''carry'' the financing for a year for about 5%, which was better than buying now and carrying the financing at about 10%. Plus the fact that the buyer wouldn't have the responsibility of maintaining the property for a year.

Every option goes on its own merits and the best deal each party can get for himself. I remember obtaining yearly options for as low as $2.00 for the year, and I also remember that the buyer went through with the purchases, and the vendors were all satisfied with the price.

Big dollars have been made with options which involved small amounts of money on the part of the buyer — the rights to the options were sold to others for a profit. But most options are obtained by buyers who have some specific plans for redeveloping the area, or converting the property to other uses. The time period in the option gives the buyer time to put everything together in his planning and financing.

If you want a property, but need time to swing it, an option just might do it for you.

46

SPECULATION

A good real estate speculator is one who knows how to make money in real estate. The definition is that simple.

The first requisite in joining the ranks of these successful money-makers is a thorough knowledge of market conditions in a particular aspect of real estate. A land speculator usually sticks with land, buying and selling it, because he knows all about it. It is the same in speculating with housing, commercial properties, and leases.

Review the chapter on ''leverage'', fully understand it, and then specialize. Not only that, but specialize in one particular urban area or county. This will require a good deal of homework on your part, because you will want to be very very familiar with the market. Nobody is going to hand you handsome real estate profits on a plate.

A sound way to start is in housing, and not only that, but a particular type of house. Take a six room brick detached bungalow for example. In the area selected, drive along every street and make a physical note of every six room bungalow with a ''for sale'' sign on it. Inspect them. Compare them. Obtain facts on recent selling prices. You will soon discover that you are somewhat of an expert on the market value of six room bungalows.

You will learn to spot the plus and minus features, and what they are worth. The attached double or single garage or carport, the extra bathrooms and washrooms, the finishing in the basements, the fireplaces, the condition of the buildings and the grounds, and a very important aspect, the reason for selling.

You will spot good, bad, tough and easy financing.

When you have spent a good solid month or so doing your homework, you will be ready to make your first offer. Before doing this review the chapter ''don't be afraid to make an offer.''

It is important to establish good rapport with a local lawyer *before* you are ready to proceed. Tell him of your plans. You will undoubtedly find that he will have some good advice for you, and perhaps he may even have access to a bit of cash for that extra few thousand you may need for an extra mortgage to swing a deal. Ensure that he sees all your offers *before* you sign them; he may show you how you can improve the offers to your advantage, and will certainly legally protect you.

It is also important to have good rapport with two or three aggressive real estate salesmen from different local brokerage houses. Tell them also of your plans. You will find that some salesmen will not pay much attention to you when they discover you are speculating because they simply won't want to bother presenting ''cheap offers,'' but don't let this deter you. By persistent viewing and meeting salesmen, you will find ones who won't mind working to flush out the good buys for you. Once you have made the first purchase through an agent, you can be sure he will stick with you like glue, because he will want more. Especially if there is a chance that he will get a piece of the action in selling your hot buy.

In searching for a profit making property, the first advice I would offer is to *check the zoning*! This cannot be stressed too strongly.

Do not assume, for example, that because there happens to be an occupied basement apartment in a house that it is a legal undertaking. It may be contrary to local municipal zoning by-laws, and this type of zoning trap can be found in many residential areas. A homeowner could be receiving rent from an illegal basement apartment for years, even unaware that it is not right, and be bothered by no one. No one, that is, until a snoopy neighbour blows the whistle on the operation with a resulting visit from a zoning inspector. Game over. Income stopped. If you spot it, and are interested in the house, quietly check the zoning for the street — you could save yourself money and a headache.

It is possible to sometimes obtain a bonus by knowing the zoning. A house on a street zoned commercial, for instance. All sorts of possibilities here. Or one with a lot large enough that when joined with a next-door property might produce three or four building lots.

Always remember that when house speculating, the house will be empty when you offer it for sale. This means that the flooring must be inspected carefully. Some houses have carpeting laid over plywood flooring, and if the vendor would decide to take the carpet, legally or not, you will be left with the prospect of replacing it because a plywood floor is just not attractive to buyers. If the floor is hardwood and bare, it would be adviseable to have it sanded and varnished.

The house you are selling must be made to look as attractive as possible to prospective buyers, which will require a very careful inspection of its interior, remembering to view it mindful of the fact that you will be selling it empty. Furniture can cover many flaws and unattractive features that will appear as soon as the vendor moves out.

The four major checks will be plumbing, heating, wiring and the roof. Buy some books on the subject of housebuilding with emphasis in these areas and make yourself familiar with these four major points.

An attractive setting is also an asset. Trees are priceless, especially if well placed.

The front door and verandah must be made to look attractive to buyers, because this is the first impression they will receive of the building when approaching it for inspection.

It has been said that there are three things to look for in speculation: Location, location, location. Near transportation and schools, for example, and know where they are when showing your house.

Don't bother looking at houses that have just been all spruced up. Someone else has done this, and they have upped the price. This is what you are supposed to do. Pretty soon you will know what is and what isn't a good buy.

Don't try to become wealthy overnight with your first purchase. This one will be your trial run, getting your feet wet. Look for a modest profit. When successfully completing your trial run, review everything about the operation and improve your performance for the next deal. After half a dozen you will be amazed at how much you know about house speculation.

Land Speculation

How much income can one realize from a vacant parcel of land? Other than leasing it to a local farmer, not much. Keep this in mind when looking at the prospects of making it with land. Mortgage payments will have to be maintained and municipal taxes paid.

One good method of land speculation is to obtain an option on the property for a minimum period of one year. The cash consideration given to the owner of the land will be about one per cent of the agreed price in the option. Then the would-be purchaser scrambles around during the option period trying to find a buyer at a higher price, or arrange for rezoning of property to greater density use, creating a higher value. If successful, money is made, and in some cases, a great deal of it. If not successful, but close to something promising, it may be possible to obtain an extension of the option for a further cash consideration. If all fails, a small loss is sustained and a lesson learned.

If the speculator had a property optioned for $100,000. and put up $1,000. cash, he is really out of pocket just the $1,000. plus the interest earning power of the thousand dollars. This is much better than sinking a large chunk of money into such a scheme by buying the property outright.

The truly big winners in land appreciation are the farmers on the fringes of the urban areas, the men who live on the old homestead and work the land. If you or I obtained a piece of land for $30,000. and someone came along and offered us $40,000. for it soon afterward, we would probably take it. This purchaser in turn would probably behave in the same manner, so that over the years the value of the land could appreciate tremendously, with the profits spread through several hands. The farmer, on the other hand, living and working with the land, possibly with his sons, resists initial bids on the land, but as time goes by and his land value soars, possibly when he is ready to retire, he would realize the entire appreciation built up over the years.

If you intend to speculate with land, be very careful not to get in too deep, and do it preferably on an option basis. Review the chapter ''optioning property.''

In searching for land, get to the *local* brokers, preferably ones who have been working your chosen area for a few years. They know local market values, trends, and can offer helpful advice. Also, subscribe to local weekly newspapers and read the ads carefully.

Commercial Building speculation

Here are five reasons for speculating commercial property:

1. The present income on the propety is just obviously too low, the leases are about ready to expire, and the situation could be drastically improved.

2. The building is in terrible condition, but structurally sound, and could be renovated to attract higher income.

3. The land under the building is obviously worth more than the entire parcel.

4. There is a good, very good, chance that the area zoning could be changed to create an inflated price on the land.

5. It can be purchased for a song.

As for the commercial property, there is a limit to the income it will produce, and if this is the true determining factor in the value of the property, with its use remaining constant, keep this in mind: Income less expenses leaves you what?

Lease Speculation

Very basic. Obtain a lease in a good location for less than the going rate, and sub-let the property for a higher figure.

This one requires particular caution. Be sure you fully understand all the clauses in the lease, especially restrictive clauses. When assured that your lease (and zoning) allows you to sub-let, be sure it will allow you to sub-let to the type of tenant you have in mind. And be sure you have the tenant, or you will be paying the rent for nothing.

Also, talk this over with a good insurance agent to be quite clear about who pays what, and ensure your sub-tenant is properly insured. Remember, in a lease, in the event of fire or damage, the rent goes on and must be paid. You are the one who pays it to the lessor regardless of whether you get it from your sub-tenant or not, so ensure the sub-tenant is a reliable one.

General

When buying and selling, always try to find the property where the vendor will help with the purchase by lending you part of the purchase price by way of a mortgage. Private mortgages can often be secured at lower than going rates, and repayment privileges can be more generous, such as repaying the mortgage before maturity without bonus or penalty. Sometimes mortgages can get in the way — a purchaser might want to buy for cash, and it is nice to know that any mortgages can be discharged without additional costs.

Don't be greedy. Anticipate a *reasonable* return on your investment.

Ensure there are no outstanding hydro or municipal work orders registered against property that interests you.

Take a good hard look at the property. What has to be done to improve it? Why are they selling? Who would buy it from you? Structure the financing to make it as easy as possible for a buyer to swing the deal.

Speculating is an interesting, educational and profitable way to spend your time and money, but it requires a very thorough knowledge of property, areas, zoning, financing and the *market*.

Speculate with your "extra" dollars, not the ones needed for necessities or bills that must be paid.

47

GOVERNMENT TAX SALES

For the first couple of years of municipal tax arrears, the property owner will receive sharper and sharper reminders to get the bills paid, and if all these reminders are ignored, the municipality naturally gets cheesed off with the delinquent taxpayer and gets tough.

Getting tough means eventual sale of the property to satisfy the municipal tax debt, but the municipality really bends over backwards and gives the property owner every reasonable opportunity to retain the property, *even after its sale.*

When all else has failed in attempt to have the tax bill paid, the owner will receive a notice of pending sale. If the owner ignores this, the notice of sale will be advertised in a publication called the Provincial Gazette.

The advertised sale will provide a brief description of the property and its location, and the date of sale, which will be by auction. It will also show the amount of tax arrears.

Contact your Provincial Government printing office and obtain a copy of an edition containing notices of sale. You may subscribe to the Gazette and have it mailed to you regularly. If you wish to bid on property, here are two suggestions:

(1) Inspect the property that interests you, before the date of sale.

(2) On the date of sale, or the day before, go to the local municipal or sheriff's office administering the sale, and see if the owner has redeemed the property by paying the tax arrears. If he has, the sale will be cancelled on your interested parcel.

If you are successful in your bid on the day of sale, you will not obtain title to the property at that time.

Your deposit money will be held in trust on the sale, until a further period of time has elapsed affording the owner to come forward and pay up. If he does, your deposit will be returned to you.

If he doesn't, you will be given title to the property.

48

BUYING AND LEASING CROWN LAND

Once upon a time when money was a scarce commodity, one could buy a quarter-section of land out west for ten dollars from the government. That's 160 acres, or about 65 hectares.

Land is still being purchased and leased from provincial governments, but not as freely as it once was. Even the governments are beginning to realize that land is not manufactured, and they are protecting what they have left. Here is a brief synopsis of what one may expect in our provinces, and the addresses of government offices to which one may write for further information.

BRITISH COLUMBIA: Prior to 1970, it was possible to obtain land by pre-emption (homesteading). That's gone, and there are now no free lands in B.C.

Only Canadian citizens are allowed the right to purchase and obtain a Crown grant leading to title. Waterfront lands can be obtained only on a leasehold basis. B.C. provides a 31 page booklet concerning the disposition of Crown lands. Write to: Director of Land Management, Parliament Buildings, Victoria, B.C. V8V 1X5

ALBERTA: To acquire a homestead sale, one must be a resident of Alberta for twelve months within three years immediately prior to the date of making application.

Land is available, and Alberta will provide you with an interpretation of the Public Lands Act and a large, interesting map of Alberta clearly showing what is and what is not available. Write to: Public Lands Division, Alberta Energy and Natural Resources, 9915 - 108th Street, Edmonton, Alta. T5K 2C9

SASKATCHEWAN: Applicant must be a Canadian citizen or landed immigrant. The Sask. Farm Ownership Act limits non-residents to having an interest in no more than 160 acres of agricultural land.

Sale policy provides only for the sale of cultivation leases to the lessee who has leased for a minimum of 5 years. Grazing leases are not eligible for sale. Write to: Lands Branch, Dept. of Agriculture, Administraion Building, Regina, Sask. S4S 0B1

MANITOBA: Policy under review. Presently one may purchase Crown lands for primary residential use or for intensive commercial development, subject to Cabinet endorsement.

Crown lands are leased for a wide variety of purposes, and the Minister's authority to lease is restricted to 21-year terms. All requests are circulated to other governmental departments and agencies for clearance prior to commitment. Write to: Chief, Crown Lands, Renewable Resources Division, 1495 St. James Street, Winnipeg, Man. R3H 0W9

ONTARIO: Cottage lots are available for purchase or lease. Leases are issued for 30 years with two additional 10-year options for renewal. Very reasonable rent.

Applicant must be a resident of Ontario during the first year in which certain lots become available. The next year, applicant must be a resident of Canada. The third year, ungranted lots may be *leased only*, to anybody including non-residents of Canada. Write to: Director, Lands Administration Branch, Ministry of Natural Resources, Ontario Government, Toronto, Ontario.

QUEBEC: Leases: Long term, 10 years or more, used when the plot of land is surveyed and classified as a permanent resort development. Short term, more than 12 months and less than 8 years, used when the plot of land is not surveyed.

Priority for renting granted to Quebec residents when a site is chosen, or when there is more than one applicant for the same land, and this, for a period of 6 months after date of receipt of the request. Write to: Ministere des Terres et Forets, Gouvernement du Quebec, Quebec City, P.Q.

NEW BRUNSWICK: It is not the policy of the Government to dispose of Crown lands, except in very exceptional cases. Homesteading is no longer provided for. Campsite leases are available, but do not convey exlusive hunting or fishing privileges. Write to: Lands Branch, Dept. of Natural Resources, Centennial Bldg. P.O. Box 6000, Fredericton, N.B. E3B 5H1

NOVA SCOTIA: Crown land no longer available and, not only that, all non-resident land owners must file a disclosure statement on their holdings in N.S. Forms for disclosure can be obtained from: Registrar of Land Holdings, Dept. of Lands and Forests, Halifax, N.S. B3J 2T9.

PRINCE EDWARD ISLAND: Provincial land resources are extremely limited, and there are non-residency restrictions. Brochures concerning the purchase and lease of agricultural lands available can be obtained. Write to: Director, Island Information Service, P.O. Box 2000, Charlottetown, P.E.I. C1A 7N8

NEWFOUNDLAND: Land is available for agriculture, residence, commercial establishments, e.g. accommodation of tourists etc., summer cottage, fishing and hunting cabins and use by religious organizations.

Leases for up to 50 years, and most reasonable rent. Title can be obtained on some types of property. Write to: Director, Crown Lands Administration, Dept. of Forestry and Agriculture, Howley Bldg. Higgins Line, St. John's, Nfld. A1C 5T7

YUKON TERRITORY: A moratorium has temporarily suspended the alienation of Crown lands for agricultural or grazing purposes. Cottage lots are available in planned recreational subdivisions only. Policies change from time to time. Write to: Supervisor of Lands, Dept. of Indian and Northern Affairs, 200 Range Road, Whitehorse, Y.T. Y1A 3V1

NORTHWEST TERRITORIES: In 1975 the disposition of lands for agricultural purposes was suspended, pending a new policy which is currently being formulated. Homesteading is not allowed.

Small parcels of land for recreational/non-residential purposes only are available, mostly in cottage lot subdivisions near major settlements. Write to: Regional Manager, Land Resources, Dept. of Indian and Northern Affairs, P.O. Box 1500, Yellowknife, N.W.T. X1A 2R3

49

BUYING AN APARTMENT BUILDING

There are buyers all over the country with $100,000. or more who are itching to invest it in an apartment building to produce the following results:

(a) Require the tenants of the property to pay all the expenses, including the interest and principal repayments on the mortgages.

(b) Provide a return of about 10% on the original investment.

(c) Provide a profit on the property in the event of a sale.

Twenty years ago I made my first sale to such a buyer, for $150,000. A well placed, solid, well tenanted 17 suite building. The buyer got it for a $40,000. down payment to a $110,000. mortgage fully amortized over 20 years.

Well, 20 years has passed. The mortgage, interest and principal, was repaid by the income from tenants. The income also paid all the operating expenses and municipal taxes, and provided the owner with a good net annual return on his investment. All paid for now, and what is today's market value of this property? Oh, I would think about $450,000. How about that?

Deals like this are being made every day across Canada, but only by people who are not afraid to get their financial feet wet, and possibly take a bit of risk. If it required little or no effort, with 100% guaranteed security, everybody would be doing it. They would not necessarily have the $100,000., or downstroke as it is called, but they would insist on getting involved through some sort of share basis. After all, 10% is much better than a lot of other investments we can think of, especially when one considers the fringe benefits and a possible whopping increase in value at the end of the line.

All these people who turn up with about $100,000. don't have it all in their own bank account. Many of them have partners; one, two, three, possibly as many as a dozen. They all have one common goal. Get involved. Make money.

Every building in Canada is owned by someone. Some people undoubtedly wish they had never become involved in owning investment real estate, for personal reasons, or a bad buy, but the majority of owners are whistling all the way to the bank. How did they get started? What makes one man a wealthy property owner, and another, who had the same opportunities, just another average Joe?

Some got their start in the building trades. They started out as labourers on a house construction job, kept their eyes and ears open, saved their money and, when the opportunity arose to purchase a couple of building lots, they took the plunge, either alone or with a partner. The demand for houses was constant, they worked hard and stuck to business, and eventually ended up being one of the big ones, or at least moderately successful.

Others did it through education. Becoming a lawyer, for example, is one of the surest ways to financial success. It not only gives one a great education into legal aspects of how other people make money, but it puts one close to these people and great opportunities to get involved.

Some people simply inherit estates. Others are talked into buying by salesmen; stumble onto a good thing; lend a man money and foreclose; marry property; obtain it by accepting real estate to settle a debt; or find themselves sitting on a gold mine due to re-zoning, and, realizing the potential, go right out and buy more. But the majority of investment properties are owned by people who went head on into it after a lot of thought, and plunged the bankroll into the financial whirlpool that is the greatest money maker of all time — real estate.

If you have worked hard for years, watched the pennies and saved diligently, it is not always an easy thing to bring yourself to write out a cheque that will seemingly wipe out your life savings. You watched that bank book balance grow over the years, and sometimes it is a bit of a shock to look at it after all these years and find it so depleted, regardless of the knowledge that it left the bank and ended up as bricks and mortar.

If you have felt the urge to get involved, and have a timid heart, or nagging doubts about going it alone, don't. Get a partner. Someone you have known for some time. Someone you feel is a very solid type, with a good clear head on his shoulders, but especially one who has the kind of money you are considering as your investment. You can always be a minor or major shareholder, but don't set the scales too far off balance. If your allowance for this venture is modest, get two or three partners. After you do buy the property, you can always sell your share to your partners under your agreement if it doesn't work out.

Before you consider buying *any* property, you naturally have to know something about it, and you should know as much about it as possible.

Have the investment listing form shown on a following page copied.

146

It will enable you to have a clear picture and record of every property you inspect. It is basically intended for listing apartment buildings, but can effectively be used for any type of investment property.

Five points: location; condition of building; income; expenses and proper financing.

The ideal location for an apartment building is close to main traffic arteries. Not right on them; close to them. Traffic creates noise, and regardless of what you have heard about ''getting used to it'', it can still create problems with tenants, who didn't realize what they were getting into. Being near the main artery provides your tenants with transportation. It is nice to take a 4-block walk to the bus on a sunny spring day, but in the winter? Proper location will provide you with a better chance of keeping the building fully occupied.

If you have had no experience with the ins-and-outs of building construction, and you find a property that seriously interests you to the point of submitting a respectable offer, get some expert advice. Buildings that have been mortgaged through an approved lender of Central Mortgage and Housing Corporation are built to its standards, so you won't have to be very concerned about the quality of construction. Sloppy maintenance and appearance of the propety can be blamed on poor management, a careless superintendent or inconsiderate tenants. This can be corrected. A badly constructed building is another matter.

Don't be dazzled by an income figure that seems great. It may be too high. You should check rental figures in the immediate area for comparable accommodation. If the figures are too high in your comparison, you could be in trouble at a later date. Work on the averages.

Despite the ''audited statement'' of expenses you may see, you should again speak to someone familiar with the expenses of operating comparable buildings. The average figures will give you an indication of what you may expect after ownership, regardless of what the owner tells you. Of course, there are many ways to cut down the expenses, and you should look critically at each item. Heat control is a good example. Some superintendents just blast away with the heat to forestall any possible telephone calls from a tenant with a complaint. The lack of storm windows is another thing to watch for in the heating bills. Is the hot water heated off the furnace or does it have its own unit? Are the garage doors properly controlled to remain closed? There isn't much point in having your financing well considered if the expenses are going to knock you right into a nil balance or debit.

When you have satisfied yourself as to the gross income and operating expenses (including taxes, which are easy to check), you have two other items to consider, which will come under operating expenses.

INVESTMENT
LISTING FORM

Bldg. Name _____

& Address _____

PRICE $ _____

CASH $ _____

1st Mortgagee _____

Amount $_____ At ____ % Due_____

Payable $ _____

2nd Mortgagee _____

Amount $_____ At ____ % Due_____

Payable $ _____

GROSS ANNUAL INCOME _____

OPERATING EXPENSES

Taxes _____

Insurance _____

Heating _____

Light _____

Water _____

Maintenance _____

Supplies _____

Elevator _____

Superintendent _____

Misc. & Audit _____

Management _____

Vacancy Allce _____

_____

_____

_____

_____ _____

Income Before Debt Charges $ _____

MORTGAGE PAYMENTS

1st mortgage _____

2nd mortgage _____ _____

Net Cash Surplus (%) $ _____

PRINCIPAL PAYMENTS

(Average_____years)

On 1st mortgage _____

On 2nd mortgage _____ _____

GROSS RETURN (%) $ _____

Estimated Capital Cost

Allowance 1st Year $ _____

SUITES ( )	MONTHLY	ANNUALLY
_____Bachelor	_____	_____
_____1 Bedroom	_____	_____
_____2 Bedroom	_____	_____
_____3 Bedroom	_____	_____
_____4 Bedroom	_____	_____
_____Garages	_____	_____
_____Spaces	_____	_____
_____Laundry	_____	_____
Sundry Income:	_____	_____

GROSS ANNUAL INCOME _____

Assessment Land:_____

Building:_____

Construction _____

Fireproof_____ Age _____

Lot_____ Laundry_____

No. Storeys_____ Refrig._____

Brick_____ Stoves _____

Incinerator_____ Inter-Com._____

Heating_____ Lobby_____

Floor Suite_____ Rec. Pl. G._____

Floor Hall_____ Air-Cond._____

Elevator_____ Balconies_____

REMARKS

148

Vacancy allowance: It was customary a few years ago to charge a minimum of 5% of the gross income as an allowance for vacancies. Recently, this figure has been reduced because of low vacancy factors. You must decide what this figure should be in view of present and foreseeable expectancy in vacancies. An argument you will undoubtedly receive today from vendors is that why should there be *any* vacancy allowance when the building is filled and with possibly a waiting list of tenants?

Management: Larger buildings will usually be managed by contract at anything from a flat fee to 3% - 5% of the gross income. Some owners spend their own time actively managing their own properties, and the owners of small buildings invariably manage their own. No matter who manages the building, the time is worth money, and this should not be forgotten in the debit side of the ledger.

Now, deducting all these expenses and allowances from the gross income, you arrive at the net income before financing. This is where the importance in mortgaging enters the picture. The more you save, or the less your outlay in mortgage payments, the more money you will have in your pocket as your net cash flow. As I have pointed out, your expense will include the principal payment as well as the interest.

There are just three ways to stretch the mortgage and make this item of expense thinner; lower interest rate, lengthy amortization, and smaller or no principal payments.

If you are going to assume an existing mortgage, there is nothing you can do about the rate of interest. If you are going to arrange a conventional mortgage, there is little you can do to lower the going, or current rate of interest. The only possible saving you might have is in the event of equitable financing on the part of the vendor. If the vendor will agree to accept a mortgage from you as part of your purchase price, you might be able to get a lower than conventional rate of interest from him. However, sometimes the only inducement for this as far as the vendor is concerned is a higher top price. So don't count on the possibility of saving money on the mortgage rate of interest.

The longer the period of mortgage amortization, the smaller the payments. The smaller the payments, the more cash in your pocket. The following will illustrate this; carrying charges per thousand dollars, per month:

10½ % mortgage, interest compounded twice-yearly

Years	Amount
5	$21.39
10	13.37
15	10.92
20	9.84
25	9.29
30	8.99
35	8.81

Of course, the longer the amortization, the longer it will take to reduce the debt to zero. Some people aren't too concerned about long term debt for two reasons; it produces a higher cash flow and gives the borrower a higher tax deduction due to the interest charges. Another reason is that future payments are made with cheaper dollars.

The difference between a 20 and a 30 year amortization plan in the above example amounts to $10.20 per year per thousand dollars. This means a plus or minus in your net cash surplus of $10.20 per year for every thousand dollars you have mortgaged. For example, on a $100,000. mortgage this amounts to a difference up or down of $1,020.00 per year to you in your hand.

The more money you owe, the more interest you pay, and the more interest you pay, the higher the figure you will show on your income tax return as a deductible item.

One thing you must remember to watch for very carefully is the *term* of the mortgage, or the length of time you have to reduce the debt using somebody else's money.

If your mortgage is *amortized* for 30 years, with a *term* of 5 years, what happens in 5 years? The balance of the debt is due forthwith. If the mortgagee doesn't feel inclined to renew the mortgage, you have to arrange to borrow funds somewhere else. This can be costly. It involves discharging one mortgage and paying the tariff for the new one. Get the longest term you can, or at least an agreement to renew the loan at the end of the 5 years.

The third means of reducing the mortgage payment expense, and thereby leaving you with more cash in your hand, is by having small, or no payments to make on the principal sum. This, of course, will mean that some day you will have a day of reckoning when the principal sum becomes due at the end of the term, but in the meantime it will provide you with more cash.

Financing is the big thing. You want to obtain a reasonable return on your investment, so you will naturally want to be clear on the four steps of investments.

1. The money you have left after deducting the operating expenses and vacancy allowance from the gross income is the *net return before financing,* or *income before debt charges.*

2. The money you have left after deducting the mortgage interest and principal payments from this figure is the *net return,* or *cash flow*, or *net cash surplus.*

3. The figure shown after you *add* the mortgage principal payment to the net return, is the *gross return.*

4. From this figure you deduct your capital cost allowance (depreciation) if it is necessary, or desirable to take it, and the figure you have left is what you will show on your income tax return as taxable income.

We have gone through the stage of arriving at the net return before financing, and we have discussed the mortgaging. Therefore, all the operating expenses of the building *and* the total yearly mortgage payments (interest and principal) deducted from the gross income will take us to the end of the second step, and leave a figure that represents the net return, or cash in your hand.

When the mortgage payments were made they included the principal payment, and, insofar as your net cash flow is concerned, they represent an item of expense. However, the government doesn't take the same attitude, and as far as Ottawa is concerned, the only expense you have in connection with a mortgage, for income tax purposes, is the interest you have paid. So now you have reached the end of the year with about 10% cash return on your investment, and the government says you made more than that as far as they are concerned, so you have to add the mortgage principal payments you made to the 10%, or net cash flow you have, to arrive at your *gross* return on your investment for income tax purposes.

The only way you can reduce this figure is by taking as much capital cost allowance, or depreciation yearly as the law allows, and deducting it from your gross, income tax return, figure. This final figure will be what you will use as your taxable figure on the operation for income tax purposes.

The Capital Cost Allowance

A Building is a term of wide range covering any structure with walls and a roof affording protection and shelter. The courts have held that the word structure includes anything of substantial size which is built up from component parts and intended to remain permanently on a permanent foundation. Portable shelters such as housing, office and other service units are also regarded as buildings if they are installed and intended to remain in a particular location.

The *Capital Cost of Property* means the full cost to the buyer and in addition to the cost of the real property includes such things as legal, accounting, engineering or other fees where they are incurred in order to acquire the property.

When purchasing an investment propery, the capital cost of the building is separated from the capital cost of the land. The reason for this is very simple — land cannot be depreciated for income tax purposes — just the building.

One popular method of doing this has been to take the ratio of municipal assessment for the property and apply it as a guide. However, the income tax department will not always accept this, so it would be advisable to obtain expert advice in placing the value on the building. Also, some Provinces are now using a "blended" assessment, which unfortunately does not show the separated value of land and building.

Assuming you purchased a small building and land for a total of $100,000., with a fair separated value of (1) land, $20,000. and (2) building, $80,000., the $80,000. would be your capital cost for income tax purposes, in determining your capital cost allowance, or "depreciation".

Depreciation allowances are not all the same. Some are greater than others. The most common is a "class 3" building, which is brick, blocks, etc. and has a 5% rate. Frame buildings have a 10% rate.

In each taxable year, you are allowed, for example, in "class 3" to take an income tax deduction of a maximum of 5% of the undepreciated balance of the capital cost of the building.

The first year's allowable depreciation on the $80,000. would be $4,000. The second year, 5% of the undepreciated balance of $80,000. minus $4,000. ($76,000.) and so on.

If, for example, the first year showed a net return to you of $3,000. on the operation of a building, you would not take the $4,000. because you would not need it. This would leave an undepreciated balance for the second year of $77,000.

You and the Government keep track of all the depreciation you have taken and on which you have not paid any income tax, because when you sell the building your day of reckoning arrives and you pay tax on it.

The tax is payable at your choice of either (1) all at once in the tax year of selling, or (2) adjusting your past returns over five years.

Depreciation cannot be taken to reduce other areas of income, as it was in the past, and it cannot be transferred to another acquired building to avoid the tax bite.

"Government rules change on the subject of depreciation, so I suggest that you check this carefully. There may be something new that would be to your advantage."

Selling the Building

The "sale price of property" means the *net* sale price after deductions of all fees and commissions paid in connection with the sale.

When you sell a depreciable property and subsequently part or all of an amount owing to you in respect of the asset is reduced pursuant to a negotiated adjustment of the sale price, or pursuant to a legal obligation under a guarantee, warranty, etc., in the agreement of sale, such reduction should be taken into account in the year of sale for the purpose of calculating the amount to be included in income or for the purpose of calculating the undepreciated capital cost of the property.

When you sell depreciable property and the proceeds of disposition include an agreement for sale, or a mortgage on land which agreement or mortgage is subsequently sold by you at a discount from its principal amount, the amount of the discount will, if the sale of the agreement or mortgage takes place in the year of disposition of the depreciable property, reduce the proceeds of disposition.

If the sale of the agreement, or mortgage, takes place subsequent to the year of disposition of the property, the discount will be deductible in computing your income for that year to the extent that the amount of the discount exceeds any capital gain (excess of proceeds over capital cost) calculated at the time of disposition.

Remember the three areas of income tax in selling an investment property:

(1) The profit on the operation of the investment for all or that part of your taxable year in which you own the property.

(2) The "recaptured" tax on the capital cost allowance (depreciation) taken during your ownership.

(3) The capital gain tax. Review the chapter "Capital Gain Tax Appraisal".

When you have a situation where the land is worth more than the present use of the property as land and buildings, and it is your intention to abandon the buildings (or demolish them) in order to avoid paying a recaptured tax on depreciation, ensure that you check with the Income Tax Department first. The rules of the game here have changed.

The Purchase Agreement

When you instruct an agent to prepare an agreement of purchase and sale, the following are points in your offer that should not be overlooked.

The initial part of the offer will cover the financing; deposit with offer, mortgage details, cash on closing (subject to adjustments), and any other financial consideration. Then you get into the property itself, and should note the importance of the following:

"The purchase price shall include all plant, machinery, attachments, fixtures and installations and equipment of every nature and kind, now on the subject property and which are not the exclusive property of the existing tenants, and, without limiting the generality of the foregoing, shall also include the master television antenna and all electrical and other appliances, fixtures and chattels.

The vendor warrants and represents that the apartment building on the subject property comprises (   ) apartments suites and that there are no outstanding orders issued by the Fire, Police, or Health Department of the City of (   ) and/or the Municipality of (   ) requiring change in or addition or alterations to the subject property.

The vendor warrants and represents that it has complied and will continue to comply with all building, zoning and other by-laws of the City of (   ) up to and including the date of closing hereinafter referred to, and that it has not committed or created a nuisance on the subject property.

The vendor warrants and represents that now and at closing, all mechancial equipment including heating, plumbing, drainage and electrical wiring systems, and elevator equipment and facilities in the subject property, will be in good working order and condition, and that the roofs of all buildings, structures and appurtenances are water-tight and that the basement is dry.

The vendor warrants and represents that Schedule "A" attached hereto sets out all pertinent information for all the tenancies in effect in respect of the subject property, and covenants and agrees that on closing, it will deliver to the purchaser the following: a proper assignment of all leases herein, all copies of all leases herein and directions to each of the tenants herein authorizing payment of rentals thereafter to the purchaser as he may direct.

The vendor covenants and agrees that on closing it will deliver to the purchaser a Statutory Declaration made by one of its officers which will contain the following and other reasonable clauses that may be required by the purchaser:

(1) That the leases referred to in Schedule "A" to the agreement of purchase and sale herein dated (   ) are valid, binding and enforceable in accordance with the terms thereof:

(2) That there are no disputes between the vendor, as landlord, and the said tenants with respect to any matter arising out of the tenancies.

(3) That all rent has been paid to the (   ) day of (   ) and that

154

there are no prepayments or rent beyond the current monthly rental: (Note: if there are, this will be settled in the adjustments on closing and credited to the purchaser).

(4) That none of the said leases have been assigned nor have any of the tenants sublet the premises leased to them:

(5) That the leases have not been amended, changed or varied in any way whatsoever, and

(6) That there are no other tenancy arrangements affecting the subject property other than those set out in the said Schedule "A" to the Agreement of Purchase and Sale dated ( ).

The vendor shall within fifteen (15) days after acceptance, supply to the purchaser all plans, specifications, sketches, drawings and up-to-date surveys of the subject property.

On closing, the vendor shall assign to the purchaser all contracts and the benefit thereof, made by it in respect of the subject property, and the vendor shall further deliver all licenses, agreements, books, records and accouts and, without limiting the generality of the foregoing, all other documents, information and papers in the possession of the vendor relating to the subject property.

The vendor warrants and represents that the gross income received by it for the fiscal year ending ( ) was ( ).

The within offer and the obligation of the purchaser to complete the within transaction is entirely conditional upon verification by the vendor to the purchaser of the fulfillment of all conditions, warranties and representations herein set out.

Provided the title is good and free from all encumbrances except as aforesaid: The purchaser is not to call for the production of any title deed, abstract or other evidence of title except as are in the possession of the vendor. The purchaser is to be allowed until closing to investigate the title at his own expense. If with that time any valid objection to title is made in writing to the vendor which the vendor shall be unable or unwilling to remove and which the purchaser will not waive, this agreement shall, notwithstanding any intermediate acts or negotiations in respect of such objections, be null and void and the deposit shall be returned to the purchaser without interest or deductions. Save as to any valid objection so made within such time, the purchaser shall be conclusively deemed to have accepted the title of the vendor to the subject property.

The sale of the subject property shall be made in accordance with the Bulk Sales Act (Province) and the Retail Sales Act (Province) and the vendor hereby, covenants, undertakes and agrees to comply with all the provisions thereof and to pay all taxes and costs in connection therewith.

This offer is to be accepted by ( ) otherwise void: and sale is to be completed on or before the (   ) on which date possession is to be given to the purchaser subject to the tenancies herein set out, and the purchaser to be entitled to the receipt of the rents and profits thereafter.

This offer, when accepted, shall constitute a binding contract of purchase and sale and time in all respects shall be the essence of this agreement.

Until completion of sale, all buildings and equipment on the subject property shall be and remain at the risk of the vendor until closing and the vendor will hold all policies of insurancce affected on the subject propery and the proceeds thereof in trust for the parties hereto, as their interests may appear. In the event of damage to the subject buildings and equipment before the completion of this transaction, the purchaser shall have the right to elect to take such proceeds and complete the purchase, or cancel this agreement whereupon the purchaser shall be entitled to return without interest of all monies theretofore paid on account of this purchase without deductions.

Unearned fire insurance premiums, mortgage interest, rentals, taxes, fuel, water rates and heating to be apportioned and allowed to date of completion of sale.

Deed or transfer and assignment of leases to be prepared at the expense of the vendor, and mortgage at the expense of the purchaser.

Any tender of documents or money hereunder may be made upon the vendor at (address) and upon the purchaser at (address) or any party acting for him or it and money may be tendered by negotiable cheque certified by a chartered bank or trust company in the City of (   ).

The offer and its acceptance to be read with all changes of gender or number required by the context.

Dated at (   ) this (   ).

Witness:

. . . .
Purchaser

Good luck!

50

BUYING A MOBILE HOME

Today's mobile home is a modern, fully equipped dwelling containing most of the services and facilities found in any single family home.

However, despite the increasing popularity in this type of accommodation, a major drawback appears to be focused on municipal by-laws. Some municipalities are prone to look upon the proposal of a mobile home subdivision as another "trailer park" which would not enhance their image of a solid community. This view is supported by the severe restrictions on such developments now in force in many urban centers in Canada. It therefore follows that if you are interested in buying a mobile home that is not part of an approved subdivision or licensed park, the zoning by-laws of your chosen municipality should be carefully checked to ensure that you can live in it once you buy it.

The modern mobile home can provide more than 600 sq. ft. (about 55 square metres), and two of them can be put together creating a home larger than many standard detached bungalows. The heating is mostly warm air, oil fired. Hot water tanks electric. Bedrooms are small and storage space limited. Walls thin but well insulated; prefinished panelling and aluminum siding — easy maintenance. They are completely prefabricated, transported to your site and installed on a concrete slab, hooked up to services and ready for occupancy.

Under Canada's National Housing Act, housing projects involving the use of the mobile home may be developed under different sponsorships:

Public Initiative: The development of mobile home parks and mobile home subdivisions may be financed under the Federal-Provincial arrangement section of the Act, or under the provisions whereby land assembly loans may be made to a province or municipality. Where the assembly of the land is carried out under either of these provisions of the NHA, it is preferable that its disposal be effected by the conveyance to the user of either a registerable freehold interest or a registerable long-term leasehold interest. If this is done, the user has the opportunity of securing long-term mortgage financing for the acquisition of his interest in the land space and the mobile unit that is affixed to it. Consideration may also be given for the use of mobile homes for public housing for rental to low-income families or to senior citizens.

Private Initiative: The development of mobile home parks and mobile home subdivisions where the purchase of individual new or existing mobile home units is included, may be financed by approved lenders under the insurance provisions of the Act.

Cooperatives: Under the National Housing Act, loans to individuals and corporations for mobile homes and mobile home parks are also available to cooperatives, and the various forms of special assistance available to families with low income are available to them also in mobile home cooperatives.

N.H.A. Financing

If the proper arrangements have been made and the appropriate legal documents executed, it is possible to insure loans under the NHA for mobile home projects on the security of mobile homes, provided the land is owned or leased by the owners of the homes. Mobile home loans can be treated in much the same way as loans for the construction of partly or totally prefabricated houses.

A loan, for example, may finance a rental project. All the housing units are then owned and mortgaged by one borrower. The land is mortgaged also, if owned by the borrower, but if the land is leased by him, the lease is pledged as security for the loan, either by means of a mortgage or an assignment of the lease.

If the housing units in a subdivision are to be individually owned, a borrower can secure one loan for the acquisition and installation of a single mobile home on a single subdivided lot owned or leased by him.

A developer-builder can obtain several such loans at one time for the development of a mobile home subdivision. Each loan need only be secured by a mortgage on the housing unit owned by the borrower together with the lot, if the latter is owned outright. If the lot is held by the borrower under a lease, a mortgage will be given on the housing unit but the borrower's leasehold interest in the lot will be mortgaged separately or assigned in favour of the lender.

If the lot leased by the borrower is already mortgaged, as sometimes is the case (usually in favour of the vendor who sold the land to the lessor, but who has not yet received payment), the lender will require that the lease not be affected by that prior mortgage. The lot may be released from the mortgage, usually on total or partial payment of the amount outstanding. Alternatively, the vendor's sale and mortgage documents or a registered amendment, may stipulate that, if the vendor repossesses the land and cancels the sale, neither the lessees nor their creditors will be affected, and that the vendor guarantees that he will honour the leases signed by the purchaser.

The interest and the requirements of the parties can usually be reconciled. However, when the borrower is to hold the land under a lease, loan insurance will be provided only after an examination and approval of the proposed lease.

Amortization periods for loans on mobile homes will be determined on the same basis as those for conventionally constructed dwellings which meet the Canadian code for residential construction.

Site planning requirements: In general terms consideration will be given to mobile home developments which integrate the mobile home into an established community as part of a planned residential development. It is, therefore, necessary that such proposals have the support of local officials and planning authorities. Scattered satellite developments which are to be located in areas not subject to planning controls or where adequate municipal services and amenities are not available will normally not be considered acceptable for NHA financing. Detailed site requirements for acceptance of mobile home developments under the NHA will be found in a CMHC "Site Planning for Mobile Homes" publication. This, and other helpful information is available at your nearest CMHC office.

Other financing is available from banks and loan companies, who will probably secure the loan under a chattel mortgage. Your dealer may also have some helpful advice for you.

There is an interesting booklet "Owner's guide to mobile home maintenance" available from the Canadian Mobile Home Association, Suite 512, 55 York Street, Toronto, Ontario.

51

BUYING A COTTAGE

There are two basic assumption errors in buying that retreat to get away from it all. The first is that ''the beach in front of the cottage is mine,'' and the second is that since a cottage is not too far away from the water, there must be acccess to the water.

Ever heard of Crown reparian rights? This is a strip of land owned by the Government along the shores of lakes and rivers, and it is public property. The public usually assumes that because the cottage is on the beach, the beach must be the property of the cottage owner. Here are some general observations to deter this thinking:

In the Yukon Territory and the Northwest Territories, the Territorial Lands Act makes it quite clear that, unless otherwise ordered by the Governor in Council, a strip of land one hundred feet in width (about 30 metres) measured from ordinary high water mark or from the boundary line, as the case may be, shall be deemed to be reserved to the Crown out of every grant of territorial lands, where the land extends:

(a) to the sea or an inlet thereof

(b) to the shore of any navigable water or an inlet therof

In Manitoba, since 1930, the Crown reserves out of every disposition of Crown land ''a strip of land one and one-half chains in width (99 feet, or again about 30 metres) measured from ordinary high-water mark. And all subdivisions abutting on navigable water must provide for a public reserve along the shore, which is vested in the responsible municipality.

In Saskatchewan, title to shorelands of a body of water is normally retained by the Crown to permit public access to and use of the water body.

In Alberta, with certain limited exceptions, the title to the shores of all rivers, streams, watercourses, lakes and other bodies of water is vested in the Crown.

In Ontario it is a very comlex subject. Some appear to own the shoreline, and some don't.

In Newfoundland, under the Crown Lands Act (1970) a strip of Crown lands not less than thirty-three feet wide (about 10 metres) around and adjoining all lakes and ponds and along each bank of all rivers, shall be reserved in all grants, leases and licences issued under the Act.

The point is, a buyer of a waterfront lot cannot assume that ownership of the shoreline goes with the lot. The odds are against it.

If the cottage lot is not on the shore, it is adviseable to ensure that at least the owner of the lot has access to the shore itself. Make this a condition of your offer in buying the lot.

When considering the purchase of a cottage, you will save yourself many hours and a great deal of frustration if you list your major requirements. A big consideration is whether the cottage is to be used simply as a summer retreat, or will there be plans in the future for year-round use or a home for retirement? The municipal by-laws may have something to say about this.

In deciding on a general location in your search, you will soon realize that some compromise will occur, and price will be the big leveler. Prices are generally dictated by distance from major urban centres, and it is understandable that the closer you are, the more you pay.

The size of the lake or river, and quality of the water has a great bearing on price. Generally, the larger the body of water, the higher the price. River frontage prices usually go at about the same price as smaller lakes. Type of terrain and summer or year-round road affect price.

When you find a property that appears to suit your needs, and pocketbook, here are a few things to think about in making the offer:

Access to water will be your prime consideration.

Check the basic structure, foundation and particularly the joists for dry rot.

It is important to ensure the roof will stand up under a heavy winter's snowfall. There will be no one there to clean it off for you and this can cause concern. Perhaps a local resident may be employed to clean the snow off the roof periodically, but remember it.

Ensure that the septic system meets municipal requirements.

If it is on a private road, who pays for its upkeep — and how much?

If the cottage is advertised as winterized, is the water system installed for winter use? A most important point.

If it is a lot only, determine from the municipality just what you can build on it, and what the septic requirements are.

If it is your intention to use the property for future year-round use, check the zoning and ensure it is not zoned for seasonal recreational use.

Before making the offer, think it over carefully, and make your offer subject to any of your doubts. The worst that can happen is that you won't get the property, but who wants to buy a dream and end up with a nightmare?

52

BUYING A MOTEL

Operating a motel, even a small one, in today's competitive market is not a job for retired persons or even for the semi-retired.

It is a full-time job which frequently demands considerable physical stamina. It demands poise in the face of pressure. It requires an aggressive, business-like approach to profitmaking. To be sure, there is a reasonably good future ahead for the motel business, and for many of those in other branches of the time-honoured calling of innkeeper. But the right starting time is not the year in which one quits work and retires.

The motel industry offers considerable opportunities to persons who are willing to invest adequate sums of money, to discipline themselves, and to adhere faithfully to proved standards of business practice.

On the other hand, anyone entering this business must bear in mind that regardless of how hard and skillfully he works, it is possible to fail anyway, because of an oversupply of motel rooms in some areas (leading to price cutting) or because of business conditions, local or national. In other words, if in your particular area there are too many motel rooms for the number of travellers, whatever the cause, one or more of the motels is going to be forced out of business.

The Basics

Your primary business as a motel operator will be renting rooms to guests, but there are other allied sources of income you may also want to explore.

Motels which have a restaurant on the premises, or nearby, generally are more popular than those which do not. As a motel owner, you may build and operate a restaurant yourself; you may erect the restaurant and lease it to an experienced restauranteur; or you may have no investment whatever in the restaurant, but refer your guests to one that is close by.

Some motels make money on gift shops, or on service stations. Vending machines add to income. So can auto or boat rentals. And there are other possible profit-producing services. Any extra income, however, is usually peanuts compared with the take from the primary source — room sales. Unless room occupancy keeps above the breakeven level, the motel itself will decline, regardless of minor secondary sources of on-premises income.

The motel industry has grown dramatically, and in many areas the competition is fierce, and yet there are other areas begging, through chambers of commerce and other development agencies, for operators to come in and build sorely-needed motels.

Pitfalls

A rude awakening for many novice motel operators occurs when they realize that they have taken on a 24-hour job with no days off.

As a host, you must see to the comfort and happiness of your guests, and as a businessman you must show a profit. These two responsibilities will keep you on the job for long hours and the work is often hard.

You not only must be a good and hospitable desk clerk, you also must be a fair plumber, electrician, advertising man, mechanic, accountant, and interior decorator. Of course, only a very few exceptionally gifted persons can be good at all these jobs, but as a motel manager you must hire personnel competent to perform these tasks, or you frequently will find you must do the best you can in situations for which you may not have been trained.

Physical stamina is essential, which makes motel management a poor choice as a retirement job. This does not mean that some middle-aged couples have not taken up motel owner-managership successfully. But it does mean that retirement is not found in the motel business.

As the operator of a small motel, you may be on your feet all morning as you go about supervising and assisting in the cleaning of rooms, repairing equipment and fixtures, and tending to highway signs. During the afternoon, you may have to get the bookeeping up to date, purchase supplies, and prepare direct-mail advertising. Meanwhile, you will have to keep smiling, and in the afternoon and evening, greet guests and see that each party is comfortable. During the night, there may be late arrivals or complaints from persons already roomed that the air conditioning has failed, that plumbing has broken down, or that guests in the next room are too noisy.

If you own and manage your motel, you may find yourself tied to it with seldom a chance for a day off. Rooms must be rented every night, and finding a person who is competent enough to manage the motel, and willing to work only on the occasions when you would like a holiday could be difficult.

Your family must be able to adjust to the confining routine. As a matter of fact, in the owner-managed motel the entire family usually works at various motel chores, and the temperament and training of each member must be considered.

There will be other pitfalls over which you may have little or no control. You may have an excellent location and do a good business — but others are aware of it and may build a bigger, better motel near yours. You may think the future looks cozy, but your Provincial highway department may decide it is necessary to by-pass your community or build a super-highway which will take away your direct access to traffic lanes.

Hazards

In fires, storms, and other natural disasters, you may find your insurance doesn't fully cover you, particularly if you count the business you lose, due to the disaster. Also, the death of a guest on your premises could result in a lawsuit which could hurtle your into bankruptcy, if your negligence is proved, and your insurance is inadequate. Or a dishonest employee may slowly rob you into insolvency through the almost invisible techniques of embezzlement.

Your biggest danger is also your greatest asset; *You*. It is your managerial abilities which will make or break your motel. It is your ability to act as a good host and a good salesman, day in and day out. It is your success in building and maintaining a high room occupancy rate at adequate price levels which will determine whether your motel will make money or lose it.

Your attitude toward your business, your dealings with your guests, with your fellow motel operators, with your suppliers, and with all other persons with whom you come in contact in the course of your business will have a direct bearing on your success or failure.

Qualities You Need

Ask yourself how well you are prepared for the essentials of motel management:

1. Ability to work long, hard hours.

2. Willingness to accept the confinement to the job (the smaller the motel, the less freedom for the operator).

3. Ability to deal tactfully with people, many of whom may have been travelling under difficult conditions all day and are not in the friendliest mood.

4. Knack of being a good host, making guests feel wanted, and anticipating their needs.

5. Constant awareness and practice of public relations.

6. Willingness to cope with all kinds of problems, which may range from a coin jammed in a soft drink machine to a guest who suffers a heart attack at 3 a.m.

7. Some knowledge of business management, personnel handling, accounting, and sales promotion, plus being a general handyman for do-it-yourself repairs and maintenance.

8. An appreciation of how important it is for you to take an active role in affairs affecting the entire motel industry, acting through joint efforts with others like yourself in local, Provincial and national motel trade associations.

9. Ambition to improve your own standards as a motel manager by studying books and journals on the subject; attending short schools, seminars and expositions; keeping abreast of current industry developments; and otherwise training yourself and your helpers.

10. Executive ability at least to the extent that you can and will be able to delegate authority.

Judging a Motel Location

Actually, only the record of a motel's profitability over a long period can be the final test of whether its location is good. The fact that you are beside a busy highway isn't enough, for a thousand passing automobiles are not worth the single car that stops and discharges guests who rent rooms.

In searching for a good motel location, keep these fundamental principles in mind:

1. The trading area must have an adequate potential. Look beyond the motel industry itself. If retail business generally is declining, if the region is losing population and otherwise slipping downward, a motel also may face a struggle for existence.

Of course, on the other hand, the area you are considering may show no immediate evidence of current progress, but still have some good petential for the near future. Perhaps you will find out that a sizeable new factory is being started, or that other industries will be expanded. Possibly you will learn that two super-highways will be completed with an intersection at a nearby point. Or perhaps your survey will disclose the fact that the proposed location is in a good spot between two growing urban areas and that highway changes between the two centers could conceivably generate business for the motel.

2. Guests should be able to get to the motel easily, and with a miniumum of confusion.

If access to your place is difficult and if the directional signs are bewildering, strangers may give up after one try at finding you and will go on and stop somewhere else.

3. You should pick your location with a view to whether it is a convenient stopping place for travellers. Locations which are an average day's drive from major centers are likely to be good. Even a motel in an inconspicuous location can succeed if it is just about the right distance from a big city. Usually, however, more business can be intercepted at well-travelled highway interchange points, and of course near airports.

4. A group of motels often can help each other. In fact, each one seems to do better when several of them are not far apart. This is partly because many travellers like to shop around before they reach a decision and sign the register. Travellers who know there are several motels at a given location will drive to that point.

Additional business develops also when there are large meetings that cannot be handled by a single motel. The delegates will occupy several in the same area.

5. Compatibility with other nearby businesses is desirable. Some types of enterprises help to build motel volume, while others drive potential guests away. Restaurants, drug stores, service stations, and similar businesses serving needs of the travelling public are assets to a location. Junk yards, railroad yards, slums and noisy or dirty neighbourhoods do not invite the traveller.

6. Although, as noted, competing motels can sometimes work together to mutual advantage, the prospective operator nevertheless should try to find out whether there will be too much competition for the business available. He should find out how many rooms there are in motels and other tourist accommodations in the area, and what percentage of them are occupied on an average night.

7. The prospective owner-manager should learn as much as he can about other possible hazards. For example, will the zoning bylaws of the municipality permit a livestock yard to be built next door? (A little extreme but you get the point.) Are there any plans for highway relocation which would result in the motel being by-passed by the bulk of the traffic?

The location will be a key factor in determining the type of motel you eventually build or buy. It will determine whether you will have a small one or a large one, whether you will offer nothing but room rentals, and whether you will need a swimming pool, restaurant, gift shop, barber shop, bellman, rooms with kitchenettes and a lot of other extra services. It will determine whether your customers will be mostly vacationers, or parents visiting children in college, or salesmen.

Remember the three most vital factors: (1) location (2) location (3) location.

166

The Established Motel

There are certain advantages in buying an established motel. New motels require from 6 to 18 months to go through a shake-down period during which daily operations are smoothed out and a regular clientele is developed. However, successful existing motel will have already been through this shake-down. Personnel will be trained and on the job. The advertising and public relations programs will have attained some momentum. The motel perhaps will have acquired a solid reputation.

You also should be aware of the disadvantages of buying an established motel:

1. What changes would you expect to make in the property and in its established ways of doing business?

2. How much extra money would be required to correct deficiences and shortcomings in the motel's construction and methods of doing business?

3. Is the motel in danger of losing its recommendation by an Association or referral agency? Why?

4. Has the motel acquired an unwholesome local reputation which may take years to overcome?

5. Are the established rates in line with others in the area? Does the motel enjoy favourable comparison with others in the area?

The Purchase Price

In evaluating the price, keep in mind these helpful points:

1. Appearance is perhaps the most important single factor in attracting business to a motel, but it might be a secondary matter in buying one. This is because external appearance can be changed, if you're willing to spend the money to do it. However, before you buy, you must get the facts about the structural quality of the buildings themselves. Are the foundations adequate? Notice whether the builder cut corners to save costs.

2. Don't be misled by gracious living quarters for the owner or by spacious and attractive lawns, a big lobby or by wide curving sidewalks. These are nice, but they won't directly produce revenue for you. They mean the present owner has put a lot of money into these extras, and that the price he will try to get you to pay will include the cost of these things.

3. Inspect the books. Pay no heed to claims of unrecorded income or to estimates of income. If the books are not made available to you, just forget that particular deal. Once you have the full financial records, you'll want to divide the gross annual revenue by the number of rooms to get the actual "per room per year" figure, one of the most accurate measurements of motel achievement. Let your accountant see the books too!

4. Consider factors not related to the books. The current owner may have had to operate under conditions you will not have to face (for example, a long period of severe weather or of highway reconstruction). Also, consider whether you'll have to spend additional money for expansion or upgrading. Place a realistic value on the motel's earned reputation, for good or ill.

5. You are accepting the new burden, so buy for yourself, not the seller. Try to find out and take into account his reasons for selling. If the price looks too low, the proposed deal should be scrutinized carefully. Remember that successful operations do not have to be sold at salvage prices. Pay for fair value. Also, be sure to obtain a satisfactory agreement that will prevent the seller from re-entering the motel business in the same area, thus becoming your competitor.

Firms which sell products may miss a sale today but sell it tomorrow for the same profit. Revenue from a motel room not rented tonight, however, never can be regained — it is lost forever. Fixed expenses continue, nevertheless.

In view of the size of the investment and the risk, one should give plenty of time and thought to reach a decision about going into this business. Do not be rushed.

53

BUYING A HOTEL

Now, I'm not talking about a Royal York or a Hotel Vancouver, or the Chateau Laurier; this is about buying a small hotel, one that you would find in the downtown area of any community in Canada, or in the countryside. These hotels usually have rooms; however, because of the general age of the properties they cater to weekly and monthly tenants, and not to the travelling public as do the motels and modern motor hotels. The main source of revenue in these hotels is derived from their food and beverage operations.

Unlike other forms of real estate transactions, few hotels are sold privately; they are generally sold through hotel brokers. The reasons are basic — because of an owner's desire not to upset his staff or customers, he will want the transaction handled discreetly. This is practically impossible on a direct sale basis which depends on the knowledge of the sale being transmitted by word of mouth by persons connected with the industry. Another reason why the hotel broker plays a necessary role in the sale of hotel properties is that potential buyers on their own do not have the opportunity to compare similar properties which are available on the market and, unlike residential properties, the hotels available may be separated by great distances, and without comparisons prospective purchasers cannot determine if the asking price is realistic.

You will notice that I said "hotel broker". There are few brokerage firms that specifically deal in the sale of hotels; however, those that do can be found by contacting the Hotel Association of the province that interests you. The association will provide you with the names of companies specializing in this form of real estate.

When you have made contact with a hotel broker, discuss your requirements with him. Be sure to outline fully your background experience, financial resources, and requirements as to location preferred, living accommodation required, etc. This information is necessary to enable the real estate agent to qualify which properties he has for sale which may appeal to you.

When you have seen the financial reports of the prospective properties that meet your requirements and you have chosen the ones that appeal to you, it is time to go and physically inspect them. It is important to have the agent accompany you. It allows him to assess your reaction first hand, to see how well he has qualified your requirements. Remember, you are contemplating making a very large purchase, and it may take time — very rarely will a purchaser buy the first property he has viewed — and often your requirements may change after seeing a couple of properties as the prerequisites you had can change very quickly as you go through your inspections. Another reason why it is important to have an agent accompany you is that with his general knowledge of the industry he is most likely to ask questions and obtain answers that you would not think of at the time.

When you have found a hotel that appears to meet all your requirements, spend some time there at different times of the day observing the physical operation of the business, but remember, be discreet. Some hotels may be quiet enough in the daytime, but when the sun goes down things can change.

Some hotel businesses have a very noisy clientelle and alcoholic beverages can bring out the worst in some people's character. However, if you have questions about the reputation of a particular establishment, the best way to get the answers is to visit the local police station. It will certainly know if a hotel has a bed reputation or not.

Have your solicitor check the municipal zoning; ensure the property conforms to all municipal zoning regulations, and make sure there is sufficient land to allow expansion. The latter may detract from the value of the property if expansion is not allowed.

The following is an overview of what one might expect to find in an agreement of purchase and sale:

The offer will describe exactly who is purchasing the property, yourself personally or a limited company of which you may be a director. Often companies are formed to purchase businesses for tax reasons, and it can be costly. Consult your lawyer and accountant as to the advantages and disadvantages of buying personally or with a limited company.

The offer will state the purchase price and the amount of down payment being offered. Remember, in hotel purchases a deposit of 5 -10% of the down payment (your cash equity) is usually required with any offer.

The purchase price will be allocated to a stated number of dollars for (1) land, (2) building, (3) chattels and equipment and (4) goodwill. For goodwill, review the chapter ''buying a business.''

The allocation to land, building, etc. is as important as the purchase price itself as it determines what depreciation (capital cost allowance) can be claimed, and will affect your tax payable on the profits of the business. For an understanding of this, review the chapter "buying an apartment building."

Hotels are very rarely sold for cash, and usually involve the vendor taking back a mortgage for part of the purchase price. Interest rates on these purchase mortgages are usually lower than rates quoted from lending institutions. The interest rate charged on vendors' mortgages has a great bearing on the value of the hotel, because prices can be adjusted according to the interest rate being charged.

Most land and building mortgages taken back by vendors will be collaterally secured by a chattel mortgage on the furniture and equipment of the hotel. The chattel mortgage will contain clauses allowing you to dispose of or replace any chattel so long as it is replaced with an item of comparable value. It will also contain a clause allowing the chattel mortgage to be transferred to a future purchaser without the approval of the mortgagee, or the acceleration of payments. This is very important, as it will allow you to transfer the mortgage without paying a bonus when deciding to sell.

The list of chattels in the chattel mortgage is compiled by the taking of an inventory. This is usually completed by the purchaser and the vendor soon after an agreement of purchase and sale is executed by both parties, and because of the difficulty in preparing this list it is usually done on the first day the hotel is not open for business following the signing. However, any chattels or equipment on loan, lease or commission basis must be referred to in the offer to purchase, as they are not included in the purchase price. For example, electronic games, laundry, linen, signs, ice cream cabinets, cigarette machines, and sometimes T.V. in bedrooms may be rented.

On closing of the transaction, just as in the closing of a house sale, there will be adjustments to be made. Such things as insurance premiums, taxes, prepaid rental contracts, security deposits, fuel oil, water, etc. In addition to these adjustments a purchaser will be required to pay for the merchantable stock which is on the premises in addition to the purchase price. The value of this stock is determined by the invoice price paid by the vendor. It is important to take into consideration these adjustments when calculating the amount one will offer for a particular property.

The foregoing is a simplified overview of some things to look for when buying a hotel. Your lawyer will certainly have more to add and say to all this.

54

BUYING A FARM

Federal and Provincial governments are anxious to keep the man on the land. Farm attrition, coupled with Canada's ever increasing population, results in the Governments' full cooperation in assisting one to get the plow moving and the cows milked as quickly as possible.

In searching, the best sources of information about farms that are for sale or rent are *farm* real estate agents, advertisements in *farm* magazines, *farm* newspapers, and rural journals.

The logical farm real estate agents will be ones in rural communities and towns. Drive around the country, pick your location, and visit nearby agents. Also, pick up a copy of the area's weekly newspaper.

If you become seriously interested in an area, or a particular farm, talk to neighbouring farmers about the land. Contact the local Provincial government agricultural agent, and talk to him about the land. You must know about the land, unless of course you are just looking for a huge building lot in the country.

Take advantage of the many services provided by Provincial and Federal agricultural departments.

The Federal department of agriculture carries on research into the physical and economic problems of agriculture. Experimental farms and research laboratories are located in many parts of Canada. The results of this work are made available to farmers by means of bulletins, posters, articles in newspapers and farm magazines, and radio and television programs. Information on markets and prices for agriculture products is distributed in daily and weekly reports on radio and television, in farm magazines, and some newspapers.

Each Province has an agricultural extension service with a representative located in each county or district. These agents interpret research data for farmers, provide assistance and advice in resolving problems, distribute extension bulletins, and give short courses on various aspects of farm management and other subjects. In addition, the extension services usually have a staff of consultants in specialized fields who may be asked for advice. Some of the extension services have home economists on staff who provide extension education services for the ladies.

Many agricultural marketing and supply firms have staff to advise farmers. For example, feed companies give advice on rations for livestock and poultry; building supply firms on building construction; chemical companies on the use of pesticides and herbicides; fertilizer companies on fertilizers and cultural practices; grain marketing companies on grain varieties and markets. Also, many colleges and vocational schools have special short courses designed for farmers.

Financial Aspects of the Farm

The amount of capital needed to start farming on a full-time basis depends on the type of farm, the productivity of the soil, the proximity of the farm to markets, and whether the farmer buys or rents.

A farmer specializing in the production of hogs or poultry requires a small acreage of land compared with a wheat farmer, but has a large investment in buildings and livestock. A cattle rancher, in common with the wheat producer, needs a large acreage of land but ranchland usually costs much less per acre than cropland. Lands near large urban centers naturally cost more than lands farther away.

The capital requirements of a beginning farm operator can be lessened if he rents land and equipment. However, competition from established operators greatly reduces the opportunities for him to obtain enough land for an efficient operation by renting. Purchasing used machinery, and hiring, borrowing or exchanging large machines are other means of reducing the initial investment, but starting with less machinery and equipment than is necessary for an efficient operation makes it difficult for a beginning farmer to compete with his established neighbours.

Volume of business is one of the chief things to consider when starting to farm. Reducing capital requirements by obtaining a smaller acreage of land or fewer livestock than is necessary for an efficient farm unit results in a small business. Unfortunately, the operator of a small farm usually finds it difficult to increase the size of his operation.

Financing the Purchase

The one selling the farm sometimes accepts a mortgage for a substantial part of the purchase price, which simplifies the financing. If this cannot be done, go after the Government.

173

Several government agencies lend money to farmers to finance the purchase. The Farm Credit Corporation of the federal government is the main source of this type of credit, and some provinces have agencies for lending provincial government funds for buying farms.

To be eligible for a government loan a borrower must be a bona fide farmer, and under provincial schemes a borrower must be a resident of the province.

An objective of all government farm credit agencies is to help a farmer establish his farm as a sound economic farm unit. The maximum loan allowed to a farmer is set by legislation and varies from province to province. Legislation of the federal government and some provincial governments provides for more credit and easier collateral to young farmers, but the farm operations are subject to supervision by the lending agency until the loan is reduced to a certain level.

Financing the Operation

Farmers may obtain short and long term credit for production, farm improvement and development from several sources.

The federal government: The Farm Credit Corporation was established to help Canadian farmers and those wishing to become farmers, purchase, develop and maintain sound farm businesses. Assistance is provided in the form of long-term mortgage credit.

Applicants must be principally occupied in farming or about to become full-time farmers at the time of the loan. Young persons under 35 years of age may retain off-farm employment while developing an economic farm business, providing farming becomes their principal occupation within five years.

A number of factors must be considered by the applicant and the Farm Credit Corporation before a loan is approved and before the actual amount of any loan is agreed upon. The applicant must demonstrate that the farm business under his or her management will generate enough income to meet all financial obligations and to allow for a reasonable standard of living. Also, the applicant's management ability and experience are taken into consideration.

Borrowers must be either Canadian citizens or landed immigrants.

Loan funds may be used to:

- purchase farm land
- make permanent improvements
- purchase breeding stock and equipment
- pay debts, or for any purpose that will facilitate the efficent operation of the farm.

174

Repayment terms are most generous: A borrower may take up to a maximum of 30 years to repay a loan, and the loan may be prepaid at any time without notice, bonus or penalty. The interest rate charged by the Corporation is set when the loan is made, and does not change during the life of the loan.

Loans are secured by a mortgage on real estate and, where necessary, on farm livestock and equipment.

Provincial appeal boards, made up of practical farmers of proven ability and judgment, are established to hear appeals from applicants who are not satisfied with the Corporation's decision on any loan application.

An application for a loan should be made at the local Farm Credit Corporation office. The address of the one nearest you may be obtained by writing to: The Farm Credit Corporation, 2255 Carling Avenue, P.O. Box 6309, Postal Station "J", Ottawa, Ontario K2A 3W9.

Provincial Governments: Most provide credit to individual farmers for purchases of farm machinery, livestock, land clearing and drainage.

Commercial Banks: For operating capital and other transactions requiring short-term credit. Banks may be the same in what they do for a living, but they are certainly not the same in how they go about laying out the carpet for borrowers. Don't ever take no for an answer if one bank manager says nay — go to another bank. They are still the best source of general borrowing, and the large growth of Canadian banks is proof that they like to lend as much money as they can.

It is also possible to obtain money from banks for farm improvement loans backed by government.

Credit Unions: Members of a credit union usually may obtain short and intermediate term credit for almost any purpose, and in the face of current rates and terms are very reasonable places to do business.

Merchants, dealers and finance companies: Credit may be obtained directly or indirectly from dealers wishing to sell their products. Finance company rates are usually higher than banks, but their loans are often easier to obtain.

Processing and supply firms: May extend credit as part of what is termed "contract farming." There are various types of contracts, ranging from simple credit deals to profit-sharing arrangements. Sometimes company supervision of farm operations is involved; protecting the investment, so to speak.

Urban smog, dirt, noise, pollution, contamination and corruption is enough to drive anyone into the country. If its your bag, I hope you make it.

55

BUYING A BUSINESS

This can be a complicated legal undertaking, requiring a good deal of financial advice from an accountant. What I can do is simply provide an overview of what may be involved here:

If the purchase of the business includes the purchase of the land and buildings, the offer to the vendor will be made describing the land and buildings first, and then go on to say it includes the goodwill, tradename, chattels, fixtures and equipment of the business which will be listed on a schedule attached to the offer.

After running through the mortgage details, it will outline the financial adjustments to be made on closing for such things as the inventory of stock in trade, insurance, service contracts, taxes, water, hydro, any local improvement commitments and mortgage interest.

Then, and here is where it can be dicey, an appraisal must be made apportioning the purchase price to land, buildings, fixtures, chattels, equipment, stock, goodwill and the trade name. See the help one needs?

How many appraisers are needed? What assurance is there that the income tax department will agree to the breakdown in the total purchase price?

Competent appraising is needed because, for example, the building will require a cost base for capital cost allowances over the coming tax years. Not only that, it will be important to establish a fair price for the "goodwill" of the business.

Prior to 1972, goodwill was not recognized as being deductible from income either as an expense or by way of capital cost allowances. It is now recognized as an eligible capital expenditure.

Taxpayers are now allowed to establish an account comparable to a capital cost allowance class for goodwill. One half of the fairly established cost of the goodwill will be included in this account, and the taxpayer may then deduct 10% of the balance of the account on a reducing balance basis.

And just what is goodwill? Here are two quotations of how courts have referred to definitions of goodwill:

(a) Goodwill is the whole advantage, whatever it may be, of the reputation and connection of the firm which may have been built up by years of honest work or gained by lavish expenditures of money.

(b) It is ''the privilege, granted by the seller of a business to the purchaser, of trading as his recognized successor; the possession of a ready-formed 'connexion' of customers, considered as an element in the saleable value of a business, additional to the value of the plant, stock-in-trade, book debts, etc.''

Goodwill cannot be divorced from the business itself. It follows the business, and may be sold with the business, but it cannot be sold separately. Generally speaking, goodwill arises as a recognizable asset only when a business is acquired at a price in excess of the going or in-use value of its net tangible assets.

So you see, you will need expert advice in these areas. Your lawyer and your accountant will be your best guide. I do not recommend taking a vendor's advice about cost apportionment, without having it completely verified.

On the date of completion an inventory will be taken of the stock at the invoice prices to the vendor, less any trade discounts.

It is customary for the vendor to make his peace with his suppliers and pay all his trade bills before closing, and to covenant to be responsible for other accounts rendered for payment for assets purchased from the vendor. You can be sure your lawyer will particularly take a good hard look at the financial details of stock and fixtures, and what's paid for and what isn't.

As for the accounts receivable in the business, it is customary for the one buying the business to purchase them from the vendor at an agreed discount. The list of receivables purchased should not include any receivables outstanding over 90 days, unless there are mitigative circumstances, with the buyer's satisfactory assurance that they will be paid.

The vendor will reveal all details of guarantees and service contracts that affect the business, and also assign rights to all franchises, if any.

It has been said that the best location for any business is right across the street from a competitor. However true this may be, the business buyer certainly doesn't want his vendor becoming his competitor lest he take all his former customers with him, so it is usual to have the vendor agree not to become the proprietor of a competing business, or be employed by one. This agreement will have a time limit, and specify an area, or distance from the business he is selling.

Don't put all your beans in one pot, which means keep some reserve cash at least for the early months of operating your new business venture. Unexpected expenses have a way of cropping up like weeds, and you will

177

want to have the ability to establish a good business name for yourself in your new location.

56

THE BUSINESS FRANCHISE (AND RISKS)

Franchising ads are currently appearing in large numbers throughout the country. While most of them offer legitimate business opportunities, some of them do not.

Be wary of advertisements which promise "get rich quick" schemes, with little effort and no risk — they can frequently lead to disappointment and sometimes to FINANCIAL DISASTER.

A good explanation of "franchise" is: A system used by a company (franchisor) which grants to others (franchisees) the right and license (franchise) to market a product or service and engage in a business developed by it under franchisor's trade names, trademarks, service marks, know-how and method of doing business.

One of the reasons for the recent enormous growth in franchising is that it has caught the imagination of the small investor and provides him the opportunity to become self-employed. For instance, the risk of failure is reduced when the franchisee starts in business under a successful corporate name and trademark and when he receives helpful training and management assistance from experienced personnel of the franchisor.

However, franchising arrangements do not always produce happy results. Franchising does not guarantee success as some promoters would have you believe. Franchising arrangements can produce severe financial loss, and on occasion have caused franchisees to lose their life savings.

Some of these franchisees have experienced disappointment and frustration by falling victim to a deceptive franchising scheme. The rapid growth of franchising has attracted a number of unprincipled operators who seek to take advantage of anyone they can. Their methods of operation and techniques are too varied to detail here but their objectives are the same, i.e., to take your money and give little or nothing in return. After the unscrupulous promoter receives payment he doesn't care whether you succeed or fail. In fact, contrary to what he tells you, you may never see him again.

179

This letter illustrates an investor's frustration after being bilked by one of these arrangements:

"My husband and I invested $15,000. of borrowed money in a restaurant franchise . . . . . . my husband is working 14 hours a day — 7 days a week for $50. per week. I work 8 hours a day for no salary. There is not enough money for my salary. The spot just doesn't bring in enough people. The franchisor refuses to take the business back and wants a royalty which makes it hard to sell the business to anyone else. He has you invest $6,000. to $10,500. as an initial investment which he pockets."

In this instance, in addition to grossly overstating the earning potential of the franchise, the franchisor misrepresented nearly every other aspect of the franchise agreement. The cost of the franchise was much higher than represented and discount supplies were not available. Moreover, the franchise was not a nationally known chain and the franchisor did not provide planned promotions or helpful training and supervision that he promised. This is a sample of the type of franchise deceptions in existence today.

Because the decision to become a franchisee may involve the investment of a lifetime of savings and effort, it is recommended that prospective franchisees carefully examine all aspects of a franchise agreement before becoming legally involved. By taking this precaution, the likelihood of financial disaster can be greatly reduced. To help evaluate a franchise opportunity it is suggested that you view the proposal in the light of the following points:

Who is the Franchisor?

If the franchisor is well-known, has a good reputation, and has a successful franchising operation, you can naturally proceed with greater confidence than if little is known about him. You should find out everything you can about the operation including:

1. Number of years it has been in existence.

2. Whether the franchisor has all the successful franchisees he claims.

3. Whether he has a reputation for honesty and fair dealing with his franchise holders.

A personal contact with franchisees is an excellent way to learn about the franchisor. Obtain the names and addresses of a representative number of franchisees in the particular area in which you are interested, travel to see them, and learn about all aspects of the operation.

In addition to gaining valuable informaion about the franchisor, it will provide you with an opportunity to view samples of the franchise products or services, equipment, advertising material, etc., and to obtain profit data and other pertinent information about the operation.

Beware of the franchisor who will not freely give you the names and addresses of his franchisees. The financial standing and business reputation of the franchisor should be of utmost interest to you. Consult the Better Business Bureau and Dun and Bradstreet.

Sometimes, a dishonest promoter will use a franchise name and trademark deceptively similar to that of a well-known franchisor. Be certain you deal with the particular franchise organization you are interested in and that the individual representing this franchise has authority to act on its behalf.

Be skeptical of franchisors whose major activity is the sales of franchises and whose profit is primarily derived from these sales or from the sale of franchise equipment or services. This may be the tip-off to an unscrupulous operator.

Remember, the more you learn about the franchisor and his operation, before making a firm decision, the less likely you will become involved in a situation that you might later regret.

The Franchise Commodity

You should determine the length of time the commodity or service has been marketed and if it is a successful promotion. Is it a proven product or service, and not a gimmick?

Decide whether you are genuinely interested in selling the commodity or service. Be skeptical of items which are untested in the marketplace and are fads. For future market potential decide whether the commodity or service is a staple, luxury, or fad item.

If a product or service is involved, be certain it is safe, that it meets existing quality standards, and there are no restrictions upon its use. Is the product or service protected by a patent or has it liability insurance? Will the same protection be afforded to you as the franchisee?

If the product is to be manufactured by someone other than yourself, identify the manufacturer and learn how your cost for the item will be established. If a guarantee is involved, determine your reponsibilities and obligations as the franchisee.

Under the franchise agreement, will you be compelled to sell any new products or services which may be introduced by the franchisor after you have opened the business? Will you be permitted under the agreement to sell products and services other than the franchise commodities, at some future date?

The Franchise Cost

Find out the total cost of the franchise. The franchise promotion may only refer to the cash outlay needed to purchase the franchise, with no mention made that it is only a downpayment and other charges and assessments may be levied against you to operate the franchise.

If other monies are involved, how is the balance to be financed? (interest rates will be important to you) Clearly establish what the downpayment is purchasing. Is it a franchise fee? Or does it purchase any other equity such as the building, etc.?

Where do you purchase equipment and fixtures necessary for opening the business? If these are purchased through the franchisor, are his prices comparable with competitive prices on the open market?

Franchisors often attempt to secure income on a continuing basis through the sale of supplies to their franchisees. If this is part of the proposed agreement, how will the price of these supplies be established? What assurance do you have that the prices will be reasonable or competitive. Does the franchise agreement prohibit you from purchasing these supplies from a source at a lower price?

Another method franchisors use to charge franchisees on a continuing basis is the assessment of royalties based upon a percentage of gross sales. Be sure these royalties are not out of line with the sales volume and expected net profits for the franchise. Don't overlook the possibility that franchisors often assess franchisees an additional percentage of gross sales to cover the franchisee's share of advertising cost.

Think about franchise costs in the light of your financial position. Consider the additional funds and operating capital you will need to get the business underway and to sustain it during the months when profits will be small and expenses high.

What Profits can be Expected?

Many franchise arrangements provide excellent income producing opportunities. Not all franchises, however, yield the fantastic profits sometimes promised. Many produce less profits than represented by franchise promoters. When deceptive promotions are involved, debts rather than profits are the usual rule.

Since ''profits'' are the overriding motive for entering a franchise business, don't take the promoter's word for granted. Verify the profits for accuracy. Ask to see certified profit figures of franchisees who operate on a level of activity that you expect to operate. Use personal contact with franchisees, quiz them regarding their financial rewards and evaluate the profit figures and comments of these individuals in the light of the territory and size of operation you have under consideration.

Training and Management Assistance

Most franchisors claim to train their franchisees. The type and extent of training varies from one day's indoctrination to a more lengthy training program. When good training is provided the franchisee enjoys better prospects for survival and prosperity.

Inexperience and lack of training can produce disappointing results. Clearly understand the specific nature of the training.

1. Will the training include more than a manual of instructions or hearing a few lectures?

2. What is the length of the training and where do you go to receive it?

3. Who will pay the expenses during the training period?

4. Will the training include an opportunity to observe and work with a successful franchisee for a period of time?

5. Do you believe that after taking the training you will be capable to operate the franchise successfully?

Will the franchisor furnish management assistance after the business is established? Spell this out specifically in your contract. If advertising aid is promised, will it be in the form of handbills, brochures, signs, radio, TV, or newspaper advertising, etc.? If you are required to furnish money for a franchisor-sponsored advertising program what specific advertising benefits can you anticipate and at what dollar cost?

Some franchisors promise management assistance with periodic visits by the supervisory personnel of the franchisor. Find out the specific nature of assistance, the frequency of the visits, and whether they will be available in times of crisis or when unusual problems arise.

The Franchise Territory

This is a critical factor to consider in evaluating a prospective venture. Here are some good questions to ask:

1. What specific territory is being offered?

2. Is it clearly defined?

3. What is its potential?

4. Do you have a choice of territories?

5. What competition will you meet in marketing the commodity today? How about five years from now?

6. Has a market survey been made of the proposed area?

7. If so, who prepared it? Ask for a copy and read it carefully.

8. What assurance do you have that your territory is an exclusive one?

9. Would you be protected from the possibility of the franchisor selling additional franchises in your territory at a later date?

10. Does the contract prevent you from opening additional outlets in your territory, or even another territory, at a future date?

11. Has the specific business site within the territory been selected? If not, how will this be decided?

Termination, Transfer and Renewal of the Franchise Agreement

Because some termination provisions can cause unexpected and sometimes severe financial loss to a franchisee, give careful consideration to this aspect of the agreement.

Some franchise agreements provide that at the end of or during the contract term if, in the opinion of the franchisor, certain conditions have not been met, the franchisor has the absolute right to terminate the agreement.

The contract generally provides the franchisor with an option to repurchase the franchise. If the franchisor should terminate the agreement under these circumstances and if the contract does not provide a means whereby a fair market price for the franchise can be established, the franchisor could repurchase the business at a low and unfair price.

On occasion, franchisors include a provision in the agreement that the repurchase price will not exceed the original franchise fee. This means that a franchisee could spend considerable effort and money building the business and be faced with selling it back to the franchisor at the price he paid for it.

Understand the conditions under which the agreement could be terminated and your rights in the event of termination. Does the contract extend to the franchisor the right of cancellation for almost any reason or must there be ''good cause''? Beware of contracts which, under the threat of cancellation, impose unreasonable obligations such as a minimum monthly purchase of goods or services from the franchisor or unrealistic sales quotas.

Keep these points in mind:

1. How would the value of the franchise be determined in the event of termination?

2. Under what circumstances could you terminate the agreement and what would it cost you?

3. Does the contract contain a restrictive covenant which would prohibit you from engaging in a competitive business in the franchise territory in the event termination occurs?

4. Have a clear understanding of contract provisions dealing with your ability to transfer, sell, or renew the franchise. What would happen to the franchise in the event of your death?

Some reputable franchisors have established fair and permanent relationships with their franchisees and have provided for an arbitration clause which allows for a fair evaluation of the franchisee's contribution in the event of termination. Under this agreement the franchisee would recoup his initial investment as well as a profit on whatever business he generated.

Franchise carrying a well-known Personality Name

When a ''name'' personality is connected with a franchise consider the degree of participation the ''name'' gives to the business. Is he a figurehead with no capital investment in the enteprise? Will he make contributions of

184

time and efffort to promote the business? What guarantees do you have that he will make appearances at your business? Does the personality have a name of lasting value in identifying your franchise with the consuming public? How sound is the franchise operation without the prominent name?

Promoter primarily interested in selling Distributorships

Be wary of promoters who primarily sell distributorships for some "new wonder product." Exaggerated income promises are common in these promotions. According to the promotion plan, the distributors solicit sub-distributors and salesmen to sell the product from door-to-door. The idea is that a large portion of the distributor's profits will be received from a percentage of his sub-distributor's sales. Unfortunately, some distributors and sub-distributors find to their mutual distress after making sizable investments of money, time and effort, that there is little profit and they are holding a large stock of unsalable products.

A Route Servicing Promotion

Be alert for deceptive route servicing promotions. These promotions are characterized by misleading representations (frequently appearing in newspaper want ads) concerning exaggerated profits and the availability of quality routes.

If equipment, such as vending machines, is to be purchased in connection with the promotion, find out if it is poorly made and highly priced. Compare the equipment and prices with those of reputable manufacturers. Carefully check out the validity of all statements made in these promotions, and remember that promoters promising assistance in locating quality routes after the contract is signed seldom deliver.

Qualifications as a Franchisee

Before you sign any franchise agreement, deterrmine if your personal traits qualify you to be a franchisee.

Are you genuinely enthusiastic about the franchise plan? Are you physically and emotionally equipped to do the work necessary to develop a successful enterprise?

Franchisees can only expect to succeed by hard work and full-time effort. Franchise plans based on part-time work generally produce only modest results for the franchisee.

Summary

Don't be rushed into signing a contract or any other documents relating to a frachise promotion. Be wary of pressure for an immediate contract closing. Don't make any deposits or downpayments unless you are absolutely certain you are going ahead with the franchise agreement. Remember, reputable firms don't engage in high-pressure tactics.

Find out all you can about the franchise. Resolve all areas of uncertainty before making a decision. Ask the franchisor for names and addresses of his franchisees. No reputable franchisor will object to giving you this information. Personally contact a number of the franchisees and discuss all aspects of the operation with them. Has the franchisor fulfilled all his promises and met his contractual obligations with them?

Check with your better business bureau. Ask for a business responsibility report on the franchisor-promoter.

Be certain that all terms of the agreement are set forth in a written contract which is not a handicap on you and not weighed unfairly in favor of the franchisor.

Consult a lawyer and have him review all aspects of the agreement before you sign the contract or any papers relating to the franchise. It may turn out to be a very sound investment!

57

BUYING AN INDUSTRIAL BUILDING

One of the plus features about owning a *residential* building is that people always have to live somewhere, regardless of the economic barometer. The multiple tenancy factor is another, which is a form of income insurance itself because the income is not dependent on one tenant.

It is for this reason that the importance of tenancy strength in an industrial building cannot be stressed too strongly. There are many fine industrial buildings, large and small, with just one tenant.

It is a common practice to lease an industrial building on what is called a "net net" basis; that is, the owner has a fixed net return on his investment, and the tenant pays for everything, the rent and all charges connected to the building, including the municipal taxes. The reason it is called a "net net" basis is to emphasize the fact that it is on a "net" basis. How about that? I have even heard it referred to as a "net net net" lease. Maybe somebody was afraid nobody heard him when he said "net", so he said NET NET NET. (Like banging the fist on the table three times instead of just once).

The reason for the net lease is very basic. If, for example, on purchased an industrial property for $100,000. cash to a $300,000. mortgage, a net, fixed, guaranteed return on the $100,000. would be required. Suppose the required return on this was 10%, or $10,000. a year.

Now, a tenant would have to be found who would be willing to pay a rental that would not only pay the $10,000. but also pay the mortgage. Here is what the annual rent would have to be:

Example:	Annual mortgage payment	$33,620.00
	(including principal and interest)	
	10% interest on $100,000.	10,000.00
	Annual Rent	$43,620.00

In addition to this rent, the tenant also pays everything else, including the municipal taxes.

The owner has a fixed (net) return on his $100,000. investment, plus a bonus in repayment of the mortgage principal by the tenant. (The amortized mortgage payments include interes *and* principal). This bonus, on an 11%, 30-year mortgage, would amount to about $9,000. over the first five years.

The owner, of course, would pay tax not only on his net investment return of $10,000., but also on the mortgage principal payment received in rent.

It is possible sometimes to obtain a commitment in the lease requiring the rent to reflect an increase to match a rise in the cost of living, which would help to keep the dollars received up to date.

Well, if the foregoing looks like a cozy deal, it could turn into a nightmare if the tenancy turned sour, and leave the owner with a migraine.

Before accepting an offer to lease a single tenancy building, be very very careful about the covenant of the proposed tenant — its responsibility to care for the property and its ability to pay the rent, not only on time, but for the entire term of the lease. This is especially directed to the new owner of a small building, who may be so anxious to get it rented he will grab the first half-decent offer he sees.

Before buying an industrial building, ensure that you are fully conversant and aware of the going rent in comparable buildings. One might also stretch the closing as long as possible to give the new owner or agent as much time as possible to find a good tenant.

The best agent to approach when looking at industrial properties is one who *specializes* in them. Such an agency has plenty of know-how on the buildings and construction, and can answer a multitude of questions to your satisfaction.

A building with a net lease can be a very attractive investment, but it must be purchased with care, and leased with care. Your best guide is an industrial broker and your solicitor.

The lease, prepared by your solicitor, will run to about twenty pages in clear understandable language. Here are some basic covenants one can expect to see:

1. The tenant will, as additional rent, in each and every year during the term of the lease, pay and discharge when due all taxes, including local improvement rates, charges, duties, fees and assessments that may be levied against the property.

2. The tenant will pay all charges for public utilities, including water, gas, electric power or energy, steam or hot water, and for fittings, machinery, apparatus, meters or other things leased, and for all work or services performed in connection with such public utilities.

3. The tenant shall operate, maintain and keep the premises in good

order and condition and promptly make all repairs and replacements. An exception to this would be reasonable wear and tear and damage by fire, lightning, explosion, riot and civil insurrections, sprinkler leakage, smoke, airplane impact, hurricane and by other insurable hazards.

4. The tenant will keep the premises well painted and clean, and at least once every four years paint the exterior of the building and the office area.

5. It will be lawful for the landlord to enter and inspect the premises at reasonable times, and if repairs are necessary that are the responsibility of the tenant, the tenant will have such repairs completed within 45 days of such notice.

6. If the tenant does not effect the foregoing repairs, the landlord may do it and charge the costs to the tenant as if the same were arrears in rent.

7. The tenant will comply with all federal and provincial statutes, laws, orders and regulations respecting the property, and comply with any lawful order of any governmental or municipal board or other competent body.

8. The tenant will not assign the lease or sublet the premises without the authority of the landlord, who is not to be unreasonable about it. Any assignment or subletting will not release the tenant of its liabilities under the lease.

9. The tenant will pay all premiums with respect to insurance placed by the landlord; such insurance will be spelled out and agreed to by both parties covering such things as ''all risk'' insurance, public liability, boiler, machinery etc., plate glass, and any special coverage dictated by the nature of the tenant's type of business.

10. The proceeds of insurance will be paid to the landlord or to any mortgagee or encumbrancer. Insurance details can be lengthy.

11. There will be clauses concerning the conditions that will cause a forfeiture of the lease.

12. The landlord will not be held responsible for accidents or damage.

13. If the tenant fails to maintain any payments on taxes, fees, insurance premiums etc. the landlord may pay such items and charge the amount to the tenant as rent.

14. The moneys provided to be paid by the tenant to the landlord shall be net to the landlord and clear of all charges, except the landlord's business and income taxes, payments of mortgage principal and interest and any expense for repairs which may be the landlord's responsibility under the lease.

58

BUYING AN OFFICE BUILDING

It can be said that the bigger and more impressive an office building, the easier it is to appraise.

Take a building in first class condition in an excellent location, one that has been well designed and recently constructed, filled with tenants with first class credit ratings who pay their rent on time, and where everything is running smoothly. What is it worth? Well, just capitalize the net cash flow at the lowest market point (%) possible, and the result will be a fair estimate of its market value. viz:

Cash flow: $\dfrac{\$100,000. \times 100}{8\%} = \dfrac{\$1,250,000.}{\text{Cash to Mortgage}}$
Fair point:

The trick is to determine just what the capitalization rate should be, which will be determined by a number of factors such as what is the lowest point at which a buyer would be satisfied with the investment, considering the tenants, length of leases and possibility of increases in revenue when the leases expire? Such a building, when exposed to the buying market, will usually carry a price tag higher than the present owner would wish to pay for it, letting the offering settle down and allowing interested buyers to tell the owner what they think it is worth.

But what about the average, small, multi-tenanted office building with tenants in a variety of occupations, some with shaky credit ratings and some with no problems. What does one look for in this one?

A first consideration will be the physical condition of the building. Major repairs or renovations will not only cost a great deal of money, but will inconvenience the tenants and their clients or customers. So give the building itself a real going over. Get professional help and be prepared to pay for the advice, which will be in writing. If you are in a hurry to get your offer presented, you could make such an inspection a condition of your offer, with a time limit of course.

Check the municipality to ensure that the building satisfies current zoning regulations. It may be possible that the building is there under legal non-conforming use and, if such is the case, have your lawyer check to ensure that on transferring the deed, the new owner can carry on with the investment as it is, without having to make any alterations or provide more parking spaces.

Check with the fire department to ensure that the building is being operated in a manner satisfactory to this body.

Check with the hydro authority and get its blessing.

Check the rents being charged in comparable buildings in the area, if possible. If the rents in the building that interests you are above the area average, find out why. If there is no logical reason for it you could be in for a shock when leases expire, finding yourself with empty space on your hands.

Check the background of the tenants. If the building contains an overly supply of lessees who could be considered risky covenants, think twice about the whole thing. You don't want any problems worrying about the income.

Review the chapter ''buying an apartment building'' and follow its useful guidelines in financing etc. Remember that the less attractive the investment, the more you are entitled to financially expect from it, and your capitalization rate will be higher.

When you are prepared to make an offer, ask the real estate agent, if there is one, to prepare the offer, and then *take it to your lawyer*. If no agent is involved, get your own lawyer to prepare the offer.

A well located, well tenanted office building is a nice investment, but take it easy and think it over very carefully before buying one.

59

INTRODUCTION TO LEASING

An agreement for a lease, or an accepted offer to lease, is not a lease. The agreement provides for the execution of a document — the lease.

The agreement contains the basic terms of the lease, the lessor and the lessee, a description of the property to which exclusive possession is to be given, the stipulated rent, and when payable, the term, and commencement date. From these essentials, the lessor and lessee carry on with their particular terms and fine print for the lease.

There are basically three types of leases:

Net Lease: The *lessee's* responsibility embraces all the municipal charges and property operating expenses.

Gross Lease: The *lessor's* responsibility embraces all the municipal charges and property operating expenses, but this is quite often watered down in the lease by requiring the lessee to pay for one or more of the operating expenses, such as heating, janitor, cleaning, hydro, and hot water.

Percentage Lease: The lessor receives, as rent, an agreed upon percentage of the lessee's gross business sales.

There are two common methods in practice:

(a) The lessee agrees to pay a fixed rent *or* an agreed percentage of his gross sales to the lessor, whichever is greater.

(b) The lessee agrees to pay a fixed rent, *plus* an agreed percentage of his gross sales over and above an agreed annual sales figure, to the lessor.

If the rent resulting from a percentage lease is greater than the basic rent, the additional rent paid is called "overage". This can sometimes produce startling and pleasant returns to the lessor, at the same time possibly giving him an inflated idea of the value of his property, but a sophisticated investor will recognize this "overage", not as a fixed return to be used as a basis of true valuation, but something subject to the vagaries of the buying public and the economy of the municipality, and certainly not guaranteed. Buying property leased on this basis, and allowing the "overage" to be used as a basis for additional property valuation, is quite often a calculated risk, and possible gamble.

192

If you are going to rent an apartment, you will usually be required to deposit a sum of money with an application equal to one month's rent. The lessor then checks your application to ensure that you will be reasonably able to maintain regular payments of rent. If he approves of you as a tenant, he will invariably shove a document under your nose and say "sign here". *Don't Do It.* Take the document to a lawyer and ask him what it is you are required to sign, and ask him to outline the rights of lessor and lessee in terms of the document. A responsible landlord can have no valid objection to waiting one or two days while you determine what you are doing.

A Form of Apartment Rent Control that Can Work

If one mentions rent control to a landlord, the suggestion will undoubtedly draw a stern look of abhorrence. On the other hand, if the landlord mentions an increase in rent, he will probably have the look returned.

There could be a solution, and a fair one to both landlord and tenant in apartment buildings.

The owner of a building, having a financial investment at stake, is being reasonable in his assumption that he should receive a fair return on his money.

One of the problems in renting an apartment, especially when it involves a lease, is the landlord's knowledge that his maintenance costs and municipal taxes are surely going to rise during the tenancy, and this is an unknown factor to him.

A commercial lease, which is usually executed for a longer period of time than an apartment lease, will likely contain agreements covering future increase in maintenance and taxes. These agreements are called escalation clauses.

This clause guarantees that the lessor (landlord) will suffer no financial loss by these future increases. If the lessee occupies 10 per cent of the area of the building, he will agree to pay, under the clauses, an increase in rent equal to 10 per cent of any increase in maintenance and taxes charged to the lessor during the term of the lease.

This enables the lessor to give a long term lease to his tenant, by ensuring that the lessor will be reasonably assured of a fixed return on his investment. If he had to bear increased taxes and maintenance over 5 to 10 years without receiving any increase in rent, he would be in a precarious financial position.

So it is with the apartment building owner. When he initially gives one a two year lease, he bases the rent on a projection that will give him a fair return. At the end of the two years, taxes and maintenance costs will have invariably increased, and he is forced to increase his rent to compensate for it.

An apartment tenant can only see the monthly increase. Moving means a new address, which is very disruptive, and inconvenient, and the tenant knows that the costs of moving will often amount to about the same as one year's increase in rent. This results in a feeling that the lessor is taking advantage of him; that the lessor is making too much money. The lessor justifies his demanded rent increases on the strength of increased taxes and maintenance costs, the current yield on money, and little else; unless, of course, he has an insatiable appetite for money.

The rent control that can work is one that the apartment owner imposes on himself and his tenants, by applying the escalation clauses to his apartment leases.

There is no secret about what any increase in taxes will be once the mill rate has been set by the municipality. It is a matter of public record.

In the happy event that a reduction of taxes might occur, the clause could also cover this, thereby slightly reducing the rent, but such a reduction would probably of offset by an increase in maintenance costs.

It could produce interesting results. The yearly statement provided by the lessor to his tenants would clearly outline the tax and maintenance costs for the initial year of the lease (when the tenants' rent is unchanged) and show adjustments to justify any increase in rent.

How could a tenant possibly have any objection to the rent structure under such an agreement; and what objections could a landlord have?

Why, they might even smile at each other!

The Offer to Lease

The balance of this chapter is basically written for lessees other than apartment dwellers. The first document you will sign is an agreement, or "offer to lease". Although the lease will be signed by both parties at a later date, it is well to keep a few points in your mind in your offer to lease. If they are not covered initially, you could be disappointed at a later date after you have made plans to move.

Ownership: It is essential that you determine at the outset just who is the lessor, and verify his authority to lease the property to you. A lease is a conveyance of an estate, and therefore title should be searched by your solicitor in the same manner and extent as though you were purchasing the property. To ensure that you are leasing from proper authority, the identical wording as in an offer to purchase could be used: "Provided the title is good and free from all encumbrances except as aforesaid and except as to any registered restrictions or covenants that run with the land providing that such are complied with''.

The reason for establishing title can be obvious if your offer to lease contains the proviso for an option to purchase the property, or your right of first refusal in the event of a prospective sale. Searching title may bring to light registered easements that you may not wish to contend with; and you will most certainly wish to be reassured of your right to possession.

Description of Property: You must first fully determine just what it is you wish to lease. Exactly. Be specific.

For single properties such as a house or small building you wish to lease intact, the municipal address will usually suffice.

Description of a duplex, or triplex, etc., should include your rights for parking, use of the grounds (you may like outdoor barbecues), laundry facilities, and basement area. You might even define your right of ingress and egress.

Commercial space should include a floor plan of the exact space to be leased, and attached to the offer. It is sometimes advisable to include a survey to properly identify the building and parking spaces, etc.

In *any* offer to lease a *part* of a building, ensure that a proper plan outling the area, floor number, etc. is included and attached to your offer.

The Rent: Paying the rent is one thing, and knowing what your financial responsibilities encompass is another.

It is advisable to outline exactly what municipal and building operating charges you will pay for, and exactly what your lessor will pay for. Be specific about these charges, *including taxes.*

Check the assessment on the property. If your lease is to contain a tax escalation clause which will require you to pay any *increase* in taxes on your assessed part of the premises, you could be in for a stiff financial jolt if the premises had been renovated and/or improved, and not re-assessed.

Your offer to lease should be checked by a lawyer for your protection and reassurance. He is going to be responsible for ensuring the cognizance of your rights and obligations in the actual lease, so do yourself a favour and let him help you from the beginning. You can be sure that the lessor is going to have a lawyer protect *his* interests!

You and the Landlord

The landlord's basic obligations are (a) covenant for quiet enjoyment, and (b) non-derogation from his grant.

Thousands of pages have been written on the subject of quiet enjoyment, many quoting judgments of higher courts in specific examples.

Basically, it is intended that you, the tenant, should be able to have undisturbed possession and enjoyment of the premises, without being *substantially* interfered with by the lessor. There would be no point in your running to a lawyer and claiming foul because of some minor irritations.

A breach of covenant for quiet enjoyment is almost always the result of some physical interference with the enjoyment of the premises.

While the covenant for quiet enjoyment is applied to a physical interference, the lessor's covenant not to derogate from his grant would be consideration at law for remedy where the covenant for quiet enjoyment would not apply.

The lessee's covenants are usually (a) to pay the rent, with the right of the lessor for re-entry if in default, and, (b) to maintain the premises in good repair. It is well for the lessee to be quite clear about who will pay the taxes, as this may be considered to be a ''usual covenant''. Spell it out.

On the question of *buying* property, you will find some good advice in the chapter *Caveat Emptor*. When leasing property, take the same attitude. Let the lessee beware! Know what you are leasing. Look the situation over from every angle. Don't take anything for granted, because once the lease is signed, it is signed, and you could find yourself on a sticky wicket.

Remember that a lease has the same effect as a sale of the demised premises for a specified term; in effect, you own the property for the term of the lease. Having the express right of quiet enjoyment, the lessor keeps out unless you agree to allow him access to your leased property, but remember that this places responsibility on your own shoulders, the responsibility that would be yours if you owned the property. The safest attitude to take is that you are in responsible possession; provide yourself with every safeguard — fire and liability insurance, proper maintenance and repair, etc., unless of course it is expressed otherwise in the lease. It is very distressing for a lessee to find that when the leased premises burn down, his business loss not only creates a severe hardship on him, but he is forced to go on paying the rent. The Chinese traders who invented insurance learned their lessons the hard way. All you have to do to protect yourself is call your insurance agent.

Nowhere in real estate is it more important to retain the services of a lawyer than in leasing. This cannot be stressed too strongly.

60

LEASING OFFICE SPACE

People have been known to walk in, take a quick look around the premises and say ''I'll take it.'' And people have been known to regret this, believe me. Don't let it happen to you.

The following is a comprehensive check list for leasing office premises, prepared by the senior leasing negotiator of A.E. LePage (Ontario), John Hudson, F.R.I., F.R.I.C.S. Before starting your search for suitable space, review this and make a note of the points that will be of special interest to you.

THE LOCATION — CHECK: -
1. Public Transportation (buses, subways, Go-train, airport).
2. Accessibility to Expressway, Parkway and Freeway.
3. Traffic congestion at rush hours.
4. Parking.
5. Restaurants, hotel and convention facilities.
6. Banks, post offices, shopping.
7. Type of neighbourhood. Is it improving, stable or deteriorating?
8. Location of residences of present staff and potential employees.
9. Accessibility for clients, customers and suppliers.

THE SPACE — CHECK: -
1. Age, quality and image of building.
2. Ownership and reputation of management (are existing tenants satisfied?)
3. Roster of present tenants.
4. How long has space been vacant? Is other space vacant? Why?
5. Number and size of floors, number of tenants (with eye to future expansion, theirs and yours).
6. What is the rental rate per sq. ft. or per sq. metre? Is the given floor area accurate? What is the basis used for measurement? Does the measurement include a percentage of the common areas?

7. Think in terms of cost per month per annum. An efficient floor layout may well bring a better building within your budget.

8. Check the width of the window module which will dictate the size of private offices. Note the size and spacing of the columns. If lessee's space is measured to the glass line, how much, if any, is lost by wall projections and heat/air conditioning induction units?

9. Allow 150 to 200 sq. ft. per person depending on "Chief to Indian" ratio.

10. Where the terms Gross and Net are used determine exactly what the lessor's definition is in each building as they relate to (a) floor area (b) services included.

11. To compare building rentals, try to determine the "effective rental rate" in each case. This may be necessary due to the variety of ways in which different owners calculate and quote their rents, escalations and allowances.

12. Does the lease contain a realty tax escalator clause, an escalator clause for operating expenses, or both? What is the "Base Year" for each or is the lessor using the alternative "Base Cost" approach? In new buildings check how the base year relates to extent of completion and percentage of occupancy. The later the base year the greater the advantage to the lessee.

13. Does the lessor do the following work or give any of these allowances: -

(a) a "turnkey deal" — defined as all lessee's interior work completed to building standards at the owner's cost;

(b) a partitioning or "leasehold improvement allowance" towards lessee's interior work. Demising walls and standard entrance doors are normally provided at owner's cost;

(c) electrical, mechanical and lighting changes;

(d) a tiled floor, a broadloomed floor or an allowance for broadloom;

(e) a number of power and telephone outlets.

14. Does the lessee pay for hydro charges, fluorescent tube replacement, ballasts and starters? This is usually the case and the cost should be in the range of 40 to 50 cents per sq. ft. per annum.

15. Type of heating and air conditioning system — does the lessor pay for its maintenance and hydro costs? Will air circulation be effective when partitions are erected?

16. Are the following included — if so, are they satisfactory? heat, water, air conditioning, janitor service, window cleaning inside and out, snow removal, landscaping, fluorescent lighting (check candle power), washrooms, drinking fountains, elevators, windows (double or single glazed?), window coverings (drapes or blinds?), wiring, soundproofing, floor

loading, underfloor ducts, services in ceiling, staff coffee and eating facilities.

17. In offices previously occupied specify all items to remain for your use, e.g. partitions, counters, shelving, broadloom, drapes or blinds, air conditioning units.

18. Parking — how many spaces and are they reserved? Are they a part of the lease or can the present monthly cost be increased? Is there additional parking in the area?

19. What is the most desirable lease term? Will longer lease protect against future rent increase or expansion by a larger tenant? Is this type of space in demand so that if necessary could readily be sublet? Has the lessee the right to sublet? Can the lessee keep any profit rental obtained in so doing?

20. Is there an option to renew? If so, at what rental? Is the space under option to another tenant at a later date?

21. Can the lessee be given notice to vacate if the building is sold or demolished? If so, is there any compensation for lessee's improvements?

22. Check if lessee is required to restore premises to their original state on termination of lease or if improvements are to remain and become lessor's property.

23. Date of possession — check this with the telephone company, contractors, movers, furniture suppliers and allow for delays. Give notice to present lessor. Make sure lessee has the right of prior entry rent free to prepare the new premises for his use.

24. What are the provisions for signs or identification?

25. What is the position regarding shipping and deliveries? Note if there are charges for use of elevators for furniture, materials or delivery of parcels.

26. Check availability and cost of storage space.

27. How is the security? Has the building 24 hour access? What time are the doors locked? At what hours or seasons are heat, air conditioning, elevator service curtailed?

28. Note if the lessor levies a fee for the supervision of the installation of lessee's leasehold improvements.

61

LEASE-BACKS

This common expression is derived from two separate and simultaneous transactions, the sale by the owner/occupant of a building to a purchaser who immediately leases it to the seller, who stays right where he is.

A benefit to the seller is that the sale provides additional cash for the business operation. This additional cash also can provide more cash, because a bank loves to see chunky bank balances, which usually makes it easier to borrow.

A loss to the seller is the loss of its real estate. All future increases in the market value now belong to the new owner.

An ideal lease-back would be one where the seller has the right to regain the real estate at a future date by purchasing it for about 20% of its selling price. This would provide the buyer with a good return on its investment through the lease, plus a 20% bonus at the end of the lease. An agreement could be incorporated in the original transaction allowing the seller to buy-back at earlier dates at specific prices. However, the majority of buyers in a lease-back won't want any part of this; they buy it to own it, period. If there is an agreement to turn it back to the seller, it would probably be at an appraised price at the time of selling.

The cash-short owner considering a lease-back will naturally explore all other avenues of raising money before getting serious about the lease-back. Mortgaging a property to 75% of lending value in a $400,000. parcel may leave the owner with a yearning for the $100,000. balance, which is tied up in equity, and which could be turned loose for expansion and other purposes. It is the converting of this equity into cash that is the prime reason for the lease-back.

There are two factors that will water down the yearning for the $100,000. If the owner had taken a capital cost allowance over a number of years in its annual tax returns, a ''recaptured tax'' will have to be paid on such deductions, if the property were sold at a price in excess of its depreciated value, which today is certainly most likely.

Another slap at the $100,000. will be a capital gain tax on disposition. Half the net gain will be taxed. So these two factors will be carefully weighed in selling to determine if it really would be a wise move.

If the owner decided to proceed, here is an example of what the agreement would entail:

If the building is new, and was constructed by a reputable builder, the costs of land acquisition and building will be the figure used to proceed with formal negotiations. If the building is a few years old, a professional appraisal will be made to arrive at its reasonable current market value, and this figure will be used.

(a) The property would be leased immediately to the now former owner on a net basis (it would pay *all* charges against the property)-for an agreed period.

(b) The rent paid would be established by the strength of the lessee's covenant (the stronger it is, the less it pays) and by the term of the lease.

(c) The lessor (new owner) would treat the investment as a sort of annuity, and it would be amortized completely, including principal and interest, over the period of time under the term of the lease, which would be what the lessee would pay as rent. The interest rate in such amortization is generally slightly higher than current, conventional mortgage rates, the reason for which is that 100% of valuation financing is effected.

(d) The long term net lease may contain a cost-of-living index, to ensure that the owner's dollar return will not be shattered by inflation during the term of the lease.

The seller will attempt to obtain two favourable considerations in the agreement:

(1) A buy-back right on attractive terms, and

(2) A renewal right in the lease at a sharply reduced rent, the reason being that the investing body will have recovered its capital cost.

The lessee, being on a net lease, and therefore required to pay all municipal taxes, local improvements, utilities, insurance, etc. will covenant to pay these charges as "additional rent", which will enable the lessor to have the same recourse for breach of this covenant as he will have for non-payment of the basic rent.

In the event of loss by fire or other cause, it will be the lessee's responsibility to rebuild, which makes it necessary to detail at length the insurance clause in the lease. It will be required to cover itself, the lessor, and possibly a mortgagee fully with a wide range of coverage. Smaller, agreed-upon claims will be settled by the lessee alone, larger amount being settled through the lessor.

A most extensive part of the lease will be that which concerns the rights and/or obligations of the lessee to repair, renovate, remodel, add to, or even completely replace the building. This will cover such aspects as performance bonds, restrictions under municipal building by-laws, etc. and the building, regardless of the approved changes, will of course remain the property of the lessor.

In case of loss or damage when the lessee will be required to promptly remedy this at its own expense, it will be bound to continue paying the rent during such period, unless otherwise provided for by moratorium in the lease.

The stiffness of the requirements of the lessee will soften as the lease approaches expiration, when it will probably have option agreements covering loss during this latter period. For instance, if the lease contains an option to purchase the property at the end of the lease, and the buildings were damaged or destroyed during this period, the lessee would normally have a clause giving it the option to rebuild, or terminate the lease by purchasing the property from the lessor, plus indemnifying the lessor for its unrecovered capital cost plus interest.

The seller deals with one body for the full treatment. No middleman looking for commissions in the transaction, which could amount to sizeable sums. The seller gets the money, and can do what it wants with it. The rent will be a tax deductible item.

If the seller had financed by conventional mortgaging, the only tax deductible part of it would be the interest on the mortgage. The rent is, in effect, a mortgage, but the principal repayment is considered a part of the rent, and is therefore also tax deductible.

However, caution must be exercised if the deal is to contain a buy-back right, because the income tax department may take the position that all the seller was doing was using the property effectively as security for raising capital. Also, in lease-back projects, the subject of the true market value of the property may be raised.

One would be well advised to seek expert accounting and tax advice in entering into any sale-lease-back contract, both buyer/lessor, and seller/lessee.

62

THE SELLING COMMISSION

Lucky you. Your house was listed with a member of a real estate board on M.L.S. (Multiple listing service) for 60 days. The listing broker and a lot of other brokers showed your house to a lot of potential buyers. A lot of time and expense went into those showings, to say nothing of the advertising costs incurred by the listing broker.

And then what? The house didn't sell and the listing expired. Lucky you — because it didn't cost you one cent. Not only that, you probably got some free appraisals out of it — the offers presented to you told you what some bona fide buyers thought your house was worth.

Tell this to a new arrival from outer space and the thing will probably think all real estate agents are nuts.

Now, why would a broker work for nothing? Well, he really doesn't, because in the real estate business *the sales pay for the no sales*.

Of all the properties listed through real estate boards' M.L.S. service, about 30% sell, which of course means that 70% of the vendors get a free ride.

Carrying this further, if a M.L.S. listing is at 6%, and 30% sell, it can be safely said that the average property is not sold for a 6% commission, but for *less than two per cent*! 1.8% to be exact.

Oh boy, have I heard them scream. House sellers that is. "What, pay 6% to sell my lovely home? Why, that's $4,200. on 70 thousand. Where do you people get off charging that kind of money?"

My first response to this is to ask the vendor what I can expect to be paid if the house doesn't sell. And you know what? That's right, nothing. Not a penny.

No real estate board in Canada will attempt to tell a broker what he should charge for selling property, unless of course some broker gets loony ideas about usury, then I imagine he would be rapped pretty fast. So the profession (and it is a professional body) uses a fee structure that it estimates will produce a respectable living for its members.

If, for example, instead of listing property at a 6% M.L.S. rate, a broker decided to lower his charges by figuring he would make it up in volume, here is what he would really be making on reduced commissions. Remember now, 30% sell and 70% don't sell.

Listing Commission	Selling Commission
5%	1.5%
4%	1.2%
3%	.9%
2%	.6%

There is a large American based organization with a policy that has worked well for years, world wide. It lists properties all over the world, and, when the listing is signed, the vendor pays the company a fee *immediately*. That's the listing fee.

The company then exposes the property for sale, and if it sells, a further fee is paid on closing.

The foregoing is an ideal system. The vendor pays some now, and some later. The broker knows that when a vendor pays a listing fee, that vendor is very serious about selling. If the property doesn't move, the broker has been paid something for his work, and if the property does move, the vendor hands over the balance.

The basic reason for this system's success is that the properties listed are owned for the most part by owners of substantial means who are willing to pay, and can pay a fee for services rendered whether or not a sale is completed.

It wouldn't work here.

Many vendors, particularly homeowners, are just not financially equipped to enter into such an agreement. They would also be undoubtedly wondering just what kind of service they would really get for the "front money".

It has often been observed that there are too many real estate agents in Canada, too many "part-timers". However true that may be, the fact remains that the average agent's annual income is less than that received by bus drivers or postmen, to give a couple of examples. If your response to that is "go drive a bus", it misses the point, which is that this business of real estate is no sinecure. Many try, and many fail, and the ones who do make it certainly earn every nickel they get.

The commission received by the broker is taken apart and passed around to all who contributed to execution of the sale, so that when you see that 5 or 6% on the bottom line, don't get the idea that the agent is going to walk away with a big chunk of your money and stick it all in *his* pocket.

The listing broker gets a piece, the selling broker gets a piece, the listing salesman gets a piece and the selling salesman gets a piece. If one broker does it all himself, as an individual, then he gets it all — but this is the exception.

It is possible to obtain the services of a broker at lower rates. All one has to do is shop around and ask; if a broker is willing to handle your business for a lower rate you may save some money.

Selling it Yourself

Here's a challenge, a chance to eliminate the commission entirely, but if you are going this route *do it properly*.

Regardless of what *you* think your property is worth, it is a sound idea to obtain professional advice. This can be accomplished by calling a *local* broker who is quite evidently active in your neighbourhood, and retain the broker to appraise the property.

There are three basic appraisals, the first of which is a verbal overview of your property. An indication of its market value.

A stronger one is a letter of opinion, not too much detail, but something in writing where the broker has expressed opinion on paper. He will be careful about what he says, because his reputation is on the line, realizing that the letter could be seen by others.

The full blown appraisal is expensive, and so it should be. A lot of work here, probably a package of several pages with everything in it from zoning, replacement and land costs to recent sales.

I suggest you use the second one, the letter. This will probably serve your purpose. If the broker has been active in your neighbourhood for a number of years he will certainly know what he is talking about.

When you have the price established, there are several things that you can do to make it easier to make your presentation to potential buyers and expedite the sale.

If you are simply going to ask all cash, or cash to the existing mortgages, you will restrict the attractiveness of the offering. Alternate financing arrangements (which are many) can be thought out beforehand with the help of your lawyer. Or you can retain the appraising broker to help you, with an understanding of a prescribed fee.

List *every* physical aspect of your property, and such things as the location of local schools, shopping conveniences, etc. You might even make a list of your favourite servicemen.

If there are guarantees concerning the property, list them also and have them available. Put everything down. Make it interesting and easy for the buyer.

The ''for sale'' sign should be properly done by a signpainter. Don't use an old piece of cardboard with some scratchy information on it — it looks terrible, and actually prompts house hunters to drive on. It leaves one with the feeling that if the seller is that cheap, there won't be much of a chance for negotiating the price.

The sign should contain the phone number and the words ''by appointment only.'' This reduces the incidence of people suddenly knocking on your door at all hours — most of which will probably be inconvenient ones.

Try to make the appointments at hours when a man will be in the house, for obvious reasons.

If you get to the point of making a verbal deal, ask the buyer to put it in writing, then take the offer to your lawyer.

Probably the earliest calls you will receive from your sign will be from real estate agents. A good local agent knows what is available in his area, including yours. After going through the private route for a while, don't be too surprised if you end up listing with a broker. He's the one with the buyers, the comparable properties and plenty of know-how.

63

THE OKLAHOMA OFFER

One of the meanest financial flim-flams devised and used by money-grabbers is the ''Oklahoma Offer''.

It is slick, professional, and to the untrained eye hard to spot. It enables one to purchase property with nothing down and make a substantial and immediate cash profit.

Unfortunately, it leaves a vendor (property seller) stuck with a mortgage, most of which is not worth the paper it is written on. If you are selling property, watch for it — here is an example of how it works:

The following are briefly the financial contents of an offer to purchase property:

1. Purchase Price: $47,000.
2. Deposit with Offer: $2,000.
3. Purchaser agrees to pay vendor $30,000. on closing.
4. Vendor agrees to hold second mortgage for $15,000.
5. Purchaser agrees to arrange, at his own expense, a first mortgage of not less than $30,000.

The innocent vendor adds it up:

Deposit:	$ 2,000.
Cash:	30,000.
Mortgage:	15,000.
TOTAL:	$47,000.

If the offer is accepted, the purchaser can go to work and arrange a first mortgage of not $30,000. but $40,000. Remember, it was agreed that the first mortgage will be *not less than $30,000.*

Out of this $40,000. first mortgage, the purchaser will pay the vendor the agreed $30,000. give himself $2,000. to get back the deposit, and put $8,000. in his pocket.

Proof?

First Mortgage:	$40,000.
Second Mortgage:	15,000.
	$55,000.
Purchase Price:	47,000.
Profit to buyer:	$ 8,000.

The vendor, having agreed to hold a second mortgage of $15,000., is now in the unenviable position of having $8,000. of the $15,000. mortgage *exceed* the purchase price of the property.

If the purchaser is a corporate shell with no assets, it could then walk away with the $8,000. profit and forget the property.

If the vendor (now the second mortgagee) ended up owning the property again, he would owe $40,000 to a first mortgagee. Here is the spot he would be in:

Property worth	$47,000.
Owing	40,000.
Equity worth	7,000.
Cash received	32,000.
	$39,000.
Selling price:	47,000.
Net loss to vendor:	($ 8,000.)
(plus headaches and legal fees)	

What this means, of course, is that it will cost the vendor (mortgagee) $8,000. out of his own pocket to regain possession of the property.

This money-making scheme is triggered by a clause in the agreement that will allow the purchaser (mortgagor) to increase the principal amount of the first mortgage "without necessarily applying the increase to reduce the principal amount of the second mortgage", which allows the purchaser to arrange and secure the $40,000. mortgage.

If questioned on this nocuous point, a glib person will say something to the effect that money obtained from such an increase will be required to improve the property, resulting in greater security for the second mortgagee (vendor). Which is hogwash! Watch it!!

Also, the purchaser may ask to assign the agreement to a third, unnamed party. This will release the purchaser from his covenant, and the assignee could be a corporate shell with no assets.

And, in *any* agreement of purchase and sale, here are two warning signs:

Be careful about accepting an offer from a buyer who shows the words ''in trust'' after his name.

''In Trust'' could be a corporate shell with no money, and when the time comes to close it would be useless to attempt to legally force a closing if the purchaser decided not to close.

It is tantamount to giving the purchaser an option on the property. Therefore, a serious consideration must be the amount of the deposit made with the offer and the length of time to close the sale. If the purchaser defaults, the vendor could retain the deposit money, which should be an amount considered to be fair compensation for the length of time the property was tied up . . .

When selling an older property, be careful about agreeing to warrant that there will be no municipal or other legal work orders registered against the property on the date of closing.

A sharp purchaser, under such an agreement, could have the property inspected by municipal fire and building departments resulting in unheard of orders to repair and/or improve the property. The vendor would be stuck with the bill.

Agree only to there being no work orders registered against the property on the date of acceptance of the agreement.

Caveat emptor? Let the buyer beware?

Let the *seller* beware!

64

SELLING YOUR HOUSE

If one has lived in the same house for years and has watched the activity of real estate brokers in the neighbourhood, it is likely that one firm will stand out in its aggressiveness by its number of "sold" signs. You will notice that I did not say "for sale" signs. There is an obvious difference.

However, most homeowners don't give this much thought until faced with a move, or the prospect of one.

Here are the basic moves. Yours will be one of them.

(1) In a hurry to sell
(2) To sell and move by a specific date
(3) In no hurry to sell
(4) To sell before buying another property
(5) To sell after buying another property

If the move has to be done as quickly as possible, it will require an all-out effort, which means listing the property on the local real estate board's multiple listing service (MLS). This opens it to all agent members of the board, who are provided with details of the listing, including a photograph of the property.

It will also require the property to be listed at the *right price*. An over-priced property is a wasted exercise — it discourages agents from showing the property. Active agents *know* the local market, and they will not waste time trying to get someone an over-the-market price. And how is this "right price" established?

Averaging. Call the offices of three local brokers who have shown evidence of being active in the neighbourhood. Don't call them all in on the same day. Ask for the sales managers. Tell each of them you are seriously considering selling and would like to discuss it with one of his top agents. Make the appointments on three half-day periods, to give the agents plenty of time to inspect the property without overlapping. Get each reaction, each valuation. Size up the agent from each office, and then put it all on your scales for averaging.

The price tags will very seldom be the same, although they will probably be close. Sometimes an owner may be unfortunate and find that one of the price tags will be much higher, and out of proportion to the other two. I say unfortunate, because this could be the work of a salesman who is simply providing an inflated price in an attempt to impress the owner with the dollar sign, get the listing, and bring the owner down to earth at a later date. Reputable salesmen will be pleased to show comparable sales records to justify the appraisal. An inflated price could also be the result of inexperience on the part of the salesman.

When you have decided on the firm that you would like to handle the sale, give the firm a listing agreement and get on with it. A listing agreement at a fair market price means that you are well on your way to a successful sale.

The MLS listing will be with one realtor, and all appointments for inspection will be made through this agent. A vendor can, of course, advise the agent that other brokers may phone directly to the vendor for appointments, but it is better to do this through the listing agent to avoid confusion, and ensure that the agent is aware of all viewings. It is necessary for the listing agent to retain a tight rein on the progress of the brokerage and to keep well informed of all progress.

Ensure that your MLS agent holds an ''open house'' date for inspections by other realtors. This is most important. On one open house I held, no fewer than 57 agents inspected the house, and it was sold very quickly. Most agents inspect properties *every day* to keep abreast of the market and have personal knowledge of the properties.

One of the distinct advantages of listing on MLS is that one of the agents may have the waiting buyer for your property, and when your listing comes to his attention it could be sold very quickly. So MLS is your best listing when in a hurry to sell.

To sell and move by a specific date can provide a bit of concern for a vendor. If an acceptable offer comes along but the moving date doesn't suit you, be careful about any thoughts of rejecting it because of this. Remember that in selling anything, it is always a good idea to ''make it easy for the buyer,'' and if everything in the agreement suits you but the moving date, you could jeopardize the deal by simply rejecting it and telling the buyer he will move when you want him to move.

Instead of touching the offer on this point, have your agent discuss it over the telephone with the buyer. This is important, because if you change the date (or anything else) on the offer, the agreement is dead unless the purchaser agrees with the change. If your buyer is adamant about the moving date, then you may be faced with interim financing, which brings up another bit of concern.

If the buyer wishes to close his purchase of your property later than you do, there are two things you must immediately consider:

The first is the amount of the deposit money placed in trust on your behalf. If the buyer has deposited $1,000. against a long closing, it then becomes your concern about whether this $1,000. would be enough compensation for you in the event that he did not go through with the deal, leaving you with an empty house on your hands.

The second is your own financing. If you have to close the purchase of another property before the closing date on the sale of your own, it will require funds to effect this. Some real estate brokers, especially the larger ones, have such interim funds available for vendors on whose behalf they have acted. Other than that, your bank may help, or perhaps your own lawyer. The foregoing points are to be carefully weighed, and the advice of your lawyer can be of great help and assurance to you.

But remember, try and avoid missing a good deal if the only thing standing between you and the purchaser is a closing date.

When one is in no hurry to sell, money can be saved by listing the propery on an exclusive basis rather than MLS. It costs less, but usually takes longer to sell.

Or no exclusive at all. Advise three or four brokers of your available property and tell them they can have an "open" listing, whereby all can work on it, but the selling broker gets all the commission.

Or list it exclusively with two brokers, on a 80/20 basis. The one coming up with the buyer gets 80% of the commission, and the other 20%. Sometimes this plan prods a couple of agents to work a little harder.

Being in no hurry also means that you can ask a little more for the property. I said a *little*. Ask too much more and you won't get much action.

To sell before buying another property is a move I would condone only if the sale has a long closing, such as 90 days or more. Providing, of course, it is your intention to buy another property. An exception to this would be a deal that is just so sweet and impossible to turn down that you would move into short term accommodation to effect the sale.

Once you have sold before buying, you will need not only time to look at other properties and find one you would like, and can buy, but you will need closing time. The vendor of the one you want to buy might want a bit of time to move himself.

So, you could spend a good four weeks finding your property, only to find that the vendor won't close for eight weeks. Total time 12 weeks. If you have sold before buying with a closing of 10 weeks, you have created a sticky wicket for yourself.

Selling after buying. Again we are faced with closing time, so give yourself a good span in closing what you buy, so you can be flexible in selling.

In buying before selling, it is often adviseable, but not always possible, to have it a part of your agreement that the purchase is conditional upon selling your own home. An advantage in selling after buying is that you know you have another home to move into.

On the other hand, an advantage of selling *before* buying is that you know exactly how much money you will have available for buying.

If you have thrown up your hands after all the foregoing, don't despair. A good agent can be very comforting.

Now, when you have listed your property for sale, and thereby retained the services of a broker, remember that you have agreed to let *him* effect the sale. You can help a great deal by not only making your property as attractive as possible to potential buyers, but also by doing your best to be as inconspicuous as possible during your agent's showings. Don't volunteer any information; it may be something the buyer doesn't want to hear. Make yourself available for answering questions, nothing more. Leave the negotiating to the agent, and when you receive offers, then *you* start negotiating.

Make every bit of information about the property available to the broker. Mortgages, site plans, surveys, municipal tax bills, heating bills, receipts for major repairs, roof and other guarantees and contracts, and leases. It would be a nice gesture to provide your own list of preferred neighbourhood shops, servicemen, and suppliers. And don't forget to mention the location of all Church denominations, and schools, both public and private.

Give the agent your fullest cooperation. By this I mean such things as bending over backwards to accept appointments at hours that may not be convenient for you. Keep the property as attractive as possible at all times for showings. Doll the place up with a few flowers, and give it the old fresh-air scent spray treatment before showings. Nothing turns a buyer off quicker than a house that reeks of unsavory odors.

First impressions are lasting impressions. So ensure that your front door, verandah and the immediate area here is attractive. When the agent is waiting for you to open the door, the buyer is standing there with nothing to do but look at that part of your house. This is most important.

Get all the junk out of the house and store it in the garage. Or better still, have a garage sale and get rid of it.

It may be difficult, but try and have the children playing outside when showing the property, or at least have them doing something *quietly*. This means leaving the TV set turned *off*.

There are many means of financing the sale.

The most common one vendors shoot for is cash to mortgage(s). You get cash for your equity, and the buyer carries on with the mortgage payments.

If the buyer "agrees to assume" the mortgage, it simply means that he agrees to maintain the payments. But if you signed the mortgage deed, you are still responsible for the debt. So you might discuss this aspect of the sale with your lawyer before you even have the property listed. He will advise you on the means available to avoid this, although if there is a good chunky amount of cash going into the property for the purhaser's equity, there would be little concern about covenant for the mortgage.

If the price is a top price, but the purchaser needs a little help with the financing, you can always consider holding a mortgage as part of the purchase price. But if you do this, try and keep the interest rate comparable to current market rates, and the term down to about three years. The reason for this is very basic; you might want to sell the mortgage, and the lower the rate and the longer the term, the less you will get for it.

If your property is clear of debt, there is usually no problem in getting all cash. Mortgaging today can be obtained with a high ratio to the selling price. You get the mortgage money on closing, plus the cash going into the deal. Or maybe you will hold that small second.

If your property has a mortgage or two against it and you receive an all cash offer, find out just how much it will cost you to remove the mortgage(s). The buyer doesn't want any encumbrance and he will expect you to pay the cost of removal. Better still, find out before you even list the property — the cost could be sizeable.

Here is something to *remember*, so read this carefully. If you are presented with an offer that is subject to the buyer selling his own home, it is customary for the agreement to contain an "escape clause" that allows you to go on offering your property for sale, and to entertain further offers. The clause says, in effect, that in the event that you wish to accept another offer on your property, you will give the purchaser 48 hours to remove the condition about selling his own property. If he does, you close with the first offer. If he doesn't, you can accept the second.

But here is the important part of this that I suggest you remember:

Ensure that the escape clause reads in such a way that you may require the purchaser not only to remove the condition, but also that he has to match the second offer. If, for example, the second offer is a couple of thousand dollars sweeter to you, you wouldn't be able to get it from the first buyer if he removed the condition unless the condition was specific on this point.

Well now, you have an acceptable offer in front of you. CALL YOUR LAWYER. If you can't see him personally, at least read it to him over the telephone. You are retaining him to close the sale, so let him protect you all the way. Lawyers have sharp eyes for sharp clauses.

214

Here are the real estate agent's duties to a vendor

1. Give the vendor a true copy of the listing agreement immediately after the execution of the agreement.

2. The agent shall give the owner an honest effort to sell the property and promote and protect his client's interest by proper guidance in matters of price, law (with limited application) and shall render conscientious service.

3. He shall offer the property at one price only, the listed price.

4. He shall accept the standard commission payable by his principal.

5. He shall inform the vendor of any and all offers to purchase the property.

6. The agent shall declare any personal interest in the transaction.

7. The agent shall be honest, loyal to his principal and shall not be negligent.

65

IMPROVING THE OFFER

Not many vendors are cool about waiting for their listing agent to present an offer. The property has been placed on the market and now the vendor wants some action.

First, there will probably be inspections of the property made by other agents, and then the showings to the househunters will begin. The grumpy one giving your home the once over could be the ultimate buyer, and the pleasant, enthusiastic couple could be nothing more than a couple of snoopers. One can never tell about buyers or who they will be in housing.

Then the phone rings. Your agent has an offer. The agent will want to present it as soon as possible, and you are naturally anxious to see it. When the agent arrives, ensure that you have a quiet and private place to inspect the offer. This could be anywhere, of course, but turn off the T.V. and shoo the kids out of the room.

The first thing you will look for and look at is the price in the offer, and this is when you can become a little upset or even uptight. After all, your agent listed it at $85,000. and here is an offer of $80,500. Such nerve, you think. How could the buyer be so greedy to expect you to drop the price by almost five grand?

But remember, this is an *offer*. Before rejecting the offer because of the price, go through the whole thing with the agent, item by item, clause by clause. After all, the agent is only doing what the law tells him to do, and that is bringing the offer to your attention.

When you have gone over the offer with the agent, ensure that the arithmetic is quite clear to you. Seeing an offer of $80,5000. with $2,000. deposit, assume a $55,000. first, pay a further $16,000. on closing, vendor take back a second, etc. you will only be confused unless it is put down in order, viz:

Price:		$80,500.
Deposit:	$ 2,000.	
Closing:	16,000.	
First Mtge.	55,000.	
Second Mtge.	7,500.	$80,500.

216

Now it is clearer. You can see that your part of it will be a total of $18,000. cash plus a $7,500. second mortgage the purchaser is asking you to hold. Her are some financial points in this offer to consider:

The buyer is prepared to put up $18,000. cash. He could very well have another $20,000. in the bank but doesn't want to put up any more, as evidenced by his asking for the second mortgage. So you ask the agent a few probing questions. A good agent will have found out all he can about the buyer, and may have some interesting answers for you.

If you do not want to hold that second mortgage, you will want it turned into cash, so remember that the shorter the term and the higher the interest rate, the more cash you will get when selling it. Ask your agent to phone his broker and see if he will give you a commitment to buy the mortgage. Get a cash figure from him, or someone, perhaps your own lawyer. If, for example, you know you can get $6,500. cash for the second mortgage, the discount of $1,000. off the mortgage now must be taken off the price from the buyer. Now we effectively have an offer of $79,500. cash to your registered mortgage.

What about a bit more cash from the buyer and a smaller second? The discount off the smaller second mortgage may bring the price up to $80,000.

If you think a second mortgage would be O.K. determine just how long you would want your money invested here. And carefully consider its rate of interest. This second mortgage could be the answer in getting yourself a sale that is to your satisfaction.

Now about that price of $80,500. If you think your asking price has been shaved too much, remember that you are just $4,500. apart, which is a little more than five per cent off the asking price — which certainly is at least a reasonable starting point. If you sign the offer back at the full price, there is agood chance you will kill the deal. Negotiate.

In cases like this, splitting the difference has created many sales. If you signed it back at another $2,250. that is being reasonable, and there may be a good chance your buyer would take it. If the agent, in presenting your counter-offer to the buyer discovered that the buyer didn't have the $2,250. perhaps he will come back to you with an offer to add the $2,250. to the second mortgage. Then you will have to sharpen your pencil again.

If there is a mortgage on your property and you receive an all cash offer with the buyer requiring you to remove all financial incumbrances, you will have to take the cost of discharging your mortgage into consideration. This probability should be taken care of at the time of listing the property. Ask your mortgagee what the interest penalty would be in such an event.

If the mortgage term has three or four years to run, and the lender wants a six months' interest penalty to discharge it, this could mean a large sum of money which *you* would have to pay. The amount would have to be deducted from the selling price of the property, so don't be hasty in agreeing to discharge your mortgage for the cash buyer.

When counter-signing an offer, be very particular about the time limit you give the other party to make up his mind about accepting it, and *ensure* that this is taken care of. Remember, when you have counter-signed, you can't accept any other offers until this one is disposed of.

A most important point about a reasonably good offer is to keep it alive. Back and forth between buyer and seller if necessary, but keep it going until all is exhausted, the offer is a sale, or it is dead and you wait for another one. One of the puzzling things about real estate is that quite often the first offer is the best offer!

Give it a chance.

66

THE LORD'S DAY ACT

The Federal Government of Canada says that it is not lawful for any person on the Lord's Day (Sunday) except as provided in any Provincial Act or law in force on or after the 1st day of March, 1907, to sell any real estate from midnight on Saturday night to midnight on Sunday night.

Furthermore, the Federal Lord's Day Act also says that it is not lawful to *offer for sale* any real estate during the above noted hours, and one cannot legally *purchase* any real estate during the period.

The penalties for breaking this law are not financially severe in themselves, but could be very severe and troublesome in other areas. A vendor or purchaser could nullify a contract that became binding on the day of acceptance, and when the deal folds in a case like this, not only the vendor and purchaser could end up in court but also the agent involved in the deal.

The safest rule is to avoid Sunday when transacting a sale, but there are some court findings on the subject which may seem to allow one to at least do part of the selling on Sunday. Remember, the contract *must be made and become binding* on Sunday for contravention of the Act. Consider the following, without of course considering it in any way to be legal advice.

A purchaser signed an offer on a Sunday, and it was accepted on a Sunday. Void? Not necessarily. The offer was conditional on the purchaser approving of the size of the recreation room to accommodate a special bar he wished to move from his present home. The buyer measured the room on Tuesday and approved of it on Tuesday. Therefore, the contract would have been completed on Tuesday.

Conversely, if the same papers were signed on a Wednesday and approval of the condition were made on a Sunday, this would mean that the contract was completed on Sunday. Watch it.

Suppose a vendor gave one an option to purchase his land, and signed the option on Sunday. Could it be void? The option is one's right to purchase the land at a future date at an agreed price, and if the vendor was advised of the buyer "exercising the option" on a Thursday, it means that the contract to buy the land was made on Thursday, and not Sunday.

But if the buyer received the option on Thursday, and exercised it on Sunday? No way.

If a buyer and seller agree to a sale and shake hands on Monday, then sign the papers on the following Sunday? The court may consider that the contract was made on Monday when the two parties shook hands.

The generally accepted rule appears to be — it's O.K. for the buyer to sign the offer on Sunday, but don't present it to the vendor until Monday — and that makes sense.

Do yourself a favour and stay away from the possible headaches that could be caused by a Sunday. Ask your lawyer about the current Provincial law on the subject.

67

PROPERTY INSURANCE

Insurance secures protection against propery loss in consideration of a payment proportioned to the risk involved.

Property insurance includes real property, buildings and contents, machinery, merchandise, household furnishings, valuables, automobiles, boats, aircraft, ships and cargoes, and in fact any insurable object in which a person has an insurable interest.

When you are going to have property insurance placed, don't call your cousin Joe and ask him for advice, unless he happens to be in the profession of placing property insurance. Consult a properly qualified insurance agent.

In the process of obtaining property insurance, you bump headlong into a matter of good faith between you and your agent. If you know something materially affecting the acceptability of the risk, and do not tell the insurer about it, that is called a "non-disclosure"; and if you tell the insurer something that is not in accordance with the facts, that is a "misrepresentation". Your non-disclosure or misrepresentation of material facts when the insurance is applied for makes the contract voidable, at the election of the insurer, upon his discovering the situation.

You must have an *insurable interest* in property, without which your insurance contract is void. An insurable interest in property is when you stand in such a legal relationship to it that you may be prejudiced by its loss or damage and stand to benefit by its continued existence. If you simply took out a policy on property belonging to somebody else in which you have no financial interest, you are merely making a bet with the insurer that the property will not be lost during the policy period, and such a contract would be void.

You do not, of course, have to be the owner of property to have an insurable interest in it. For example, those who have possession of the property of others, such as bailees, pledgees, pawnbrokers, warehousemen, carriers, jewellers, furriers, tenants, etc., have an insurable interest. Their interest arises out of their potential liability to make good loss or damage to the property in their care. Others with an insurable interest are executors, administrators and other trustees, mortgagees, lienholders, vendors under conditional sales agreements; and lessees and other users of property which they employ for gain and who may therefore suffer business loss if it is damaged or lost.

Your indemnity, up to the limit of the policy, is to be fully indemnified for what you have actually lost in money value, but you can make no profit out of the occurrence in case of loss. Your loss is the cost of restoration or repair in the event of partial loss, with due allowance for betterment, and, in the case of total loss, it is the depreciated actual cash value of the property at the time of loss — the insurer pays the true *pecuniary* loss, no, more, no less.

A *valued policy* is one covering loss or damage to chattels under which, on *total* loss of the insured property, a fixed sum is payable which has been agreed upon between you and the insurer at the inception of the contract. Generally speaking, and subject of course to gross or fraudulent over-valuation, the stated amount is payable by the insurer without reference to your actual monetary loss. Generally, your insurer requires you to obtain an independent valuation of the property before entering into such a contract.

The first form of insurance was marine insurance on ships and cargo. Next came fire insurance, and today fire insurance accounts for about 20% of all insurance business written in Canada.

A fire insurance policy will cover you in the event of your property being destroyed or damaged by fire, lightning, or an explosion of natural, coal or manufactured gas, without allowance for any increased cost of repair or reconstruction by reason of any ordinance or law regulating construction or repair, to an amount not exceeding, *whichever is the least*, of:

(a) The actual cash value of the property at the time of destruction or damage.

(b) The interest of the insured in the property.

(c) The sum set opposite an applicable item in the policy, and subject to any pro rata provisions.

The policy does not cover:

(a) Loss, destruction or damage to goods occasioned by or happening through their undergoing any process involving the application of heat.

(b) Loss, destruction or damage caused by riot, civil commotion, war, invasion, act of foreign enemy, hostilities (whether war be declared or not), civil war, rebellion, revolution, insurrection or military power.

(c) Loss, destruction or damage to electrical devices or appliances caused by lightning or other electrical currents unless fire ensues and then only for such loss, destruction or damage as results from such fire.

(d) Loss, destruction or damage caused by contamination by radioactive material.

(e) Money, books of account, securities for money, evidences of debt or title; automobiles, tractors, and other motor vehicles; aircraft; watercraft.

(f) Loss, destruction or damage to a building or its contents during alteration of or addition to the building and in consequence thereof, unless written permission therefor has been previously granted. Normal repairs are allowed without permission.

(g) While the building insured or containing the property insured is to the knowledge of the Insured vacant or unoccupied for more than thirty consecutive days or, being a manufacturing establishment, ceases to be operated and contunues out of operation for more than thirty consecutive days.

(h) While to the knowledge of the Insured there is situated or used in the building insured or containing the property insured gasoline, benzine, naphtha or other substance of an equal or lower flashpoint, in total quantity greater than one gallon in addition to that contained in tanks of vehicles.

(i) Loss directly or indirectly, proximately or remotely, arising in consequence of or contributed to by the enforcement of any by-law, regulation, ordinance or law regulating zoning or the demolition, repair or construction of buildings or structures, which by-law, regulation, ordinance or law makes it impossible to repair or re-instate the property as it was immediately prior to the loss.

The cardinal principle being that the contract of property insurance is a contract of indemnity, you will not recover more than the actual value of your property at the time of the loss.

A provision of your fire policy is that in no event shall the insurer's liability exceed what it would cost you to repair, or replace, the property with material *of the same kind and like quality*. This is not the proper measure of damages which you may invoke, but, rather a limitation on the insurer's liability.

The term "value" is difficult to define with exactness, and as a result several interpretations have developed. Establishing value is, to some degree, a matter of opinion, but several concepts are useful in arriving at the true meaning of value as used in insurance contracts. One of the basic concepts of value is "actual cash value", which is defined as replacement cost less depreciation. This concept is useful in that it establishes a value which is designed to restore you to the same financial condition you were in prior to the loss.

A problem arises here because you usually must replace the damaged or destroyed property at full cost, and so must pay for the cost of the depreciation at that time. On certain types of property it is often possible to

223

avoid this situation by insuring on a *replacement cost basis* so that the value will be determined on the actual amount required to restore your property without having to take into consideration the item of depreciation.

Interrelated to actual cash value and replacement cost are the concepts of: (1) value in use, and (2) value in exchange. Value in use refers to the benefits you derive from property in the form of shelter, income, health, or pleasure. Value in exchange is a measure of goods which can be valued in terms of the price at which the property would have sold, not exceeding the cost of replacement.

There are two primary and fundamental obligations which you must assume if a fire insurance contract is to be effective and binding upon the insurer. You are responsible for the determination of the amount of insurance. for which the policy is written, and for proving a claim in case of loss. Unless you meet these obligations, the effectiveness of the policy is jeopardized and its purpose is materially affected.

Misunderstanding by you as to your responsibility for these two points would probably be partly due to the fact that insurance is future indemnity; purchased today against loss, which may or not be realized. Loose thinking could also be a factor. The amount of a fire policy relates to the value of the property to be insured. You should insure for the full value of the property in order to get the best protection. At the time the contract is purchased a properly qualified appraiser should enter the picture.

Remember that your insurance policy will cover you to the extent of the actual cash value of your property at the time of loss, but not exceeding the amount which it would cost to repair or replace the property with materials of the like kind and quality, and not exceeding the amount of the insurance you have effected. You must realize that premium cost for the protection is based not only on the value you put on your property, but also upon its type and character. Indemnity payable at time of loss is based upon a specified type of value at that time.

Judges and lawyers have expounded on the meaning of actual cash value, but are still confronted with new and exceptional interpretations of it. It is not book value, historical cost, purchase cost, trended costs, nor the result of cube or square foot computation, although this information when properly applied can assist in its determination. Remember that the intention of the contract is to place you in the same position after the loss as you were before.

In many instances when an insured business suffers a severe loss from fire and additional perils that may be covered, the insurance settlement falls short of the loss. Primarily the reason for claim settlements coming into this picture are (a) insufficient coverage against the background of the present day values and (b) the insured's misunderstanding of the basic fundamentals of a standard fire contract.

There are several advantages in securing an appraisal beyond the point of satisfying an insurer's enquiry as to whether insurance to value has been written. Primarily, appraisals for fire insurance are invaluable for the following reasons; (a) to insure proper coverage without over or under insurance; (b) to provide immediate proof of loss in the event of fire, as required by the conditions of the fire policy, and (c) to facilitate settlement of claims through availability of a written record covering inventory of destroyed property with itemized values. Appraisals will also help you in the following:

(a) Sale or purchase — to assure the seller that he is receiving a reasonable price under current market conditions, and to provide the purchaser with an analysis of the value of the property, both from the standpoint of current market and long term investment value.

(b) Financing — to provide the lending institution with an unbiased statement of value which could be accepted to expedite a loan.

(c) Expropriation — to ensure adequate compensation for actual value of property taken in whole or in part for public improvement, or expropriation.

(d) Reorganization or merger — to establish, through the opinion of a disinterested appraiser, a fair value of the assets, thus assuring equitable distribution of the assets to the interested parties.

(e) Litigation — to provide an expert opinion as to the value of the propety to assist the Court in ascertaining value, and the assurance of the availability of expert testimony if required in the process of litigation.

(f) Liquidation — to provide accurate estimate of the sum that may be realized from liquidation of assets.

(g) Accounting — to provide an estimate of the cost of replacing assets under current conditions, and to establish present worth of assets.

The appraisal will be paid for by you, and if you don't have it done, you are being ''penny wise and pound foolish''. Without it, in the event of partial or total destruction of your property, you will undoubtedly find that to furnish a proof of loss, stating the exact value of the property to the satisfaction of the adjusters, may present a serious problem.

You should review your insurance coverage priodically. *All of it.* It is something we are sometimes guilty of ignoring until it is too late. Place a bookmark in this page to remind you to call your insurance agent. Or, better still, never mind the bookmark. Call him now!

68

PROPERTY PROTECTION

The first thing you must do to start protective measures for your home is make a note of your police department telephone number. Keep it near the telephone, clearly visible. In an emergency dial ''0'' ask for police and immediately give them your name and address.

Protection of the home begins with you. In the home. It cannot be effectively carried out without your assistance and co-operation.

No home, whether apartment or house, can be burglar-proof. However, the security of every home can be improved to the point that a burglar will not risk the chance of detection which is ever-present in a well protected home.

1. Have your doors mounted so that the hinge bolts are not exposed on the outside.

2. Have your locks properly mounted, of good quality, and able to be dead-locked.

3. Have your doors equipped with a chain-type doorstop, to prevent the door being pushed open suddenly when unlocked.

4. You should know where all the keys for your locks are distributed, and don't distribute them indiscriminately.

5. Don't leave a key under the welcome mat at your front door; a stranger might take it literally. Don't ''hide'' it outside the door. It won't be hidden from a burglar.

6. It is not a good idea to have car and house keys in the same key case, if your name and address is in the case. In case of loss, and discovery, someone knows where they can gain easy access to a home.

7. If you have lost or mislaid keys, you should have your locks changed.

8. Have your window locks and catches in good working order, and be sure to use them.

9. Windows that provide easy access to your home should be protected with extra locks.

10. When inspecting your home for weak points, keep in mind that burglars will use ladders, garbage pails, trellises and low roofs to reach windows and doors that are not normally accessible.

11. Consider also these other openings into your home:

(a) The milk chute which may allow someone to enter by crawling through, or which may provide access to the door-lock.

(b) The coal or wood chute, again a way of entering.

(c) Openings which contain air-conditioning units or exhaust fans which can be pushed in to gain entry.

12. Your garage should be kept locked to prevent burglars using your tools and equipment to break into your home, and to prevent theft.

13. When going out for the evening, leave lights on in one or two areas in your home, *and a radio playing.*

14. When going away for extended periods of time, you should:

(a) Arrange with your neighbours to watch your home, and notify the police department if they see anything suspicious.

(b) Arrange to have all deliveries stopped, including bread, milk, newspapers, and in addition, *have a neighbour pick up handbills and circulars.*

(c) Have some type of equipment, such as an automatic timing device, to turn light on and off at designated times.

(d) Arrange to have the grass cut regularly.

(e) Leave instructions with a neighbour or your building superintendent where you can be reached in an emergency.

In other words, when you are going away, leave your home so it has that ''lived-in appearance'', which helps to frighten off the burglar.

15. If you are an apartment dweller, you should:

(a) Refer unknown persons seeking entrance to your building to the superintendent and never let them in with *your* key.

(b) Let your superintendent know at all times when your apartment is usually vacant.

(c) Report the presence of suspicious persons to the superintendent or to the police department.

16. If you live in a house:

(a) Have a close neighbour who knows when your home is usually vacant who could report to the police any suspicious person around it.

(b) You should report the presence of suspicious persons or automobiles in the neighbourhood to the police department.

17. If your doors are solidly constructed, have a ''peep-hole'' device which will enable you to identify a caller without opening the door.

18. Your valuables and extra cash should be kept in a safety deposit box at your bank or trust company.

19. You should keep a record of serial numbers and other identifying marks on your valuables in the event they are stolen.

20. Do not trust your memory with such things as license numbers. Write them down.

21. Always verify the identity of hydro, gas and other service men who seek entry to your home.

Now that you have read this chapter, there are two things you can do right now.

(a) Place the telephone number of your police department on your telephone, clearly visible.

(b) Read this chapter again, and check the points one by one to see how much safer you can make *your* home for you and for your family.

Most Important: If you employ a babysitter, have your *address* clearly posted near the telephone. In case of emergency, a babysitter could panic and not remember the address. When I say address, I mean the address where your children and the babysitter are located.

69

FIRE PROTECTION

Read this chapter carefully, and when you have read it, read it again. It could save your life, and the lives of your loved ones.

In Case of Fire

Shout ''Fire'': to arouse persons nearby if you see fire, or smell smoke or gas. If you believe the fire to be in a room, a cupboard or in a basement section, keep the doors closed. Quickly shut any doors and windows that will help confine the fire, cut down the draft and prevent spread of deadly gases. This will give everyone more time to escape.

Out You Go: Save lives by getting everyone out of the building involved as quickly as possible. Don't wait to dress yourself or children — wrap them in blankets.

If you have to go upstairs or away from exits to rescue children and you are unable to return to the ground floor, or if you are otherwise trapped, get to a room with a window, quickly shut the door between you and the fire, and shout for help. Don't jump from upper storey windows except as a last resort — wait for help.

Remember, the air is usually better near the floor in a smoke-filled building.

Summon the Department: by telephone *only* after all are out.

Never go back into a burning building. It can be totally involved in flame in seconds.

Try to hold the fire in check with equipment at hand while the fire department is responding. Fight the fire only if you are not endangered.

Don't waste time or your life.

Plan in Advance: Have your plan of escape from fire worked out in advance. Everyone should know the plan, and the reasons for each part of it.

Alternate escape routes are a *must* because one or more of the ways out may be blocked off by fire.

229

Escaping from one-storey buildings is relatively simple — there are alternate routes through any of the windows to the outside. But remember, storm and screen windows may be difficult to get through. Make sure there is something such as a chair available to smash them out.

Two-storey buildings require more planning because the stairway may be blocked off by fire, smoke or hot gases. Be prepared to use upper windows, perhaps to the roof of an adjacent building, by having ladders strategically located, or by means of a rope with knots at every two feet anchored to the inside of windows.

Remember, in the event of a fire during sleeping hours, a closed bedroom door may save your life.

If conditions permit, gather everyone together into one room before attempting to escape. Children are easily lost in the confusion.

When escaping *never* open the window before the door is closed behind you. This cuts down the draft which would help to spread the fire into your area of escape.

Fire drills should be carried out often enough so that everyone's role becomes automatic.

Methods of evacuating children and sick or aged persons should be studied particularly.

Everyone, including children, should know how to telephone the fire department and the number to call.

If in doubt, have your local fire chief check over your escape plan with you.

How to Fight Home Fires: When you blow out a match you extinguish a fire. It is easy to do at this stage. However, small fires can grow and join to destroy an entire city. The first five minutes are vital. Keep calm, don't panic! Remember, each fire is different.

Clothing Fires: Don't run, it fans the flame. Act quickly to smother the fire. Make victims lie down, then roll them up in a rug, coat, or blanket with the head outside. Gently beat the fire out. Give burn or shock first aid.

Cooking Fires: (involving fat, grease or oils): Turn off the stove or appliance and cover the pan, or close the oven, or pour baking soda on the fire, or use an approved type of fire extinguisher. Never use water! It will spread the flame.

Electrical Fires: (motors, wiring, etc): Unplug the appliance if possible. Use an approved type of fire extinguisher, or throw on baking soda. Never use water on live wiring, or you may get an electrical shock.

Fires in Ordinary Combustibles: Keep near the door so that you can escape if necessary. Stay low out of heat and smoke. Aim a stream at the base of the fire. For floor fires sweep from the edge in, for wall fires sweep from the bottom up. Stay outside closets, attics, etc., and shoot the stream in. Ventilate the area only after the fire is out. Remember, if the fire is large, get out and close the doors behind you.

Home-type fire-fighting tools are very effective against small fires. Brooms, or mops soaked in water, blankets, rugs, buckets and garden hoses are good examples. A threaded hose connection on each floor of the house (in bathroom, kitchen and basement) and a good length of garden hose properly coiled is a good fire protection.

There are numerous fire extinguishers on the market suitable for home use. Make sure that you use a type listed and labelled by a nationally recognized fire testing laboratory, such as the Underwriters' laboratory. Otherwise you cannot be sure it is reliable.

Home fire-fighting equipment will not be of any help unless you know how to use it. You will not have time to learn how after a fire breaks out. Read the instructions on the fire extinguisher *now* and be sure that everyone in the house knows how to use it and the other equipment as well.

The equipment is of no use unless it is in good working order. Check with the dealer or your local Fire Chief regarding maintenance of your type of extinguisher.

Do not risk your life unless it is to save another life. The house can always be rebuilt, and unless it is a small fire you probably cannot extinguish it by yourself anyway.

Instruct Your Babysitter: During your absence the babysitter is responsible for the safety of your children and your property. Impress upon her that in the event of fire, the first and most important thing to do is to get the children out quickly and stay with them. Tell her to wrap them in blankets, not take time to dress them. The following rules will assist you in advising her:

Show her through your house so that she will be familiar with each part of it, and leave *your* municipal address by the telephone.

Be sure she knows the quickest way out for the children if she has to get them out because of fire.

Show her the alternate escape routes in case the regular route, such as the stairway, is blocked off by fire.

Show her how to control the heating equipment in case this should be necessary.

Give her the telephone number of a nearby friend who can come to her assistance quickly, as well as one where you may be reached if possible.

She must call the Fire Department as soon as possible from a neighbour's house.

A Safety Fire Test

Can you answer ''yes'' to all these questions? Questions which receive a ''no'' answer indicate potential danger spots which need prompt attention and correction. Inspect your home yourself — today!

In Case of Fire: Is the number of the nearest fire department posted near the telephone?

Have you instructed your family in a plan of action if fire breaks out?

Have your family been instructed and drilled on the location of exits from the house and how to close all windows and doors in case of fire?

Do you keep exit routes clear — expecially of such things as room heaters and stoves which might start a fire and block your escape?

Are bedroom windows large enough and sufficiently unobstructed to serve as emergency exits?

Care of Children: Do you make it the rule never to leave small children alone or unattended?

Do you show your babysitter the escape routes from your home, and give instructions on the right way to call the fire department?

Do your babysitters (and you) know the first rule of safety in fire emergencies: get everybody out fast, and don't go back in?

Are your children trained to keep a safe distance from flame and spark sources?

Electrical: Has wiring been checked by a qualified person since installation?

When new appliances were added to the load, was wiring inspected and any necessary new wiring installed by a qualified electrician?

Do you check your fuse box regularly to see that only specified sizes are being used?

Are all electric motors kept oiled, clean and free from dirt accumulation?

Lightning Protection: Has your radio or television antenna been equipped with a properly grounded lightning arrestor?

Heating Equipment: Have your stoves, furnace, chimney and smoke pipes been checked and cleaned where necessary within the past year?

Are furnaces and stoves at least 18 inches from any exposed woodwork?

Do any stove pipes run through attics or concealed spaces?

Are smoke pipes, when running through combustible partitions, protected by a double ventilating metal thimble?

Do you prohibit the use of gasoline or kerosene for starting or quickening fires in your home?

Does your fireplace have a metal screen in front of it to prevent sparks from flying onto the carpet or furniture?

Are all portable heaters of a type listed by the Canadian Standards Association?

Is your portable oil heater always placed on a level floor to ensure proper operation?

Do you always refill the fuel tanks of portable heaters out of doors and in the daylight?

If you use a wick-type portable oil heater, do you trim the wick and clean it regularly?

Do you always turn your portable oil heater out upon retiring at night or when moving it from one part of the house to another?

Flammable Liquids: Are small quantities of gasoline stored in safety cans?

Have you made it a rule never to use flammable liquids like gasoline or kerosene for cleaning clothes or starting fires?

Are oil saturated or paint rags properly disposed of or stored in metal containers?

Smoking Habits: Are approved design ash trays provided?

Is smoking in bed strictly against the rule in your home?

Do you make a bedtime check for smouldering butts lodged in chesterfields and also upholstered furniture?

Are you careful how you dispose of cigarettes, cigars and pipe ashes?

Are matches and lighters kept out of the reach of children?

General: If you use L.P. gas, are the cylinders outside the building on a solid foundation and located away from windows and basement doors?

Do you keep rubbish cleaned out of the attic, basement, closets, garage and yard?

Do you use extreme care when using lighter fuel to ignite your barbecue?

Do you spray your hair only away from open flames or lighted cigarettes?

Fire Protection: Have your fire extinguishers been checked and recharged if necessary within the past year?

Do you have approved fire extinguishers?

Do you have enough garden hose supplying water?

Like many of the tragedies in life, fire, or at least its worst effects, can be avoided if we only think about it beforehand, and act wisely. Remember — if you learn the rules, and never need them, you lose nothing: If you never learn them and need them, when fire occurs, you may lose everything — including your life.

Hundreds lose their lives each year in Canada as the result of fire — most of them children.

SMOKE DETECTORS: Visit your local fire station and ask for recommendations; not only for the detector, but the number required for your home.

Do it soon . . . . .

70

METRIC REAL ESTATE

As the majority of Canadian residents know, conversion of weights and measures to the metric system of measurement in Canada is, of course, approved federal government policy, endorsed by all provinces and currently is being implemented nationally.

Canada's "target" for operating substantially in metric is 1980. Most programs are either on schedule or, ahead of projections.

Consumers already have been at least partially conditioned to recognizing and working with the metric system. Products such as film, cameras and related photographic equipment; skiis, other sporting goods, drugs and medicines have been available solely in metric sizes for decades. Since 1975, temperature and weather forecasts have been reported in metric values.

Metric dimensions are now appearing on articles of clothing and hardware items. Approximately fifty per cent of food products are now packaged and marketed in metric containers.

For the past year, Canadians have been driving their automobiles at speeds and distances measured in kilometres.

In the real estate industry, conversion to the metric system of measure will eventually require all construction and all real estate transactions to be expressed in metric units and terms. This will include, but will not be limited to the appraisal, leasing, purchasing and selling of real property.

The date proposed by federal authorities for construction and real estate transactions to be conducted primarily in Metric was January 1, 1978.

On January 1, 1978, Public Works Canada along with many provincial government agencies began tendering all construction, lease, sale, and purchase of real property with dimensions expressed solely in metric. Central Mortgage and Housing Corporation (CMHC) as of May 1979, will accept mortgage applications and related documentts for processing only if all dimensions are identified in metric units.

Prior to the voluntary deadline of January 1, 1978, several real estate boards operating a Multiple Listing Service (MLS)* on behalf of the their members had converted to operating in metric units and terms. Currently, approximately 85 per cent of all listings processed by members of the Canadian Real Estate Association have structure dimensions and lot sizes indicated solely in metric or, expressed in metric units along with Canadian/Imperial equivalents.

The real estate industry has perhaps a special or almost unique problem when adapting to the metric system of measure. For many industries conversion is a one time proposition. Individuals active in the real estate industry, however, will be working with land titles, surveys, and other historical documents which originated and date back over periods from one to hundreds of years. Unless and until these documents are amended to show dimensions in metric equivalents, the industry must, of course, convert the existing dimensional references to metric.

Accordingly, since real estate brokers and salespersons are working directly with the public, it is a never ending process of educating — or at least assisting — vendors and purchasers in becoming knowledgeable and comprehending dimensions with regards to their real estate transactions.

It has been suggested that perhaps the largest challenge to metric conversion in the real estate industry and indeed all industries, is not the metric education or commitment by industry and business. Instead, the challenge and opportunity is the education and acceptance of the metric system by the public at large.

Real estate personnel must and will, be in the "metric public familiarization business" long after they themselves have accepted and become familiar with metric units and terms.

Canada's commitment to changing to the metric system of measurement is no longer a debatable issue. It is a rational and required, modern contemporary fact of life. For the real estate industry, it will be an ongoing challenge and opportunity to assist the public to learn and work with metric units.

The real estate industry has historically adapted to change. Real estate practitioners will continue this tradition by adapting to the metric system as it has adapted to various other changes affecting the industry in the past.

There are literally thousands of volumes of metric related publications, conversion tables and charts available for individuals wishing to obtain reference and resource information. Following is a portion of the material

*Multiple Listing Service and MLS are two of several Certification and Design Marks registered federally, owned by the Canadian Real Estate Association, and reserved for the exclusive use of members in good standing.

appearing in the ''Metric Guide for Real Estate'' brochure, published by the Canadian Real Estate Association, endorsed and approved by Metric Commission Canada. This material, reproduced with the express permission of the Canadian Real Estate Association, is intended to serve as a guideline only.

Specific application of metric measurements and metric terms to real estate advertising and all real estate related documents, will be as required by local custom and existing regulations.

Measurement Units

LENGTH

Metre (m) — is the basic unit of length in the metric system and is used for most real estate measurements. The metre replaces the foot and yard.

The metre can be described as equal to a long pace. An average door is approximately two metres (2 m) high.

Kilometre (km) — equals one thousand metres (1000 m) and is used for most distance measurements, replacing the mile. Sixteen kilometres (16 km) is approximately ten miles.

AREA

Square metre (m²) — is the basic metric unit for area measurement and is used to measure the area of individual rooms, entire buildings and building lots. The square metre replaces the square foot and square yard.

Note: Never express an area as being so many metres square. There is a difference of 90 square metres between 10 square metres and 10 metres square.

Hectare (ha) — is used to express the area of larger parcels of land for example; subdivisions, farm and recreational properties.

A hectare is equal to a square measuring 100 metres by 100 metres or stated another way, 10,000 m². The hectare replaces the acre.

Square kilometre (km²) — is used to measure only very large areas of land, such as a district or entire county. The square kilometre replaces the square mile and is equal to 100 ha.

VOLUME

Litre (L) — replaces gallons. The litre is used to express volume of hot water supply and fuel tanks.

Cubic metre (m³) — replaces cubic feet, cubic yards, and is used to measure storage and warehouse volumes.

Application and Accuracy of Metric Units

In other metric countries, metric measurements related to real estate advertising have been rounded off and applied on the following basis. This custom is being followed in Canada.

Residential:
Lot size and room dimensions — expressed in metres to the nearest 0.1 m.
Areas — given in square metres to the nearest 5 m².

Commercial:
Dimensions — metres to the nearest 0.1 m.
Areas — square metres to the nearest 1 m².

Industrial:
Dimensions — metres to the nearest 0.5 m.
Areas — square metres to the nearest 10 m².
Volume — cubic metres to the nearest 100 m³.

Land:
Dimensions — metres to the nearest 1 m.
Areas — square metres to the nearest 5 m².

Larger properties:
Areas between:
  1 hectare and 10 hectares — to the nearest 0.1 ha.
  10 hectares and 100 hectares — to the nearest 0.5 ha.
  100 hectares and 1,000 hectares — to the nearest 1 ha.
  1,000 hectares and 10,000 hectares — to the nearest 10 ha.
Areas over 10,000 ha (100 km²) — to the nearest 1 km².

Rounding of Numbers

In the metric system, the rounding of measurements follows the same principle as previously used in the Canadian system.

For example:
8.2503 m becomes 8.3 m to one decimal place
8.3492 m becomes 8.35 m to two decimal places
8.3257 m becomes 8.326 m to three decimal places.

Note: The rounding of a number should be made in one step. For example, 9.1948 m correctly rounded in one step becomes 9.19 m. If the same number (9.1948) is rounded in two steps, an error occurs. 9.195 m (first step) and 9.20 m (second step).

As area or volume measurements are calculated by multiplying, rounding is always applied *after* the calculation is completed.

Writing Metric

There is a unique and easily recognized symbol for each metric unit.
These symbols remain constant in all languages and for each application. A

few of the basic rules for the use of symbols are:

- Use symbols instead of writing out full unit names.
  (3 m *NOT* 3 metres — 9 ha *NOT* 9 hectares)
- Never pluralize symbols (1 m, 5 m *NOT* 5 ms).
- Always insert a full space between the quantity and the symbol.
  (3 m *NOT* 3m — 9 ha *NOT* 9ha).
- Always use decimals when writing metric — *NOT* fractions
  (9.5 m *NOT* 9½ m — 0.5 km² *NOT* ½ km²)
- Separate long lines of digits into more easily read blocks of three digits, with regard to the decimal point.
  (96 343.581 583 *NOT* 96343.581583).   A space is optional with a four digit number. (4567.1234 or 4 567.123 4)
- Do not use a period after symbol, unless the symbol occurs at the end of a sentence.

Simplified Conversion Tables

Until such time as all real estate surveys, deeds and legal records have been converted into metric units, conversion of Canadian system units to (and from) metric system units will be unavoidable.

The following table provides conversion factors for most Canadian units used previously to express measurements relating to real estate.

Note: When converting existing Canadian units to metric units, do not use numbers which imply a greater accuracy than was acceptable in the past.

Dimensions should be expressed in metric units to the minimum number of significant figures — consistent with the need to express them with sufficient accuracy to serve their purpose.

Length

> 1 m = 39.370 inches
> 1 m =   3.280 84 feet
> 1 m =   1.093 61 yard
> 1 inch = 0.0254 m
> 1 foot = 0.3048 m
> 1 yard = 0.9144 m
> 1 km = 0.621 371 mile
> 1 mile = 1.609 344 km

Conversion factors for other Canadian units of length.

> 1 pole or rod = =   5.0292 m
> 1 chain   = 20.1168 m
> 1 arpent   = 58.4713 m
> 1 furlong   =   0.2012 km

Area

1 m^2 = 10.7639 square feet
1 m^2 = 1.1960 square yards
1 ha = 2.471 05 acres
1 km^2 = 0.386 102 square mile
1 square foot = 0.092 903 m^2
1 square yard = 0.836 127 m^2
1 acre = 0.404 686 ha
1 square mile = 2.589 988 km^2
= 258.998 ha

Conversion factors for other Canadian units of area.

1 rood = 1 011.714 m^2
1 arpent = 0.3419 ha
1 quarter section = 64.752 ha
1 half section = 129.504 ha
1 section = 258.998 ha

Volume

1 m^3 = 35.3147 cubic feet
= 1.307 95 cubic yards
1 cubic foot = 0.028 317 m^3
1 cubic yard = 0.764 555 m^3
1 litre = 0.219 97 gallon
1 gallon = 4.546 09 litres

Price Conversion/Comparisons

$100 per m^2 = $9.29 per square foot
$10 per square foot = $107.64 per m^2
$1,000 per ha = $404.69 per acre
$100 per acre = $247.10 per ha
$1,000 per km^2 = $2,590. per square mile
$1,000 per square mile = $386.10 per km^2

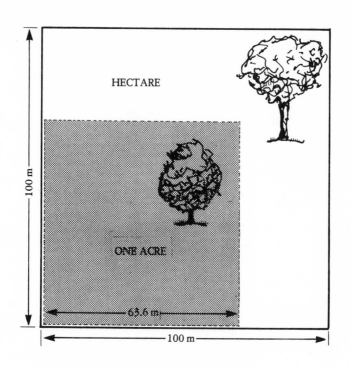

HECTARE

ONE ACRE

63.6 m

100 m

100 m

71

CAPITAL GAINS TAX APPRAISALS

Most Canadians are not affected by capital gains tax on their real estate. A gain on the sale of your residence will not be taxed as long as you use it only as your principal residence.

Generally speaking, real estate, other than one's principal residence, when sold will be subject to a capital gain or a capital loss.

The gain would normally be when the property is sold for more than it cost. The net gain, after all deductions, will be subject to our capital gains tax.

When a net capital gain is established, half the gain will be free of tax, and the other 50% will be added to your income tax return filed for the year of disposition. The capital gains tax payable will therefore be determined by your tax bracket for the year.

For example, if a net gain is $5,000. and your tax bracket is 40% after adding your gain, here is what will be *tax free* of the $5,000.

50% of $5,000.	$2,500.
60% of $2,500.	1,500.
Tax Free:	$4,000.

As a rule, half of certain capital losses, *allowable capital losses*, are deducted from half of all capital gains, *taxable capital gains*, for the year, with the remainder added to your income when you file your income tax return. If the total of your allowable capital losses for a year exceeds the total of all your taxable capital gains for the year, you may deduct up to $2,000. of the excess from your other income for that year. Any remaining loss over and above that amount may be deducted from income of the immediately preceding year and the following years. If you are in a loss situation, contact your local income tax office for the detailed application of this to your total capital loss.

A capital gain or capital loss occurs when you dispose of your real estate (other than your principal residence). A capital disposition, however, is not limited to a sale. Other transactions or events may also give rise to a capital disposition, such as:

A. The exchange of real estate

B. Giving some real estate to another

C. Expropriation of your real estate

While as a rule a capital gain or loss occurs whenever there is a change in the ownership of a property, there are other situations in which a capital gain or loss occurs even though there is no actual change in ownership. These *deemed dispositions* may occur when:

1. The owner of property becomes a non-resident of Canada

2. The owner of property changes its use (for example, he starts to rent a house in which he lived)

3. A person dies (he is ''deemed'' to have disposed of all his capital property immediately before his death).

Valuation Day

The inclusion of half of capital gains in income began on January 1, 1972, necessitating a method for ensuring that no tax would be assessed, or losses allowed, for any capital gain or loss which arose before that date. This was accomplished by establishing a starting point, *Valuation Day*, for calculating capital gains and losses.

When a taxpayer disposes of real estate held on December 31, 1971, its value on Valuation Day is used to determine the capital gain or loss since that date.

Valuation day is important only for property acquired before January 1, 1972. There are no Valuation Day implications for property acquired on or after that date.

Valuation Day will affect those who on December 31, 1971, owned real estate (other than a principal residence) such as cottages, land and rental property.

To determine any capital gain or loss when you dispose of these properties, you must know its fair market value at Valuation Day. You do not have to establish or report the Valuation Day value of your property to Revenue Canada, Taxation, until you dispose of it, nor will any value be considered or accepted beforehand.

Although you may not be planning to dispose of your property for several years, it is to your advantage to determine the Valuation Day fair market value of the property now; if you wait, the value becomes increasingly difficult to establish.

You should keep in mind that all property will eventually be disposed of for income tax purposes. Even if it is never sold or otherwise disposed of, disposal will be deemed to have occurred on the death of the owner.

It is your responsibility to establish the Valuation Day fair market value of your property. Determining the value may be a simple matter, which you may wish to do yourself, or the size and type of the property may make it sufficiently difficult that you require a professional appraiser.

Note, however, that the cost of appraisal fees is not deductible from your income and cannot be deducted from any capital gain on eventual disposition of the property.

There are two methods for determining the fair market value of real estate on Valuation Day:

(1) Obtain from a professional appraiser a fully documented appraisal with supporting data which adequately explains the investigation carried out. It should include a detailed explanation of the basis used to arrive at the estimated value. Remember that these figures may not be required for several years, when the appraiser may no longer be around to explain his method.

(2) Establish the value yourself. Collect information on sales of similar properties in the same area around December 31, 1971. This will help you to arrive at the fair market value of your own property. To support your valuation, you should retain documents containing the following information:

a. A brief description of the property, including location, lot, building size, and date and type of construction.

b. The cost and date of purchase.

c. The cost of any additions or improvements.

d. The property assessment for municipal tax purposes.

e. Insurance coverage.

Keep receipts for the cost of labour or materials for any improvements, and tax assessment notices. These documents will help to support your estimate of the value. Additional information may be required for certain types of property. For example:

Farm Property	a. The type of land (arable, bush, scrub)
	b. The type of farming done.
Rental Property	a. The gross annual rental income
	b. The net annual income before depreciation (capital cost allowance).
Commercial/Industrial	a. The type of business for which the property is used.
	b. The gross annual income derived from it.

> c. The net annual income before
> depreciation (capital cost allowance).

Remember, any capital gain on the sale of your home is not normally subject to tax. Thus your home need not be valued, provided you use it only as your principal residence. Any type of structure you own and ordinarily inhabit may qualify as a principal residence. Shares of capital stock of a cooperative housing corporation may also qualify.

If you use your home partly for producing income, capital gains may be taxable when there is a change in use of part of the property or when the property is sold. This rule applies where part of the home is used as the residence of the owner and the remainder is rented or used for carrying on a business. In this case, a valuation of the home would be required and the valuation must be apportioned between the part used to produce income and the part occupied as a principal residence.

If your principal residence is part of a farm, you should establish the value of the principal residence separately in addition to the value of the farm as a whole. An option is available in computing any capital gain on the sale of a farm, which requires a Valuation Day value for the home as distinct from the value of the remainder of the farm property. Contact your local tax office for details of farm disposition options.

The income tax department has set up a Real Estate Data Bank containing information to assist in verifying Valuation Day values reported in income tax returns. This bank contains records of real estate transactions which took place in 1971 and 1972, and information in it has been computerized and kept in district tax offices. Taxpayers who are disposing of property may obtain information from the Data Bank.

The disposition of real estate other than your principal residence will usually result in a capital gain and require a Valuation Day value. Cottages, summer homes, second residences, residential rental property, farms, commercial and industrial land and buildings are included in this type of real estate.

If you own property purchased before Valuation Day, you would be well advised to get its Valuation Day value established now.

72

QUICK APPRAISALS

An appraisal is an opinion of value, and it logically follows that the better qualified the appraiser, the higher the rating of the appraisal. A good arbiter of an appraisal is the buyer, the one who agrees with an appraisal to the point of paying the price.

The most recognized appraiser in Canada is the one with the designaion "A.A.C.I." (Accredited Appraiser, Canadian Institute). If one were to seek a real estate degree of qualification that carries with it an assured professional income, this is the one to shoot for. It is a degree recognized by our courts, requiring years of application to obtain.

There are professional appraisers from coast to coast, and if you require a highly regarded opinion of value, call one. But there are times when all you want is a rough idea of value of your property, which is where this chapter can help.

In appraising *any* property, the first thing one must establish is its legal use. Check the zoning. There would be no point, for example, in trying to establish the value of a house as a rooming house operation if the zoning stated that the area is strictly designated for single family dwellings.

The three generally accepted areas of appraisal are:
1. Comparable sales
2. Replacement value
3. Capitalization of a cash flow.

Housing

Comparable sale values are most commonly used in housing, and are reasonably reliable. If three houses of a similar plan and condition to yours sold recently for about $75,000. there is little point in expecting that you could get a few thousand more for yours, although some try. Usually an overpriced house is easy to spot — the "for sale" sign has been there for more than three weeks or so. In an active market there is a buyer for every

246

house, if it is priced right, and a house that is priced right certainly won't take any more than 3 weeks to move.

An excellent opinion of the market value of your home can be obtained from a real estate agent who has been active in your neighbourhood for two or three years. The agent is on top of local values and has a full knowledge of what every house for blocks around sold for.

Many brokers will provide a verbal opinion of value without charge, obviously because they think that sooner or later they will get your listing. The easiest way to get it is to simply call an active local broker and say you would like to talk about the possibility of selling. He, or one of his salesmen will be there lickety split, believe me.

This is your free ''appraisal'', but if you want the price with a view to selling, it is better to obtain a figure from about three different agencies and average the results.

The homeowner who has done quite a bit of renovating, such as finishing a recreation room, installing a bar, laid top grade broadloom, decorated with expensive wallcoverings etc. may be of the opinion that all these costs can be recovered in selling. Forget it; they can't. Even if one is fortunate enough to find a buyer who thinks all these extras suit him just fine, the buyer won't feel like paying any more than about half the costs of the work. So keep this in mind when pricing your home.

If the house is in an overall average price range for your area, a quick stab at pricing can be to work on average price increases over a number of years. Average increases, even to local areas in a municipality, can often be obtained from a member of a real estate board.

If the home is something out of the ordinary, not a standard plan, it will take something more than sales comparisons to establish value, because there won't be any comparisons to use. This is where replacement value can come into play, and requires a heavier inspection and examination than one of a standard plan. Which will cost money, because it will call for the work of a fee appraiser, who certainly won't work for nothing.

Commercial Buildings

Capitalizing the cash flow is a common method of appraisal here. Study the chapter ''Capitalization'' and then go to work on it.

Annual Gross Income:	$100,000.
Annual Operating Expenses:	50,000.
Income before debt charge:	$ 50,000.

The operating expenses will include everything, including municipal taxes. The $50,000. is the cash return for the year. If the property is clear of mortgage debt, this figure could be capitalized at the local going rate. If it is 8%, then one could say the property is worth $625,000. But the buyer probably won't agree with this because he won't be buying for cash. He will finance the purchase with a mortgage or two, and the mortgage payment will have a large bearing on what he will pay.

If current mortgage rates are 12% on such a building, and the buyer reasoned he could get a $400,000. mortgage through his connections, here is what the financing will show. The mortgage is amortized over 25 years.

Annual Gross Income:	$100,000.
Annual Operating Expenses:	50,000.
Income before debt charge:	50,000.
Annual mortgage payment:	49,531.
Cash flow:	$ 469.

See the problem? Nothing left but petty cash. The mortgage lender would take a look at this and probably say no way man. Too close to the vest. If a vacancy occurred in the building, there would be a debit cash flow. Zilch.

So the buyer takes a look at a $350,000. mortgage. Same rate and amortization.

Income before debt charge:	$50,000.
Annual mortgage payment:	43,339.
Cash flow:	$ 6,661.

Now the buyer will capitalize the cash flow at 8%, which will produce a figure of $83,262.

This $83,262. will be added to the principal amount of the mortgage ($350,000.) and the result is what a buyer will say the property is worth: $433,262. or round it out at about $435,000.

So you can see that the costs of financing will be the criterion in establishing market value of the property.

If the property has a mortgage on it at a lower rate, say 9%, then the price will go up, with reservation. I say this because if the 9% mortgage has just two or three years to run, then the buyer will be faced with renewal or refinancing, and of course he couldn't be sure that he would do it at 9%. A long term, of course, is a different matter.

Other factors in this appraisal could be the possibility of increasing the income if the majority of leases were to expire soon. The value of the land itself, without the building, may also be an overriding factor.

Industrial Buildings

A good appraisal here can be done by determining the *rental value* of the property on a *net* basis. Study the chapter "buying an industrial building."

After a little probing, if it can be reasonably assumed that the building could be leased at $1.25 per square foot per year, and the building has a net rentable area of 10,000 square feet, the net annual rental income would be $12,500.

Now, I ask you to first review another chapter, "Capitalization."

The strength of the tenancy can have a bearing on the price; it is reasonable to assume that the stronger the covenant, the less the rent. For an example, let us assume that with a good tenant, one who we know will pay the rent promptly and behave in a responsible manner in caring for the property, a satisfactory rate of return would be 9%.

Capitalize the projected net return of $12,500. at 9%:

$$\frac{12,500}{9} \times \frac{100}{1} = \$138,888.$$

So a reasonable assessed market value of the property will be $138,888.

However, remember that not many buyers will purchase a vacant industrial building unless they are getting what they consider to be a very good deal. The arithmetic of the buyer of the vacant building will be worked in a similar manner to the foregoing, but he may be a little tougher because the building is vacant.

With a building tenanted to a good covenant, the value is comparatively easy to establish.

Vacant Land

Again, we look at the zoning. What can the land be used for? Its maximum use. By that I mean that if the zoning will allow a 20,000 s.f. building to be erected, complete with parking facilities etc. then it will be appraised on that basis, and not on anything less.

However, remember that to realize the appraised price, a buyer will have to be found who would be willing to buy it on that basis. The eventual selling price of anything is the proof of the appraisal. If a buyer cannot be found for maximum use, we have to hang in there until we find one, or lower our sights and look for offers.

Take a piece of land that the zoning says its o.k. to construct a nice little three storey building with 10,000 rentable s.f. on each floor. Complete with parking.

Step one: Estimate a reasonable rental figure. A gross figure — one where the owner pays the building expenses. Do a little probing of other buildings in the area. If it is determined that the gross rental would be $10. per s.f., then the gross income would be $300,000. (plus a bonus in the rental income of the parking spaces).

Step two: Take about 50% of the gross income and allow the figure ($150,000.) for operating expenses, including taxes.

Step three: Determine the construction costs for such a building. This figure can be obtained possibly from your local real estate board, or from a firm of quantity surveyors. Assume the costs of average $30 s.f.

Step four: The building should show a net return of about 10% as an investment, so we will capitalize the net return of $150,000. at 10% and this will be the allowable cost for the project, including land. ($1,500,000.) Remember, this is a quick appraisal, so we won't go into the mechanics of mortgaging. You can doodle with that later.

Step five: Deduct the construction costs from the allowable cost:

Allowable:	$1,500,000.
30,000 sf @ $30.	900,000.
	$ 600,000.

The $600,000. is the quick appraisal of the land value. When you have all this worked out, call a commercial and industrial real estate broker and ask him what adjustments should be made in your figures. The foregoing is only an example of the mechanics of the appraisal — the location of the land will have a lot to say about it, which is where the advice of the local broker can be invaluable.

With vacant land zoned industrial, use the same principal, but assess the rental on a net basis, as mentioned before.

With other vacant land, building lots, farms, bush, swamp, etc. call a *local* broker and seek his advice. Always call the local brokers. They know what they're talking about (most of the time).

73

TITLE INSURANCE

Title insurance is corporate indemnification against title losses, whether arising out of matters of public record or matters not of record, such as forgery, fraud, concealed marriages, etc. The insured may be anyone who has an interest in real estate including home owners, mortgage lenders, industries and leaseholders.

From a legal standpoint, it may be defined as a contract of indemnity against loss or damage arising out of defects in, or liens upon the title to real property. A definition would be "the application of the principles of insurance to risks incident to real estate titles".

Title insurance is not a gamble, or is it guesswork. Just as the life insurance company bases the issuance of its life policies upon physical examinations made by competent doctors, so does the title insurance company base the issuance of its title policies upon carefull examinations of titles made by experienced title lawyers.

Every lawyer who examines titles is aware that there may be defects in titles of which he cannot take cognizance in his opinion: defects arising from fraud, forgery, conveyances by minors or persons of unsound mind, demands of missing heirs, rights of divorced persons, deeds by defective corporations, errors in registration and copying and many other like circumstances that are liable to occasion serious financial loss to investors in real estate or real estate securities. Title insurance is protection against financial loss through such defects as these and all other matters adversely affecting the title as insured.

Under the terms of a title policy, should the title be attacked, the insurance company through its approved lawyers will defend it in court at its own expense. Should loss be suffered, the insurance company must protect the assured.

There are three basic policies available:

Owners Policy: This policy is generally used in insuring all estates of ownership, occupancy and possession and remains in force as long as the insured or his heirs have any interest in the property. In addition, when the property is sold the owners policy continues to protect the insured against any action for recovery by a subsequent purchaser.

Mortgagee Policy: This policy is used to insure estate or interests held by lenders as a pledge or security for the payment of a debt. Such estates or interests exist in many different forms, dependent largely under the laws and customs of the local area. Liability upon the mortgagee policy is reduced as payments upon the mortgage are made, and terminates upon satisfaction of the debt, whereas liability upon an owners policy is perpetual and indeterminate.

The coverage of the mortgagee policy is designed to meet the security needs of mortgage lenders. This coverage is broader than that of the standard owners policy.

The mortgagee policy provides continual protection to each successor in ownership of the mortgage. Loss payable under a mortgagee policy is automatically transferred to the assignee of the debt and security. In the event of foreclosure and purchase by the holder of the security, the policy automatically becomes an owners policy and insures the purchaser as owner of the fee, against loss or damage arising out of matters existing prior to the effective date of the policy.

Leaseholder Policy: This policy protects a leaseholder against loss or damage sustained by reason of eviction or curtailment of his leasehold interest through title difficulties. Such policies are usually written on long term industrial or commercial leases.

Premiums for most other forms of insurance are recurring and must be paid periodically. Title insurance policies continue in effect for a *single premium.*

There are many practical advantages of title insurance which arise directly as a result of title defects against which a lawyer cannot or would not certify, and for which he is not responsible in the event of a loss suffered by real estate investors.

The possibility of human error that may result in financial loss is always present. Registry office employees can err in copying and indexing deeds, mortgages and other instruments that affect the titles to real property. Nor is any lawyer infallible. In spite of the high reputation enjoyed by that profession, to err is human. Because of the growing number of exposures to risks due to pressure and complexity of present-day real estate conveyancing, title insurance can provide for safety, security and complete insurance indemnification.

After deliberate consideration, no broadminded counsel can for a moment believe that his own opinion of title, based upon a search however properly made, can give his client the security that a title insurance policy will provide.

252

No lawyer, regardless of his ability, can assure his client that all signatures affixed to the instruments making up a chain of titles are genuine, or that none of the signatures affixed to instruments constituting a chain of title was fraudulently or wrongfully obtained, but a title insurance policy insures against forgery, fraud, duress and misrepresentation.

Some people may be of the opinion that a title insurance policy would not help under the "Torrens" or "Land Titles" system of registration, but it is interesting to note that approximately 50% of title insurance policies issued in Canada cover titles registered under this system. A policy provides indemnity against the following matters, for which compensation may not be available without it under provincial land titles acts.

(a) Provincial taxes, succession duty and municipal taxes, charges, etc.

(b) Any right-of-way or other easement.

(c) Adverse possessory title by encroachment.

(d) Leases not exceeding three years.

(e) Mechanics' liens.

(f) Expropriation rights and public highways.

(g) Errors in survey or description.

(h) A prior certificate of title.

(i) Instruments executed by legally incompetent persons.

(j) Fraud, when not participated in or known to the insured.

(k) Any amount due in excess of that recoverable from the fund.

(l) All costs and legal fees involved in any action or preparation therefor regardless of the success or otherwise of the action or preparation therefor, being related to title matters within the coverage of the title insurance policy.

74

INTEREST RATES

Remember, the more frequent the compounding, the greater the yield to the *lender*. The tables on the following pages will provide helpful information in determining interest calculations for a number of mortgage loans:

(1) Interest only loans

(2) A fixed principal payment, plus interest

(3) A blended payment (interest and principal)

The last column on each page shows the effective annual yield to the lender.

However, before calculating interest, ensure that you are familiar with the Federal Interest Act, and its effect on mortgages. If you cannot obtain a copy locally, write to the Queen's Printer, Ottawa, Ontario, and get one.

Interest only loans: simply use the rate applicable to the compounding frequency and the period of payment.

Fixed principal payment, plus interest: On the first payment, use the appropriate rate for the entire amount of the loan. On subsequent payments, use the appropriate rate and apply it to the outstanding principal balance of the loan.

Blended payment (interest and principal): Calculate the interest using the appropriate rate. The payment will include interest and principal, so the balance of the payment will be the amount of principal to be deducted from the principal balance owing.

For example, a $10,000. loan, 10%, compounded half-yearly, repayable $100. monthly. The first month's interest will be $81.64 on the $10,000., so the balance of the payment ($18.36) will be applied to the prinicipal. Deduct this $18.36 from the $10,000. when estimating the second payment, so the interest on the second payment will be $9,981.64 × 0.816485, or $81.50. The balance of this month's payment of $100. will be $18.50, which will be applied to principal. Repeat this throughout the loan.

COMPOUNDED MONTHLY

	Payable Monthly	Payable Quarterly	Payable Semi-Annually	Payable Annually
10	0.833333	2.520891	5.105331	10.471307
10¼	0.845167	2.584450	5.235695	10.745514
10½	0.875000	2.648036	5.366192	11.020345
10¾	0.895833	2.711647	5.496825	11.295801
11	0.916667	2.775285	5.627592	11.571884
11¼	0.937500	2.838950	5.758496	11.848594
11½	0.958333	2.902640	5.889533	12.125933
11¾	0.979167	2.966357	6.020706	12.403901
12	1.000000	3.030100	6.152015	12.682503
12¼	1.020833	3.093869	6.283459	12.961736
12½	1.041667	3.157665	6.415039	13.241605
12¾	1.062500	3.221487	6.546754	13.522108
13	1.083333	3.285335	6.678605	13.803248
13¼	1.104167	3.349210	6.810592	14.085026
13½	1.125000	3.413111	6.942715	14.367444
13¾	1.145833	3.477038	7.074975	14.650502
14	1.166667	3.540992	7.207371	14.934203
14¼	1.187500	3.604972	7.339902	15.218546
14½	1.208333	3.668978	7.472571	15.503535
14¾	1.229167	3.733011	7.605375	15.789169
15	1.250000	3.797070	7.738318	16.075452
15¼	1.270833	3.861156	7.871397	16.362382
15½	1.291667	3.925267	8.004612	16.649962
15¾	1.312500	3.989406	8.137965	16.938195
16	1.333333	4.053570	8.271454	17.227078

COMPOUNDED QUARTERLY

	Payable Monthly	Payable Quarterly	Payable Semi-Annually	Payable Annually
10	0.826484	2.500000	5.062500	10.381289
10¼	0.846973	2.562500	5.190664	10.650758
10½	0.867453	2.625000	5.318906	10.920720
10¾	0.887930	2.687500	5.444723	11.191176
11	0.908390	2.750000	5.575625	11.462126
11¼	0.928846	2.812500	5.704102	11.733571
11½	0.949293	2.875000	5.832656	12.005511
11¾	0.969732	2.937500	5.961289	12.277947
12	0.990163	3.000000	6.090000	12.550881
12¼	1.010586	3.062500	6.218789	12.824311
12½	1.031001	3.125000	6.347656	13.098240
12¾	1.051407	3.187500	6.476602	13.372667
13	1.071805	3.250000	6.605625	13.647593
13¼	1.092194	3.312500	6.734727	13.923019
13½	1.112576	3.375000	6.863906	14.198945
13¾	1.132949	3.437500	6.993164	14.475372
14	1.153314	3.500000	7.122500	14.752300
14¼	1.176927	3.562500	7.272628	15.074166
14½	1.194020	3.625000	7.381406	15.307664
14¾	1.214360	3.687500	7.510976	15.586101
15	1.234693	3.750000	7.640625	15.865042
15¼	1.255017	3.812500	7.770351	16.144487
15½	1.275333	3.875000	7.900156	16.424437
15¾	1.295641	3.937500	8.030039	16.704893
16	1.315940	4.000000	8.160000	16.985856

COMPOUNDED HALF-YEARLY

	Payable Monthly	Payable Quarterly	Payable Semi-Annually	Payable Annually
10	0.816485	2.469508	5.000000	10.250000
10¼	0.836478	2.530483	5.125000	10.512656
10½	0.856452	2.591423	5.250000	10.775625
10¾	0.876405	2.652326	5.375000	11.038906
11	0.896339	2.713193	5.500000	11.302500
11¼	0.916254	2.774024	5.625000	11.566406
11½	0.936149	2.834819	5.750000	11.830625
11¾	0.956024	2.895578	5.875000	12.095156
12	0.975879	2.956301	6.000000	12.360000
12¼	0.995715	3.016989	6.125000	12.625156
12½	1.015532	3.077641	6.250000	12.890625
12¾	1.035329	3.138257	6.375000	13.156406
13	1.055107	3.198837	6.500000	13.422500
13¼	1.074866	3.259382	6.625000	13.688906
13½	1.094605	3.319892	6.750000	13.955625
13¾	1.114325	3.380366	6.875000	14.222656
14	1.134026	3.440804	7.000000	14.490000
14¼	1.153708	3.501208	7.125000	14.757656
14½	1.173370	3.561576	7.250000	15.025625
14¾	1.193013	3.621909	7.375000	15.293906
15	1.212679	3.682207	7.500000	15.562500
15¼	1.232243	3.742470	7.625000	15.831406
15½	1.251830	3.802697	7.750000	16.100625
15¾	1.271397	3.862890	7.875000	16.370156
16	1.290946	3.923048	8.000000	16.640000

COMPOUNDED ANNUALLY

	Payable Monthly	Payable Quarterly	Payable Semi-Annually	Payable Annually
10	0.797414	2.411369	4.880885	10.000000
10¼	0.816485	2.469508	5.000000	10.250000
10½	0.835516	2.527548	5.118980	10.500000
10¾	0.854507	2.585489	5.237826	10.750000
11	0.873459	2.643333	5.356538	11.000000
11¼	0.892372	2.701079	5.475115	11.250000
11½	0.911247	2.758727	5.593560	11.500000
11¾	0.930082	2.816279	5.711873	11.750000
12	0.948879	2.873734	5.830052	12.000000
12¼	0.967638	2.931094	5.948101	12.250000
12½	0.986358	2.988357	6.066017	12.500000
12¾	1.005040	3.045525	6.183803	12.750000
13	1.023684	3.102598	6.301458	13.000000
13¼	1.042291	3.159577	6.418983	13.250000
13½	1.060860	3.216461	6.536379	13.500000
13¾	1.079391	3.273252	6.653645	13.750000
14	1.097885	3.329948	6.770783	14.000000
14¼	1.116342	3.386552	6.887792	14.250000
14½	1.134762	3.443063	7.004673	14.500000
14¾	1.153145	3.499481	7.121426	14.750000
15	1.171492	3.555808	7.238053	15.000000
15¼	1.189801	3.612042	7.354553	15.250000
15½	1.208075	3.668185	7.470926	15.500000
15¾	1.226313	3.724237	7.587174	15.750000
16	1.244514	3.780199	7.703296	16.000000

75

REAL PROPERTY DEFINITIONS

Abstract	A written, condensed history of title to a parcel of real property, recorded in a land registry office.
Abuttals	The bounding of a parcel of land by other land, street, river, etc. A boundary.
Acceleration Clause	On mortgage payment default, the entire balance of the loan is due and immediately payable.
Administrator	One who has charge of the estate of a deceased person who died without a will, or one who did not appoint an executor. Appointed by Court order.
Adverse Possession	When someone, other than the owner, takes physical possession of property, without the owner's consent.
Agent	One who legally represents an individual or corporate body.
Agreement of Sale	Written agreement whereby one agrees to buy, and another agrees to sell, according to the terms and conditions in the agreement.
Agreement to Lease	Written agreement whereby one agrees to lease real property to another, according to the terms of the agreement.
Amortization	To extinguish a loan by means of a sinking fund.
Appraisal	A written estimate of the market value of real property, made by a qualified expert.
Appreciation	Increased market value of real property.
Appurtenances	Additional rights that are an adjunction to real property.
Assessed Value	Value of real property set by a municipality for taxation purposes.

Assessor	Person employed by a municipality or other Government body empowered to place valuation on property for taxation purposes.
Assignment	Legal transfer of interest in real property or a mortgage from one person to another.
Assumption Agreement	An agreement whereby a person other than the mortgagor covenants to perform the obligations in the mortgage deed.
Attornment of Rent	Taking of rents by Mortgagee in Possession to protect his rights in case of default by mortgagor.
Blanket Mortgage	Single mortgage registered to cover more than one parcel of real property.
Bond	A binding agreement to strengthen the covenant of performance.
Broker	A person who legally trades in real estate for another, for compensation.
Certificate of Charge	Provincial Government acknowledgement of registration of mortgage in a Land Titles office.
Certificate of Title	Provincial Government acknowledgement of registration of title deed in a Land Titles office.
Chattels	Moveable possessions, such as furniture, personal possessions, etc. A furnace, before it is installed, is a moveable possession. Once installed, it is not.
Chattel Mortgage	A mortgage on moveable possessions, personal property.
Closing	The time at which a real estate transaction is concluded legally in a registry office.
Cloud on Title	An impairment to title of real property, such as executed judgment, mortgage, lien, etc., registered legally against the property.
C.M.H.C.	Central Mortgage and Housing Corporation, a Crown agency administering Canada's National Housing Act.
Commission	Financial remuneration paid to an agent for selling or leasing property, based on an agreed percentage of the amount involved.
Consideration	Something of value for compensation.
Contract	An agreement upon lawful consideration which binds the parties to a performance.
Conveyance	Transmitting title of real property from one to another.

Covenant	Solemn agreement.
Convenantee	Lender in a (mortgage) deed.
Covenantor	Borrower in a (mortgage) deed.
Date of Maturity	In mortgages, the last day of the term of the mortgage.
Deed	A document containing an agreement that has been signed, sealed, and containing proof of its delivery; effective only on the date of delivery. (Mortgage deed, title deed, etc.)
Demise	To transfer or convey an estate for a term of years, or life.
Deposit	Money or other consideration of value given as pledge for fulfillment of a contract or agreement.
Depreciation	Reduction in market value of property. Also used to indicate capital cost allowance.
Derivative Mortgage	Mortgage on a mortgage. Mortgagee assigns his mortgage to lender to secure loan.
Dower	Rights of wife or widow in freehold property owned by her husband.
Easement	A right acquired to use another's land or buildings, generally for access to some other adjoining property.
Encroachment	Undue or unlawful trespass on another's property, usually caused by a building, or part of a building, or obstruction.
Encumbrance	Any legal claim registered against property.
Escheat	Conveyance of property to the Crown (Government) due to intestate person dying and leaving no heirs.
Escrow	A deed or contract delivered to a third party to be held until the payment or fulfillment of the agreement by the grantee.
Estate	One's interest in lands and any other subject of property.
Equity	The financial interest of a property owner in excess of any encumbrances, limited by its market value.
Executor	Person legally appointed by testator to carry out the terms of his will.
Exclusive Listing	An agreement granting sole and exclusive rights to an agent to sell property.
Fee Simple	Absolute ownership of property.

Fee Tail	Property ownership, limited to some particular heirs.
First Mortgage	One that takes precedence over all others. (Mortgage seniority established by date and time of registration.)
Fixture	Permanent improvements to property that remain with it.
Foreclosure	A legally enforced transfer of real property ordered by a Court to satisfy unpaid debts. The most common is a foreclosure by a mortgagee.
Freehold	Property held in fee simple (untrammelled tenure) or fee tail (for the term of the owner's life).
Frontage	Property line facing street.
Gale Date	The date on which interest is charged.
Grant	An instrument of conveyance transferring property from one to another.
Grantee	Person to whom a conveyance is made; one who receives legal transfer of property from another; the buyer.
Grantor	Person who makes a conveyance; one who transfers property to another; the seller.
Hereditament	Property that may be inherited.
Hypothec	Lien on real estate (Quebec).
Hypothecary Creditor	Mortgagee (Quebec).
Hypthecary Debtor	Mortgagor (Quebec).
Indenture	An agreement between two or more parties. Originally, indentures were duplicates placed together and cut in a wavy line, so that the two papers could be identified as being authentic by corresponding to each other.
Instrument	A writing instructing one in regard to something that has been agreed on.
Intestate	Not having a will.
Joint Tenancy	Ownership of real property by two or more persons; when one dies, his share automatically passes to the survivor(s).
Judgment	Binding decision of the Court.
Landed Property	Having an interest in and pertaining to land.

Landlord	A lessor. One who allows another to occupy his land or building for a consideration.
Lease	Binding contract between a landlord (lessor) and tenant (lessee) for the occupation of premises or land for a specified period of time, and a financial or other consideration.
Leasehold	Property held by lease.
Leaseholder	Tenant under a lease.
Lessee	The tenant. One who pays rent.
Lessor	The person granting use of property to another.
Lien	A legal claim affecting property.
Lis pendens	Notice of commencement of Court action, recorded against title of property.
Market Value	The Courts have defined this as being the highest price estimated in terms of money which a property will bring, if exposed for sale in the open market, allowing a reasonable time to find a purchaser who buys with knowledge of all the uses to which it may be put, and for which it is capable of being used.
Mechanic's Lien	A lien filed and registered against property by a person or corporate body, for labour and/or materials supplied for the improvement of the property.
Moratorium	Provincial statute deferment of mortgage principal payments during depression. Non-existent now.
Mortgage	Read chapter 10 in this book.
Mortgage Bonds	Bond holders are represented by trustee, who is the mortgagee. Bonds can be traded, making them more flexible than individual mortgages.
Mortgaged Out	Situation whereby total mortgage debt on property equals or exceeds market value of property.
Mortgagee	The lender in a mortgage deed. The one receiving the mortgage.
Mortgagor	The borrower in a mortgage deed. The one giving the mortgage.
N.H.A.	National Housing Act
Option	An agreement whereby one has the exclusive right to purchase another's property at a specified price, with a time limit.

Personalty	Personal property, chattels.
Postponement Clause	In mortgaging, the agreement of an equitable mortgagee to allow the mortgagor to renew or replace a senior mortgage that becomes due before such equitable mortgage.
Power of Attorney	Legal authority for one to act on behalf of another.
Prepayment Clause	In a mortgage, an agreement giving the mortgagor the privilege of paying additional sums off the principal balance over and above the agreed payments.
Principal	A person or corporate body employing an agent.
Principal Balance	In a mortgage, the outstanding dollar amount owing on the debt.
Quit Claim Deed	A full release of one's interest in property to another, usually executed between mortgagees and mortgagors.
Real Estate	Landed property (land).
Real Property	Land *and* buildings thereon, and rights thereof.
Realtor	Certification mark being the property of the Canadian Real Estate Association. Designates broker-member of Association.
Realty	Real Property.
Rest	The date upon which the amount between the parties to a mortgage is altered. It is not necessarily the date upon which payment is made, unless so agreed in the mortgage deed.
Sales Agreement	Purchase of property without obtaining title deed until a specified further sum of money is paid to the vendor.
Socage	A tenure of land held by the tenant in performance of specified services or by payment of rent, and not requiring military service (history).
Straight Loan	In mortgaging, a mortgage with no principal payments. Interest only.
Survey	Surveyor's report of mathematical boundaries of land, showing location of buildings, physical features and quantity of land.
Tenancy in Common	Ownership of real property by two or more persons, whereby on the death of one, his share is credited to his own estate.

264

Tenant	The one who pays rent for the right to occupy land or buildings.
Tenant in Tail	Holder of an estate limited to the heirs of his body. The line of heirs is called entail.
Tenement	Property held by tenant.
Tenure	The right of holding property.
Title Deed	Proof of legal ownership of property.
Title Search	Research of records in registry or land titles office to determine history and chain of ownership of property.
Usury	An unconscionable and exhorbitant rate of interest.
Zoning	Specified limitation on the use of land, the construction and use of buildings, in a defined section of a municipality.

76

BUILDING DEFINITIONS

Central Mortgage and Housing Corporation has provided us with a comprehensive list of building terms in construction, including the areas of electricity, heating, plumbing and the roof.

Construction Types

Adobe Construction
A type of construction in which the exterior walls are built of blocks that are made of soil mixed with straw and hardened in the sun.

Block Construction
A type of construction in which the exterior walls are bearing walls made of concrete block or structural clay tile.

Brick Construction
A type of construction in which the exterior walls are bearing walls made of brick or a combination of brick and other unit masonry.

Brick-Veneer Construction
A type of construction in which the wood frame or steel structural frame has an exterior surface of brick applied as cladding.

Dry-Wall Construction
Interior cladding with panels of gypsum board, fibre board, plywood or gypsum plaster, a dry operation as opposed to wet plaster.

Fire Resistive Construction
Floors, walls, roof, etc., constructed of slow-burning or non-combustible materials recognized as such by building codes or local regulations applicable to the type of building proposed.

Monolithic Concrete Construction
A type of construction or process in which the concrete for the wall, floor, beams etc. are poured in one continuous operation.

Plank Frame Construction	A type of construction in which the structural framework is composed of solid wood plank uprights and horizontally placed planks laid on edge, with or without sheathing.
Post and Beam Construction	A type of construction made with load-bearing posts and beams in which the enclosing walls are designed to support no loads other than their own weight.
Prefabricated Construction	A type of construction so designed as to involve a minimum of assembly at the site, usually comprising a series of large wood panels or precast concrete units manufactured in a plant.
Reinforced Concrete Construction	A type of construction in which the principal structural members such as floors, columns and beams are made of concrete poured around isolated steel bars or steel meshwork in such a manner that the two materials act together in resisting force.
Skeleton Construction	A type of construction in which all external and internal loads and stresses are transmitted to the foundations by a rigidly connected framework of metal or reinforced concrete. The enclosing walls are supported by the frame at designated intervals, usually at each storey.
Steel Frame Construction	A type of construction in which the structural parts are of steel or dependent on a steel frame for support.
Wood Frame or Frame Construction	A type of construction in which the structural parts are of wood or dependent upon a wood frame for support. In codes, if brick or other incombustible material is applied to exterior walls, the classification of this type of construction is usually unchanged.

Electrical Terms

Alternating Current	A flow of current which constantly changes direction at a fixed rate.
Ampere	A measure of electric current.
Cable: Armored Cable	Insulated wire having additional flexible metallic protective sheathing — often referred to as BX cable.
Ceiling Outlet	An outlet for ceiling lighting fixtures.
Circuit	Continuous conducting path through which current flows.

267

Circuit Breaker	An automatic mechanical device which serves the same purpose as a fuse, i.e., to prevent overheating in a circuit through overloading.
Conduit, Electrical	A protective, pipelike covering for electrical wiring.
Convenience Outlet	An outlet into which may be plugged portable equipment such as lamps or electrically operated equipment.
Current	A flow of electricity.
Direct Current	A flow of current constantly in one direction.
Fuse	A device for interrupting an electric circuit under conditions of overloading or short circuiting, comprising a fusible element which fuses at predetermined excess loads so as to open the circuit.
Insulation, Electrical	Nonconducting covering applied to wire or equipment to prevent the flow of current to contiguous materials.
Kilowatt Hour	A unit of measurement of the consumption of electric energy at a fixed rate for 1 hour; specifically, the use of 1,000 watts for 1 hour.
Meter	A device used for measuring the amount of electric energy consumed.
Outlet	A point on an electric circuit designed for the direct connection of lighting fixtures, appliances and equipment.
Panelboard	A center for controlling a number of circuits by means of fuses or circuit breakers, usually contained in a metal cabinet. Switches are sometimes added to control each circuit.
Power Circuit	A circuit transmitting electric energy to a motor or to a heating unit too large to be served by an ordinary circuit.
Radio Outlet	An outlet having connected thereto an aerial and ground for the use of a radio.
Special Purpose Outlet	An outlet used for purposes other than ordinary lighting and power.
Switch	A device to open and close a circuit.
3-Way Switch	A switch designed to operate in conjunction with a similar switch to control one outlet from two points.
Transformer	A device for transforming the voltage characteristics of a current supply.

Voltage	A measure of electric pressure between any two wires of an electric circuit.
Watt	A unit of measurement of electric power.
Wiring: *Knob-And-Tube* *Wiring*	A method of exposed wiring using knobs and tubes of nonconducting materials to insulate the wiring from the surfaces on which or through which it is installed.

Heating

Air *Conditioning*	The process of bringing air to a required state of temperature and humidity, and removing dust, pollen and other foreign matter.
Baseboard *Heaters*	A radiator shaped like a regular, decorative baseboard, but having openings at top and bottom through which air circulates. Provides convected and radiant heat.
Conduction	The transfer or travel of heat through a body by molecular action.
Convector	Have removable front. Air enters through the arched opening near the floor, is heated as it passes through the heating element and enters room through the upper grill.
Hot Water *Heating*	The circulation of hot water through a system of pipes and radiators either by gravity or a circulating pump.
Indirect *Heating*	A system of heating by convection.
Panel Heating	Coils or ducts installed in wall, floor, or ceiling panels to provide a large surface of low intensity heat supply.
Panel *Radiator*	A heating unit placed on or flush with a flat wall surface, and intended to function essentially as a radiator.
Radiant *Heating*	A heating system in which only the heat radiated from panels is effective in providing the heating requirements.
Radiation	The transfer of heat from a substance by the emission of heat waves.
Radiator	That part of the system, exposed or concealed, from which heat is radiated to a room or other space within the building; heat transferring device.
Space Heating	The methods of heating individual rooms or living units by equipment located entirely within these rooms or living units, such equipment consisting of single unit without ducts, piping, or other mechanical

269

means of heat distribution exterior to the room in
in which situated.

Steam Heating	The circulation of steam through a system of pipes and radiators by any of the numerous methods employed.
Two-Pipe System	A heating system in which one pipe is used for the supply of the heating medium to the heating unit and another for the return of the heating medium to the source of heat supply. The essential feature of a two-pipe system is that each heating unit receives a direct supply of the heating medium which cannot have served a preceding heating unit.
Warm-Air Heating System	A warm air heating plant consists of a heating unit (fuel-burning furnace) enclosed in a casing, from which the heated air is distributed to various rooms of the building through ducts.
Warm Air Heating System, Forced	A warm air heating system in which circulation of air is effected by a fan. Such a system includes air cleaning devices.
Warm Air Heating System Gravity	A warm air heating system in which the motive heat producing flow depends on the difference in weight between the heated air leaving the casing and the cooler air entering the bottom of the casing.
Warm Air Heating System, Perimeter	A warm air heating system of the combination panel and convection type. Warm air ducts embedded in the concrete slab of a basementless house, around the perimeter, receive heated air from a furnace and deliver it to the heated space through registers placed in or near the floor. Air is returned to the furnace from registers near the ceiling.

Plumbing Terms

Backflow	The flow of water into a water-supply system from any source except its regular one. Back siphonage is one type of backflow.
Building Drainage System	All piping provided for carrying waste water, sewage or other drainage, from the building to the street sewer or place of disposal.
Building (House) Subdrain	That portion of a drainage system which cannot drain by gravity into the building sewer.

Building Main	The water-supply pipe, including fittings and accessories, from the water (street) main or other source of supply to the first branch of the water-distributing system.
Catch Basin	A small underground structure for surface drainage in which sediment may settle before water reaches the drain lines.
Cesspool	A covered pit with open-jointed linings into which raw sewage is discharged, the liquid portion of which is disposed of by seepage or leaching into the surrounding porous soil, the solids or sludge being retained in the pit.
Downspout	A pipe which carries water from the roof or gutter to the ground or to any part of the drainage system (synonymous with the conductor, leader, rainspout).
Dry Well	A covered pit with open-jointed linings through which drainage from roofs, basement floors, or areaways may seep or leach into the surrounding porous soil.
Dual Main system of Water Supply	The use of two underground conduits, pipes or lines, each to supply one side of a street.
Main	The principal artery of the system to which branches may be connected.
Plumbing Fixtures	Receptacles which receive and discharge water, liquid or water-borne wastes into a drainage system with which they are connected.
Plumbing Stack	A general term for the vertical main of a system of soil, waste, or vent piping.
Plumbing System	A system of pipes including the water-service line and building drainage lines from their several connections within the building to their connections with the public mains or individual water-supply and sewage-disposal systems, together with fixtures, traps, vents and other devices connected thereto. Storm-water drainage pipes may be considered a part of the plumbing system when connected to a public sewage system.
Roughing-In	The work of installing all pipes in the drainage and venting systems and all water pipes to the point where connections are made with the plumbing fixtures.
Septic Tank	A sewage settling tank intended to retain the sludge

	in immediate contact with the sewage flowing through the tank, for a sufficient period to secure satisfactory decomposition of organic sludge solids by bacterial action.
Sewage	The liquid or water-borne wastes carried away from buildings with or without such ground or surface water as may be present.
Sewer	A conduit, usually closed, designed or used for carrying sewage from buildings and/or ground and surface water to sewage-disposal plants or to natural bodies of water.
Sewer System	A system comprising all sewers (sanitary, storm, and combined), culverts, and subsurface drains needed to conduct sanitary sewage and storm water from a site.

Sewer Types

Building (House) Sewer	That part of the horizontal piping of a building drainage system extending from the building drain to the street sewer or other place of disposal (a cesspool, septic tank, or other type of sewage-treatment device or devices) and conveying the drainage of but one building site.
Sanitary Sewer	A sewer designed or used only for conveying liquid or water-borne waste from plumbing fixtures.
Storm Sewer	A sewer used for conveying rain or subsurface water.
Sewerage	The composite parts of a sewer system including conduits, pumping stations, treatment works, and such other works as may be employed in the collection, treatment or disposal of sewage.
Soil Pipe	Any pipe which conveys the discharges of water-closets, or fixtures having similar functions, with or without the discharges from other fixtures.
Tile Field	The system of open-joint drain tiles laid to distribute septic tank effluent over its absorption area. A tile system laid to provide subsoil drainage for wet areas.
Trap	A fitting or device so designed and constructed as to provide a liquid trap seal which will prevent the passage of air through it.
Vent	A pipe installed to provide a flow of air to or from a drainage system or to provide a circulation of air

within such system to protect trap seals from siphonage and back pressure.

Vent Types

Back Vent

A branch vent installed primarily for the purpose of protecting fixture traps from self-siphonage.

Vent Stack

A vertical vent pipe installed primarily for the purpose of providing circulation of air to and from any part of the building drainage system.

Water Closet

A plumbing fixture consisting of a bowl for the reception of fecal discharge and equipment for flushing the bowl with water. A minor enclosed space in a building equipped with such plumbing fixture.

Water Distribution system

All water mains and service lines, outside of building lines (or to a point near the building line), needed for domestic water supply and fire protection.

Water Supply System of a Building

All the water-service pipes, the water-distributing pipes, and the necessary connecting pipes fittings and control valves.

Roof Types

Curb (or Curbed) Roof

A roof in which the slope is broken on two or more sides; so called because a horizontal curb is built at the plane where the slope changes.

Deck Roof

Having sloping sides below and a flat deck on top.

Flat Roof

A roof which is flat or one which is pitched only enough to provide drainage.

Flat-Pitch Roof

A roof with only a moderately sloping surface.

Gabled Roof

A ridge roof which terminates in a gable.

Gambrel Roof

A gable roof each slope of which is broken into two planes.

Hip Roof

In general, a roof which has one or more hips. A roof which has four sloping sides that meet at four hips and a ridge.

Lean-To Roof

A roof which has a single sloping surface that is supported at the top by a wall that is higher than the roof. A roof which has a single sloping surface.

Mansard Roof	A type of curb roof in which the pitch of the upper portion of a sloping side is slight and that of the lower portion steep. The lower portion is usually interrupted by dormer windows.
Monitor Roof	A type of gable roof commonly used on industrial buildings, which has a raised portion along the ridge with openings for light and/or air.
Pavilion Roof	A roof which in plan forms a figure of more than four straight sides.
Pent Roof	A roof, other than a lean-to roof, which has a single sloping surface.
Pitched Roof	A roof which has one or more sloping surfaces pitched at angles greater than necessary for drainage.
Polygonal Roof	A roof which in plan forms a figure bounded by more than four straight lines.
Pyramid Roof	A hip roof which has four sloping surfaces, usually of equal pitch, that meet at a peak.
Ridge Roof	A roof which has one or more ridges.
Shed Roof	A roof with only one set of rafters, falling from a higher to a lower wall, like an aisle roof.

77

COMPLAINING ABOUT A BAD DEAL

The majority of real estate complaints are related to (1) the purchase of new dwelling units, (2) building additions for existing dwelling units, and (3) repairs to existing dwelling units.

For the unhappy consumer with complaints regarding the foregoing, here are the addresses of Provincial Government Consumer Protection Bureaus who will give you a sympathetic ear. However, if you write a complaining letter to a Government office, remember that the office can only act within statute authority.

Office de la Protection du Consommateur,
Ministere des Consommateurs,
700 est, boul. St.-Cyrille, 15e etage,
Edifice Place Hauteville, QUEBEC.
G1R 5A9

Consumer Bureau,
Dept. of Provincial Secretary,
P.O. Box 6000, FREDERICTON, N.B.
E3B 5H1

Director, Research and Education,
Dept. of Consumer Affairs,
P.O. Box 998, HALIFAX, N.S.
B3J 2X3

Consumer Services Division,
Dept. of the Provincial Secretary,
P.O. Box 2000, CHARLOTTETOWN, P.E.I.
C1A 7N8

Dept. of Consumer Affairs & Environment,
2nd Floor, Elizabeth Towers,
ST. JOHN'S, Nfld.
A1C 5T7

The Director, Consumer Information Centre,
Ministry of Consumer and Commercial Relations,
555 Yonge St., TORONTO, Ont.
M7A 2H6

Co-Ordinator, Consumer Communications,
Manitoba Dept. of Consumer Affairs,
1023 - 405 Broadway Ave.
WINNIPEG, Man.
R3C 3L6

Director, Consumer Affairs Resource Centre,
Dept. of Consumer Affairs,
11th Floor, SPC Building,
2025 Victoria Ave., REGINA, Sask.
S4P 0R9

The Director, Resource Centre,
Alberta Dept. of Consumer & Corporate Affairs,
10065 Jasper Avenue,
10th Floor, Capitol Square, EDMONTON, Alta.
T5J 3B1

The Director, Consumer Resource Centre,
Ministry of Consumer & Corporate Affairs,
838 Fort Street, VICTORIA, B.C.
V8W 1H8

Complaints against a real estate agent can often be satisfied by confronting the agent and/or his employer. Nobody wants any flack in his business, so start here.

If this route fails, take the matter to your local real estate board, if the offending agent is a member. Real estate boards are very conscious of the ethical responsibility of its members, and tolerate no nonsense.

If the agent is not a member of a real estate board, or if he is, and you are not happy about the result of your complaint, here are the addresses of Provincial Government officials responsible for the licensing of agents. Your complaint will be handled with dispatch.

The Superintendent,
Service du Courtage Immmobilier du Quebec,
Ministere des Consommateurs Cooperatives
    et Institutions Financieres,
Hotel du Gouvernement, QUEBEC, P.Q.

Corporate Services Officer,
Dept. of the Provincial Secretary,
P.O. Box 6000, FREDERICTON, N.B.
E3B 5H1

Director, Consumer Services Bureau,
Dept. of Consumer Affairs,
5639 Spring Garden Road,
P.O. Box 998, HALIFAX, N.S.
B3J 2X3

Director, Division of Consumer Services,
Dept. of Provincial Secretary,
P.O. Box 2000, CHARLOTTETOWN, P.E.I.
C1A 7N8

The Superintendent of Real Estate
Dept. of Consumer Affairs and Environment,
P.O. Box 999, ST. JOHN'S, Nfld.

Registrar, The Real Estate and Business Brokers Act,
Ministry of Consumer and Commercial Relations,
555 Yonge Street, TORONTO, Ont.
M7A 2H6

Registrar, The Real Estate Brokers Act,
The Manitoba Securities Commission,
1128 - 405 Broadway Ave., WINNIPEG, Man.
R3C 3L6

Director, Licensing & Investigations,
Dept. of the Provincial Secretary,
Room 308, Towne Square, 1919 Rose St.
REGINA, Sask.
S4S 0B3

Deputy Superintendent of Real Estate,
Consumer and Corporate Affairs,
9th Floor, Capitol Square,
10065 Jasper Av. EDMONTON, Alta.
T5J 3B1

Director, Real Estate Council of B.C.
Suite 608 - 626 West Pender Street,
VANCOUVER, B.C.
V6B 1V9

78

THE LAST WORD

Ten years ago a man purchased the first edition of this book. He studied it, got interested in the subject, and got involved.

Today that man's *equity* in his real estate holdings is worth nearly ONE MILLION DOLLARS. And that's a fact. An outstanding example of what one man did in the short space of ten years!

On the dust jacket of that first edition my advice was to get into the country and buy one hundred acres of land for one's future financial well-being. Well, we all know what happened to the price of 100 acres of land. Oops, I mean 40.469 hectares.

Well, you say, that was over the past ten years. What about the next ten?

In 1969 I provided a chart for some University students on the cost of real estate. The chart started at the lower left hand corner at 1939 and went up to the upper right hand corner to 1969. All the way up there was a wavy line, dipping and climbing, but mostly climbing. And how it climbed.

I advised the students to make their own chart, with 1969 at the lower left hand corner, and 1999 in the upper right.

That chart is still climbing. A bit wavy at times, but climbing, and I can't see any reason in the foreseeable future for it to stop climbing.

My last word is like my first word.

GET INVOLVED
BUY SOME REAL ESTATE

Don't dream. Don't procrastinate. Get a piece of the action — even a little piece. And to the 60,000 or so real estate agents in Canada who spend most of their time creating financial real estate success for others, while living on hopeful commissions, I have this piece of advice:

If YOU want to make it over the long haul, you'll very seldom do it on your commissions. You MUST get involved.

As we all know, the Federal Government has provided a very generous pension plan that is tied to the cost of living. It must surely be the world's greatest pension.

Well, in the likely event that you will not retire on a Federal Government pension, what are you doing about your old age? The young generally don't like to think about 30 or so years ahead, its just too far off. But with good health it will come just as surely as death and taxes.

Here is my suggestion: After you buy your house, go into the country, find a nice piece of concession-corner land you can buy with about $3,000. down, mortgage the balance for what you can carry without hurting yourself too much (which will dictate the purchase price) and then . . .

Forget it until you are 55 or so. Sell it, and live off the interest. That's your assured pension.

Don't think for one minute that land in this world is going to get cheaper. It won't. Not because I say so, but because of what the late Will Rogers reminds us all — "buy land, they're not making any more of it."

If you follow this advice, and a couple of years later someone offers you double your equity, DON'T SELL. Resist the temptation to take the profit and buy that new car or take that vaction. This is YOUR PENSION that buyer is tampering with!

Go on, get a little piece of land. Enjoy it. Grow some vegetables on your pension. Rent it to a farmer. Stand on it and look around, you're a landowner!

Hang onto your pension.

The foregoing piece of advice may not go down too well with some economists, but what I am attempting to do here is have you take some of that money you will be pouring down your drains of frivolity and bury it in land.

In 1942 the author was a Flight Sergeant stationed at an air observers school in Malton, Ontario. That same year, a young man (not me, unfortunately) purchased 97 acres of land near the air station for $12,000. with $2,000. down.

I had access to $2,000. at the time, but buying a parcel of land was the furthest thing from my mind. There were too many week-ends in Detroit to take care of!

Well, that same man sold this land about 25 years later for One Million, Three Hundred Thousand Dollars ($1,300,000).

The next time you get some urge to go flying off on some expensive holiday, or feel the need of an expensive piece of tin on wheels, forget it. Just once, forget it, and buy a piece of land.

Believe me, you will not regret it.